DEEP SOUTH DISPATCH

DEEP SOUTH
DISPATCH

MEMOIR OF A CIVIL RIGHTS JOURNALIST

JOHN N. HERBERS

with ANNE FARRIS ROSEN | Foreword by GENE ROBERTS

University Press of Mississippi / Jackson

Willie Morris Books in Memoir and Biography

www.upress.state.ms.us

Designed by Peter D. Halverson

The University Press of Mississippi is a member of the Association
of American University Presses.

First printing 2018

∞

Library of Congress Cataloging-in-Publication Data

Names: Herbers, John, author. | Rosen, Anne Farris, author.
Title: Deep South dispatch : memoir of a civil rights journalist / John N. Herbers
with Anne Farris Rosen ; foreword by Gene Roberts.
Description: Jackson : University Press of Mississippi, [2018] | Series: Willie Morris
books in memoir and biography | Includes bibliographical references and index. |
Identifiers: LCCN 2017049188 (print) | LCCN 2017050504 (ebook) |
ISBN 9781496816757 (epub single) | ISBN 9781496816764 (epub institutional) |
ISBN 9781496816771 (pdf single) | ISBN 9781496816788 (pdf institutional) |
ISBN 9781496816740 | ISBN 9781496816740 (cloth : alk. paper)
Subjects: LCSH: Herbers, John. | Journalists—Southern States—Biography. |
Civil rights movements—Press coverage—Southern States.
Classification: LCC PN4874.H47 (ebook) | LCC PN4874.H47 A3 2018 (print) |
DDC 070.92 [B]—dc23
LC record available at https://lccn.loc.gov/2017049188

British Library Cataloging-in-Publication Data available

Contents

Foreword

JOHN HERBERS WAS ONE OF AMERICA'S MOST IMPORTANT NEWS REPORTers in the second half of the twentieth century. Few, if any, covered as many important stories as solidly or as vividly as Herbers.

First for United Press International, then the *New York Times*, he was present with his notebook at an astonishing array of journalistic hot spots. He sat in a tense courtroom for days reporting the iconic trial of the murderers of Emmett Till, a fourteen-year-old black boy who was beaten and shot to death by two Mississippi white men and thrown in a river because he may have whistled at a white woman. Herbers also chronicled the rise of the White Citizens' Councils in Mississippi as they marshaled economic pressure against school desegregation and black voter registration.

Later, while working at the *Times*, he rushed to Dallas just hours after President John F. Kennedy was assassinated and as federal and state lawmen searched frantically for the shooter. In Birmingham, Alabama, he raced to the Sixteenth Street Baptist Church just minutes after a bomb shook the building and watched in horror, thinking of his own daughters, as the bodies of four young black girls were pulled from the wreckage. In St. Augustine, Florida, he watched angry whites roam the streets and attack civil rights demonstrators at will, pouring muriatic acid into a swimming pool to prevent blacks from using it. At the first Byron De La Beckwith trial for the assassination of NAACP leader Medgar Evers, he carefully recorded the exchange when the district attorney asked a potential white juror if he thought it was a crime for a white man to kill a black man in Mississippi. "What was his answer?" the judge asked after a long silence; and then came the reply from the district attorney: "He's thinking it over."

Herbers endured the long Mississippi Freedom Summer of 1964 in which hundreds of out-of-state students swept into Mississippi to confront white supremacy head on, and almost immediately three civil rights organizers were slain and their bodies hidden in an earthen dam. He watched as FBI agents and one of the suspected killers unearthed the bodies. Few reporters had more exposure to Martin Luther King Jr. than Herbers, who reported on him from Atlanta to Birmingham to Mississippi and finally for weeks at Selma, Alabama, as diehard segregationists attacked demonstrators so viciously that they paved the way for the Voting Rights Act of 1965. Toward the end of the Selma movement, the *Times* transferred Herbers to Washington, DC, where he became a key player in the paper's Washington bureau, covering the Watergate turbulence and the administrations of six presidents.

I am in a unique position to assess Herbers's brilliance and acumen. I succeeded him in 1965 as the *New York Times'* chief southern correspondent when he was transferred to Washington. I read and reread his stories in the *Times'* files, followed in his footsteps to several civil rights battlegrounds, and marveled at the quantity and quality of his coverage and at his courage. White mobs heckled him. He was repeatedly threatened.

Clearly, Herbers had a story to tell, although he waited until late in his ninety-three-year life to do it; but then, with assistance from his daughter, Anne Farris Rosen, he focused on his southern reporting years with a here's-what-I-saw-and-heard narrative that speeds you through the chapters. He died early in 2017 on the eve of the funeral of his beloved wife, Betty. His book had been written and accepted by the University Press of Mississippi at the time of his death but not yet printed.

Future historians and anyone who wants to know more about the civil rights years can be grateful, indeed, that John and Anne raced with death to complete the manuscript. It's quite a book. And it could not be more timely as the nation now witnesses another period of racial upheaval. Never have Herbers's writings been more critical and immediate than since he first penned them. His historical retrospective—eerily similar to today in many respects when he describes the rise of white supremacy groups and race-baiting diatribes by white leaders—provides us with a deeper understanding of America's constant struggle to achieve racial equity.

How did Herbers become the man he was? The book is also a personal journey, a poignant coming-of-age story about a young man's struggle as

he questions his southern heritage and the prescribed laws and mores of a
segregated society in the 1950s and 1960s. How did a skilled and exceptionally
gifted reporter emerge from a depression-wracked Mississippi household
where the prevailing wisdom was that blacks were put on earth to be servants to whites? The short answer: by degrees. John goes from high school
into the army upon graduation, and in the midst of World War II, thanks to
good army libraries, he becomes a serious reader. After the war he enrolls
at Emory University in Atlanta and joins the staff of a student newspaper,
where two other students also go on to become journalists who write about
civil rights—Claude Sitton for the *New York Times* and Reese Cleghorn for
the *Atlanta Journal* and the *Charlotte Observer*.

After college graduation in 1949, Herbers headed for Mississippi, not
because it was a potential site of racial turmoil but because it was home;
his parents were growing old and they needed him. He landed a job on the
Morning Star in Greenwood, Mississippi, and then on the *Jackson Daily
News*. Even though the US Supreme Court's school desegregation decision
was still three years away, he became aware that "race was rising to a low boil
in Mississippi." It was apparent even at the *Daily News*, where racism was
permeating the building as surely as the smell of printers' ink. He was feeling
uncomfortable with both the paper's tone and with his low pay when, in 1952,
he married his girlfriend, Betty, and jumped to the three-person United Press
Jackson bureau for a five-dollar increase in weekly salary.

It was not until the Emmett Till trial, which shocked America with its
racial unfairness, and Rosa Parks's refusal a hundred days later to give up her
bus seat in Montgomery, Alabama, that it became clear that white supremacy
was now a national story. When Herbers became UP's Jackson bureau chief
and had the authority to decide what to cover, he put an increased focus on
racial stories. He got no pushback from his editorial bosses in Atlanta and
New York but plenty from the small-town radio stations and newspapers,
especially the Jackson TV station WLBT. "You are an integrationist," the
station manager shouted at one of Herbers's reporters. "You know you are."

Herbers's staff "did not write opinion pieces or display an ideology," but
simply covering racial stories was enough to rankle news clients in a state
where only a small handful of journalists were firmly open to writing about
race no matter which way the chips fell. Even had he not been a remarkable
reporter, his determination that UP would cover both sides of racial turmoil

in Mississippi would make him a memorable figure in southern journalism. The heat from news clients was so persistent that Herbers found himself wondering as he got up in the morning, "Is something wrong with me?"

Herbers left Mississippi to accept a Nieman Fellowship at Harvard University and soon after was transferred to the much larger Washington UPI bureau. But he did not have as much journalistic freedom as he had in Jackson, and he began to miss the South and the racial story. A dream came true when the *New York Times* called in the summer of 1963 and asked Herbers to join Claude Sitton, the *Times*' southern correspondent, to expand the paper's presence in the South. He couldn't have been more eager.

It was the peak of the civil rights era, when steam was gathering for the Civil Rights Act of 1964 and the Voting Rights Act of 1965. There was barely a time out for family life. Herbers was, for instance, on his way to the Birmingham airport on Sunday, September 15, 1963, to celebrate his eleventh wedding anniversary with Betty when he heard on the radio that a bomb had exploded at the Sixteenth Street Baptist Church. He quickly made a U-turn.

Herbers and his daughter, Anne, chose to frame this book around his southern years, but, if the clock had not run out, they could have written another book on his Washington years. He covered, variously, the White House, Congress, urban affairs, and national political campaigns. His coverage was exceptional. In addition to his news stories, he wrote four books on civil rights, urban affairs, and the White House press corps, choosing national issues over his personal story.

Finally, under Anne's prodding, he decided at last to write of his years covering the racial story in the South. As this book demonstrates in chapter after chapter, they were indelible years—for Herbers, for the South, and for the nation.

GENE ROBERTS

Preface

THIS BOOK IS THE PRODUCT OF TWO GENERATIONS OF WRITERS—MY father and myself. Twenty years ago, after retiring from the *New York Times*, my father composed his memoir, inscribing some of his more personal thoughts and experiences on paper for the first time. During his decades-long career, he had written more than four million words describing trends in American government, politics, and society. His dispatches about other people were mostly written with the sterile eye of a self-effacing observer. So, when I read the memoir, I was surprised and fascinated to find how revealing he was with his own story.

It was a sensitive and introspective narrative, but it failed in one major respect. It ended with two paragraphs about the infamous Emmett Till murder trial in 1955, the mere starting point of his fifteen years reporting about civil rights. "Daddy, what happened to the rest of the story?" I asked him. "I've already written all that," he answered. He was right. During his years in the South, he had produced hundreds of articles chronicling the marches, protests, beatings, and deaths that he had witnessed. Now in his later years, he had no interest in finishing the memoir, and, instead, went for an ocean swim before tending to the turnip greens in his garden and preparing a gourmet dinner. He also had a deadline to meet for an article in *Governing* magazine about the continuous shift of federal power to the states. The incomplete memoir was relegated to the bottom drawer of his file cabinet.

Ten years ago, while helping him clean his office, I came upon the faded manuscript. I dusted it off and suggested we try to breathe new life into it. He still wasn't very interested, but I was. I unearthed hundreds of his articles, and he and I worked elbow to elbow to slowly distill them into a more complete account. In the process of revising it, I learned new things about him, including his formative childhood circumstances, that he had interviewed the parents of the children killed in the Birmingham church bombing on the night of their deaths, and that one of his first assignments as a young reporter in 1951 was to cover the brutal execution of Willie McGee, a black man in Mississippi found guilty of raping a white woman.

I also realized that he had prepared me all my life to work with him on this book. He took me to my first civil rights rally at age five. By first grade, I had graduated to accompanying him to a KKK march that he covered, and my family was forced by angry vigilantes to leave St. Augustine, Florida, when I was in second grade. My summer vacation during middle school was visiting seventeen American inner cities after racial violence, and my father and I were teargassed on the US Capitol lawn when I accompanied him during a Vietnam War protest he was covering. In college, I typed the final manuscript of his book on the demise of the civil rights movement.

When I became a journalist, he was my mentor, giving me advice when I sought it on my own articles about government, politics, and race relations. My father often marveled over how his notebook, typewriter, and newspaper ink had been replaced by smart phones, computers, and Twitter, and that news today is told in real time by many citizen journalists. In 2015, he spoke at my journalism class, News Coverage of Racial Issues, at the University of Maryland and helped students understand how history informs the current racial situation in America. The nation had elected the first black president, but my father expressed dismay over the untrod roads that lay ahead. He reminded students that our country had made three major attempts to repair its record of racial suppression, including a strong but unsuccessful drive during the early 1800s to bar the importation of slaves and the expansion of the plantation system, the short-lived period of post–Civil War Reconstruction, and the civil rights movement beginning in the 1950s. Now there is a fourth effort in response to a rash of publicized killings of black people by police officers and a resurgence of white supremacy forces. My father died in 2017, unable to bear witness to a new generation of struggles. But he hoped that the legacy of his words might serve as a foundation for the next piece of history in the nation's unfolding quest for justice.

ANNE FARRIS ROSEN

DEEP SOUTH DISPATCH

CHAPTER 1

An Old Secret Revealed

IN 1969, I WAS FORTY-FIVE YEARS OLD AND WORKING IN WASHINGTON, DC, as a national reporter for the *New York Times* when my mother called from Crystal Springs, Mississippi, to say my father was dying from complications from Parkinson's disease. Mother said Pop had been asking in his sleep for his parents, which was surprising and disturbing because Pop had not enjoyed a happy childhood.

I hurriedly flew to Memphis, Tennessee, and drove one hour south to Crystal Springs, the last refuge for my parents, who had moved like nomads from town to town in west Tennessee and north Mississippi, opening and then closing failing variety stores. They never accumulated enough wealth to stay anywhere long or put down roots, and they reared my three sisters and me in genteel poverty.

Their house was one of the hundreds of thousands built across the nation after World War II to accommodate a home-starved population. Unseasoned timbers supported small rooms, asphalt shingle siding, and acrid paint trim of grays and blues. A few rattling window air conditioners provided little respite from the oppressive August heat. I found Pop with his head sunk deep in the pillows of a massive, ornately carved oak bed. Built for the grand scale of Mother's childhood estate, it now monopolized their small, crowded bedroom. He smiled at me and we grasped hands. We talked about his illness, which had progressed so that he could not leave his bed. But in the stoic spirit of men of his generation, Pop talked of his malady as something of passing unimportance. Mother's remark about him calling for his parents weighed on my mind, and I asked him casually why he had rarely talked about them when I was growing up. His reply hit me like a bolt:

"My mother was shot and killed by a spurned suitor in the lobby of a hotel in Hot Springs, Arkansas," he said. "The man then shot and killed himself."

I was dumbfounded and yearned to know more. But my questions went unanswered as Pop drifted into sleep, and I never had another opportunity to pursue the subject with him.

Pop, eighty-four, died alone a few days later at a country hospital near his home as Hurricane Camille ravished the Mississippi Gulf Coast with a destructive fury. I felt that the violent storm was an allegory for his troubled life: childhood neglect, his mother's murder, back pain he endured most of his adult life, and his inability to make a better living for his family in the ravages of the Great Depression.

Pop's life was an uphill struggle with few plateaus of optimism. His father had been a prosperous wholesale liquor dealer in Memphis, a brawling river port. Despite the family's wealth, Pop was a street urchin left to his own devices because he was an only child of parents consumed with their business and social status. Street gangs picked on him, he once swam across the raging Mississippi River on a dare, and he endured beatings by priests in Catholic schools. To me, his stories of childhood sounded exciting because they contrasted with my own happy but sheltered upbringing.

Not all his stories were harsh. One day, a crowd gathered around the stage door of the ornate Orpheum Theatre to see Lillian Russell, the celebrated operetta singer. When the great lady emerged in full beauty and glamorous attire, she spotted Pop in the crowd and said, "What a darling red-haired, freckled-face little boy. I am going to give you a dime." She bent down, kissed his blushing forehead, and placed a dime in his palm as the crowd cheered in approval.

But where was his mother as he roamed the streets of the ruffian riverboat city as a young boy? The most vivid portrayal of Pop's parents and one of the few he recounted was his earliest recollections of them arguing, loudly and often. I was told only that Pop was still a child when his parents divorced, that his mother remarried a well-to-do businessman, and that she moved to Chicago. She was a subject hushed up before it could be brought up. Few relatives spoke about her during our long hours reciting family stories even though they knew her personal history well. Pop never mentioned her in any detail. I never met her, and so she remained in my mind a mysterious, ancient ancestor.

After Pop died, I did not want to question Mother during her grief about the mysterious murder, but I wanted to know more about my lineage even if a search of my past kin could possibly produce relations to robbers, gamblers, or prostitutes. When one of my aunts discovered during an earlier genealogical tracing that we were related to a woman hanged in New England for being a witch, she declared the entire process to be corrupt and abandoned the search.

Once I was back in Washington, I kept thinking about my grandmother's tragic end in Hot Springs, and knew I must learn the details, no matter how scathing or gory. Learning more about Pop would help me appreciate the meaning of his life. I was never close to Pop, partly because parents in those times were not friends but authority figures, and probably because he was distant, struggling to cope with his tumultuous past. Yet, despite his anguished upbringing, Pop never faltered. He worked into his seventies, running an ever-shrinking store and delivering wholesale merchandise to other stores in his tiny Corvair. No one ever described Pop as heroic. His stolid sacrifices were expected in a time marked by war and economic upheaval. I regretted that I had never thanked him for all the sacrifices he had made for our family. But I would not have known how to reach beyond his heartache even had I tried.

The next summer, I traveled to Hot Springs to find some answers. My heritage stemmed from a different place: Memphis and the quiet and shrouded villages of the southern Delta, where children were imbued with a strong dose of optimism and self-reliance. This protected childhood had masked my harrowing family history in Hot Springs, so I knew little about the town. The distance from Memphis to Hot Springs is less than two hundred miles, but the two cities could hardly be more different. Memphis, perched on the banks of the Mississippi River, is surrounded by vast floodplains, fertile plantations, muddy rivers, poor black families, and ultraconservative politics. Hot Springs, however, sits in mountains with inhospitable farms, rushing clear rivers, poor white families, and a streak of populism blended with fundamentalist religious sects.

I discovered that at the turn of the twentieth century, Hot Springs was the jewel of the Ozark foothills, a famous spa town that called itself America's Baden-Baden. Nestled in an alluring narrow valley, the town hosted forty-six springs pouring eight hundred thousand gallons of steaming, mineral-infused water each day into bathhouses that promised cures and relief from every disease known to humankind. Railroads penetrated the surrounding forests and brought vacationers, bathers, celebrities, cultured socialites, and industrialists from the East and North who spent money lavishly. It also served as one of the first spring training destinations in the South for many major-league baseball teams including the Boston Red Sox, Brooklyn Dodgers, and New York Highlanders (now the Yankees). Babe Ruth trained there nine times.

Yet even in its rich heyday of the early 1900s, Hot Springs was a raucous frontier town. Posh hotels sat next to saloons and gambling dens. Al Capone had a regular room in the town's most prestigious hotel overlooking the neoclassical and Renaissance-revival bathhouses. Police arrested the New York Giants' manager in Hot Springs for gambling. Several saloons used upstairs rooms as brothels and hideout apartments for gunfighters and hit men. Western-style shootouts were common on the streets. One dispute over the outcome of the 1899 mayoral election took the lives of five men, including the police chief, two officers, and a sheriff's son.

When I visited in 1970, Hot Springs remained a living museum untouched by the present day. Time had forgotten this place, partly because it was surrounded by forests designated as a national park. It was obvious why it had appealed to those seeking a cool summer retreat and soothing mineral vapors when medical science was still in its infancy. Most of the eight massive Gilded Age bathhouses that lined the downtown Central Avenue were now abandoned and closed, but the National Park Service had renovated and reopened one with traditional spa services.

I found a historical account at the public library describing the town's past. The most elaborate drinking establishment was at the entrance to the opera house, where Sarah Bernhardt, Enrico Caruso, and Lillian Russell performed. The report said there were also about fifty less-elaborate saloons and pool halls that catered to "railroad men, cowboys, and the rough-and-tough . . . where the shooting, fistfights and arguments usually took place." An inevitable clash rose between the local, poor, mountain people and the sophisticated, affluent visitors from the North whom they served.

It was in this milieu that Pop's mother, a beautiful woman about thirty years old calling herself Miss Anna Myers, arrived around 1900. Why she moved to Hot Springs was not clear except that she was looking for a new life. She was recently divorced at a time when severed marriages were considered taboo, and she left behind in Memphis her only child, my father, John (Jack)

Norton Herbers, who was twelve years old and in the care of his father, John Alexander Herbers, and Catholic boarding schools.

The chosen last name of Myers was an alias and reflected her scattered and inconsistent past. Census records showed that Anna was the daughter of English-born Joseph Harper and Sarah Blackwell Harper, who married and lived in Memphis. When Anna was seventeen, she married John Alexander Herbers, a union unacceptable to both of the couple's families. The Herbers were staunch Roman Catholics who peddled liquor on the Mississippi riverfront; the Harpers were active Protestants steeped in strict Calvinist traditions who rejected Catholic beliefs and practices. The marriage confirmed that Anna, a dark-haired beauty with translucent skin and fine features, was the family rebel. A year later, Pop was born.

In Hot Springs, Anna easily blended with well-to-do visitors at the spas who enjoyed music, theater, and fine dining. So many prominent wealthy families arrived from Chicago that they established their own private gathering and dining quarters called the Illinois Club, which newspapers described as "palatial." One of the Illinois Club's patrons was a wealthy mining prospector from Chicago, Charles H. Eder, known as an "avid sportsman." Charles and Anna met in Hot Springs and were married, which immediately initiated Anna into the Chicago society set of Hot Springs. She also gained the legitimate name of Anna Eder.

Although my family rarely spoke about her, there were a few sketchy accounts that made it clear that Anna was independent and outgoing and cared little for protocol. One story was that when she and Charles attended a concert in Chicago, the band played "Dixie," and she alone stood and cheered, to the embarrassment of her husband and friends.

Documents in Hot Springs about Anna were as elusive as my relatives' recollections. The county courthouse that once kept data had burned down, and the town library contained nothing about her death. I consulted professional researchers, who were of little help. Like Las Vegas today, the town kept quiet unpleasant behavior, especially among the rich. Even the Illinois Club, where Charles and Anna kept an apartment, had been replaced in the 1940s by a commercial building. The only information I could find on her murder came from yellowed, faded pages of out-of-town newspapers from February 1909. These confirmed her death in graphic detail.

The *Memphis Commercial Appeal* reported in the florid language of the day:

HOT SPRINGS, Ark.—A sensational double tragedy was enacted at
10 o'clock tonight in one of the palatial private cafe apartments of the
Illinois Club, when William Garner, a former officer of the city, shot
and instantly killed Mrs. Charles Eder and fired a 45-caliber bullet
through his own head.

Three shots from a 45-caliber pistol rang out, and M. Goldsmith,
first to reach the scene, found the two bodies lying apart on the deep
carmine rugs, the lifeblood flowing out. Neither spoke after the shots
were fired. The woman was fully dressed, still wearing a veil, gloves
and topcoat when found. She had been fatally shot through the right
lung and bled to death without uttering a word.

Mrs. Charles Eder lived at 135 Central Avenue. Her husband had
been absent from the city about two weeks. He is engaged in mining
enterprises, and was prominent in the sporting world. Garner was 35
years of age, and Mrs. Eder about the same age.

The affair is one of the most sensational that has happened here in
years, and was widely discussed as theater and dance parties heard of
the tragedy.

In Garner's pocket tonight the following blood-stained note was
found:

"Kid—You have fooled the last man you will ever fool. Bury me
alone in some desolate spot.

"Signed: W. P. GARNER.

"P.S.—May God bless and care for my two dear boys."

The next day, another article appeared in the same paper:

HOT SPRINGS, Ark., Feb. 10—"Don't do it, dear. I never meant what
I said." These words, by Mrs. Charles Eder, just after receiving a fatal
shot from a 45-caliber pistol in the hands of William P. Gardner, just
before he turned the weapon on himself and inflicted a fatal wound.

Mrs. Eder died a few minutes after being fired on, and Garner died
this morning at 10 o'clock.

The verdict of the coroner's jury was that Mrs. Eder was killed by
Garner, who afterward committed suicide in a jealous rage. After the
verdict was rendered the bodies were turned over to the relatives for
interment.

Aside from the numerous friends and relatives of the principals, thousands of visitors gathered about the morgue throughout the day.

Mrs. Charles Smith and Miss Edna Wilson, both neighbors of Mrs. Eder, testified at the inquest that Garner often visited her in her apartment, and that he had lately threatened her life when they had quarrels. Mrs. Eder had stated to witnesses that she feared Garner might carry out his threats and end it all in a tragic affair. The coroner's verdict was that Garner killed the woman and himself while crazed with jealousy.

(T)he body of Garner was conveyed this afternoon by his aged father, to rest in the country churchyard, a "desolate place," in accord with the note found on Garner's body after the shooting.

Charles Eder, husband of the woman, was located at Pine Bluff, and arrived tonight to take charge of his wife's body.

Jack Herbers, a young man 20 years of age, is the only son of the dead woman.

The boy was not sent for.

This sensational story of ill repute blurred my mind but explained so much, especially the last sentence, "The boy was not sent for." Anna's sordid affair and devastating end was such an affront to the moral standards of the day that no one summoned Pop. He was the victim of a conspiracy of silence, and I realized that I would never find enough information to judge fully her life and character. I found one letter in Pop's belongings that Anna wrote him from Chicago six months before she died. "My darling boy," she wrote. "I don't like it here for I am alone so much, but if you were here to run around with me to the five-cent theatres it would be alright . . . Lovingly, Mother." Perhaps there was a side to her that I could honor if only her descendants had not been so tightly controlled and fearful of a puritanical society that could bring shame and ruin to our family.

I never knew much about Charles Eder either, but Pop spoke of him as a kind man. For years when we were growing up, Mr. Eder would send packages from Chicago containing a delicious cake or other food we could never afford to buy. He apparently loved Anna deeply because he took her body to Memphis and buried her in the Harper family cemetery plot. A graceful and elaborate marble border circles her body, and a headstone reads:

In Loving Memory
Anna Lilly
wife of
Charles H. Eder
July 17, 1867, Feb. 9, 1909
"He died that we might live."

The final line is from a popular Christian hymn reminding sinners that Jesus died for them so that they might live for righteousness. But did that quotation on the tombstone mean that Mr. Eder thought that his wife died as a sacrifice to appease a sinner who did not deserve her favor? I do not know. I do not even know whether Pop attended the funeral or when he learned the details of her death. In the tenor of the times, it was considered sufficient to say only, "The boy was not sent for."

CHAPTER 2

A Small-Town Cocoon

GRAPHIC REPORTS OF ANNA EDER'S DEATH IN THE LEADING MEMPHIS newspaper must have been humiliating for Pop and his family. The Herbers were German bourgeois who had settled and prospered in Memphis before the Civil War. They were a rich and established family thriving off a boisterous city that claimed the country's highest murder rate. That notoriety was not surprising given the city's violent and turbulent past. Memphis was incorporated in 1826 and was a Confederate military center during the Civil War until the city eventually fell to Union forces despite a failed and bloody raid to recapture it by Confederate General Nathan Bedford Forrest.

During Reconstruction, when the national government was attempting to extend civil liberties and voting rights to freed slaves, mobs of white Memphis citizens went on a rampage, killing forty-six black men, wounding seventy more blacks, and raping five black women. They burned four churches and twelve schools. The raids enraged members of Congress and helped secure passage of the Constitution's Fourteenth Amendment, which sought to ensure equal protection under the law.

During a yellow fever epidemic, at least five thousand Memphis residents died in 1878 alone. Half the city's population fled to escape the illness. A decade later, the city became an industrial center and the national leader for shipping cotton and hardwood. Cotton grown on farms extending from Texas to Virginia was graded and shipped through the Memphis port for worldwide distribution. The city hosted the largest cotton market in the country.

With that trade came a boon to entertainment: vaudeville and concert halls for the well-to-do; saloons and brothels for all classes; and a new form of music from the cotton fields called the "blues" that made W. C. Handy and other performers famous nationally even though the local newspaper derided them as "syncopated chop-suey noise-makers."

By 1900, Memphis had 102,320 residents, half black and half white. Those numbers swelled on Saturdays when farm folk from miles around arrived by wagon and horseback to buy groceries, clothing, and liquor. Protestant cries for prohibition had not yet reached the mid-South in much force, and my grandfather enjoyed a lucrative business selling copious amounts of alcohol from his liquor store. Country folk told their children that when they died, the pearly gates of heaven would open at Memphis along the Mississippi River shoreline.

At the time of Anna's death, Pop was living with his father and working as a salesman for dry goods stores and the American Tobacco Company. I came to learn that the psychic damage to Pop over Anna's death was inestimable, and Pop endured it as an indelible burden for the rest of his life. Shortly after the murder, Pop's father brought his girlfriend home to live with him and Pop. This violation of the marriage bed during a time of arch Victorian standards was considered in the Christian community to be an egregious sin, and the full weight of society's judgment only exacerbated Pop's suffering. Pop was so offended by his father's action that he immediately moved out of the house in protest. Pop's father was so equally offended by this move that he disinherited Pop from his will, leaving his substantial estate to a cousin.

Pop told me about his disinheritance when I was eleven years old as we walked home from his variety store on a red clay road in Somerville, Tennessee. It was during the Depression, and we rented an eighteenth-century house on the edge of town that was held together with wooden pegs and had no plumbing. We also had no car. Our home was half a mile from the store unless we took a shortcut through the town cemetery. On our walk home, I asked him how much the store had taken in that day. He said two dollars and sixty cents. I knew that our house rent was twenty dollars a month, groceries ran even more, and although we raised chickens, a pig, and a cow and planted a large garden, we still could not make ends meet. Why, I asked him, were we so poor? He blamed the economics of the Depression but also explained to me that he had been disinherited. But he left out the most vital information about Anna's death, the falling out with his father, and why he never legally challenged his father's action to claim his inheritance.

When Pop left his father's home, he lived with an aunt in Memphis who persuaded him to abandon the Catholic Church and join the Alabama Street Presbyterian Church, where he sang in the choir. He had Anna's good looks, and he was something of a dandy dresser, changing his shirt in summer several times a day. Life outside his father's home was a new world to him, and he enjoyed it, especially when he met Mabell Clare Foster, a product of a high-society finishing school in Memphis. Mabell Clare was the oldest of seven children born to Bettie Paschall and Andrew Foster, a railroad station manager who prospered in the lumber business.

The Paschalls originally hailed from a proud Kentucky family that produced enough eccentrics to fill a William Faulkner novel. Newton J. Paschall, the patriarch and Mabell Clare's grandfather, lived in Fulton, Kentucky, on the Tennessee border and was a captain in the Confederate army serving in General Forrest's cavalry. During the war, Fulton was divided between supporters of both the Confederacy and the Union even as the town was most often controlled by the Federals. During the height of the war, Captain Newton J. Paschall fell in love with a young woman named Sarah Jane Wilson, who left no doubt where she stood in the divisive war. "Although of immature age, I was very decided in my preference of the political situation," she wrote in her diary. "So with South Carolina blood tingling in my veins, I donned the secession badge. I wore mine pinned on the left breast as the pride of my heart."

Sarah Jane further explained her loyalty in no uncertain terms:

Readers could better understand this hasty rashness could they understand the terrorizing that the people had to suffer for years before in consequence of malice that had been inculcated into the negro minds by malicious anti-slave people until many ignorant negroes thought their only chance for freedom was to kill all the slave owners. Plots and preparations for an uprising of the negroes against the whites being frequently detected gave rise to many untrue rumors that agitated the minds of people in some communities. So they lived in constant dread of what might happen. Hence my aversion to the Republican Party or anything or anybody favoring anti-slavery. And my faith now is that Abe Lincoln and John Brown (of Harper's Ferry, Va.) and many others of like presumptions will reap their reward in the second judgment.

As the war dragged on, neither Captain Paschall nor Miss Wilson wanted to put off their marriage. When Confederate forces withdrew from Fulton in 1864, Captain Paschall devised an elaborate scheme to sneak a contingent of soldiers on horseback through the Union lines to the home of his fiancée. She disguised herself as an old lady in a sunbonnet, and the soldiers ushered her to a nearby county courthouse where Paschall ordered the clerk at gunpoint to issue a marriage license. He also found a preacher brave enough to perform the marriage ceremony on the spot. Federal troops sent out a company of a hundred men to search for Paschall and take his bride as a prisoner. But Paschall secured the services of a gray-haired man with an old white mare to return his bride to her family, and Paschall and his men escaped from enemy territory under the cover of night.

That story became a legend in Fulton. After the war, Paschall earned a medical degree in St. Louis, went back to Fulton as a family doctor, and founded a drug store. The Paschalls reared nine children in a spacious home known for its sumptuous holiday feasts. The Paschall home was described in my ancestors' diaries as having "early red raspberries, peacock feather dusters, cream too thick to pour, turkey gobblers that chased you, deep blue violets very fragrant, and cold biscuits in a jar in the kitchen cabinet." The home also had a former slave the family named Uncle Tom, who was very young when the war ended and stayed on with the family after the war.

My mother, Mabell Clare Foster, the beautiful darling of the Paschall family, was well groomed for a brilliant marriage among high society. Instead, she became a schoolteacher and fell in love with Pop, who proposed marriage. There was nothing unpretentious about the Paschalls, so they were aghast when they learned of Mabell Clare's choice in a future husband. Not only was he the son of a liquor dealer but he was also born a Catholic, a forbidden religious combination in the eyes of the Protestant Paschalls. It didn't seem to matter that Pop was now a Presbyterian with a promising job. Yet perhaps the worst strike against him was his mother's scandalous death, which everyone in Memphis knew about because they had read about it in the newspaper. Pop would not conform to the rigid expectations of marital rites, and the proposal set off vocal opposition from the Paschalls in Memphis and Fulton.

At the same time, Pop's father died of acute lobar pneumonia at the age of sixty-three while in the care of the cousin who inherited his wealth. Pop was advised that, as the only child and closest descendant, he could under

Tennessee law contest the will and win his inheritance. But he declined to do so, knowing that the publicity from the trial would only strengthen the Paschalls' opposition against him. He forsook the money for love. Even with this sacrifice, it took him two years to wear down the Paschalls, and he and Mother were finally married in 1917 among a circle of friends for whom Pop sang and Mother played the piano. As might be expected of the clannish Paschalls, they eventually accepted Pop as part of the family, but I didn't learn all these details until after Pop died from a long-lost Paschall relative I found living in Fulton.

At some point in his career, Pop decided that he could never again work for anyone else. He would pay a price for that decision, for he was highly regarded as a talented worker who knew merchandise and markets. Instead of working for stable employers, he scraped together enough savings to open a variety store outside Memphis. For a while he did well, but the store eventually did not prosper, and my parents moved to Whiteville, Tennessee, a tiny farming town sixty miles east of Memphis. It was a strange decision. He was not an adventurous person, he was averse to change, and he avoided risks. Both Pop and Mother were urban people who knew nothing about small towns, where the economy and culture were attuned to agriculture and a close association of families and neighbors. But retail trade was flourishing in small towns, and Memphis held too many memories for Pop. He was searching for some calm and a sanctuary removed from an upbringing that contributed to his neurosis.

My parents learned that the only profitable days for small-town merchants were Saturdays, when farm folk came to town, and Christmas Eve if the weather was good. After one cold, rainy Christmas Eve with lots of merchandise still on the shelves, Pop reluctantly carried out a promise to sing a solo in church. Paralyzed with his usual stage fright, his performance of "Oh, Beautiful Christmas Eve" sounded "like a sick cow," according to Mother.

By the time my parents had four children, they had established a pattern of moving from one small town to another to open what would eventually become another failing store. Wherever we lived, we always rented houses, some with plumbing, but all with wood stoves for heating and cooking. Mother constantly complained that the sinks were always too high for women of average height because they had been designed by men who never bothered to consult the women who used them.

We were always on the brink of bankruptcy because of Pop's mismanagement, expansion overreach, or economic conditions beyond his control. If one of us had a serious illness, my father begged the doctors to reduce their fees. He also begged wholesalers to give him credit with no proof he could pay them. My parents could not afford to buy me more than one pair of shoes each year, so I wore no shoes in the summer.

Mother flourished in these small-town settings. She was a gregarious woman, polished in the social graces, and endeared herself to people in all walks of life, including the town's ruling matriarchs. She was an active member in the women's circles of afternoon teas and church auxiliaries. She often found time to counsel troubled poor people, black and white, who sought her out in the store. Pop had no life outside his work, the church, and the vegetable garden that reduced our grocery bills. I do not remember our parents ever hosting or going to a dinner party, although Mother would have liked nothing better.

Pop was extremely jealous of Mother, becoming deeply disturbed if she seemed too friendly with another man, although no one else would suspect her of infidelity. He had chronic back problems no doctor could diagnose. He had all his teeth pulled, thinking that would solve the problem, but the pain persisted, and in his forties, in the depths of the Great Depression, he suffered a nervous breakdown. But he was very good at concealing his psychological state, and despite his health problems and hypochondria, he never missed a day's work. In my eyes, he was a kind and loving father who had the respect of our relatives and was liked by all the merchants on the town square.

He spent long hours listening to classical music on the radio, and he had a sense of humor that broke the monotony of his pain. In one store, he noticed that a mouse he named Oscar would habitually run by his cash register and then emerge moments later on a pipe along the ceiling. If a customer noticed Oscar by the cash register, Pop would say, "That's Oscar. Oscar, you run on upstairs now." Then he would point to the ceiling, and the customer would be amused to see Oscar scampering along the pipe to the attic. On Saturdays, almost everyone came to town in wagons, trucks, and automobiles to shop and socialize. Although there were rigid differences between class and race, Saturdays in Pop's store allowed a grand mixing of every type of person.

Not all families were the same, but the so-called "good white families" usually treated their black servants in what they thought was a humane and generous manner. But these families never questioned why blacks were assigned only menial jobs and entered a white home only through the back door. Instead, they adhered to a biblically based belief that blacks were innately inferior and were willed by God to be servants. As children, we were taught not to question those habits and beliefs.

Everyone abided by a strict community standard. Elizabeth Spencer, a novelist who grew up in Carrollton, Mississippi, wrote in her 1998 memoir, *Landscapes of the Heart*, that her family's beloved cook was severely beaten by a white man whose wife accused the cook of being disrespectful to her on the street. The family quietly arranged to get the cook out of town to protect her but made no effort to see that her attackers were punished. Spencer wrote that seeing the beaten cook was the greatest horror she had ever experienced.

My family had no black servants, and we children never knew of any physical cruelty to black people. We never read a local newspaper, but even if we had, we would not have found reference to the lynchings that were occurring throughout the South. Nor would we have read about cruelties or unfairness toward blacks in our textbooks at school. And we most certainly would not hear about this from the white church pulpits. I learned only after I became a newspaper reporter in the 1950s that lynchings had occurred near the small towns where we lived.

Although we brushed shoulders daily with blacks and they shopped in numbers in our stores, they were largely nonexistent in our social life, education, and religion. The schools were segregated so we never attended school with black children. What little we knew of their ringing spirituals and blues songs came to us from the radio. It was not until the beginning of the civil rights movement and the publication of classic novels like Ralph Ellison's *Invisible Man* that blacks became of interest to southern whites. As a child, I was unaware that for blacks, the barriers erected and maintained by whites were a daily obsession dating back to slavery. We were never taught how their lives were shaped even though they nursed us, cleaned our houses, washed and ironed our clothes, and performed menial tasks all over town. I would not know how they really felt about us until the civil rights movement burst on the scene in the 1950s.

The differences among the residents of our small southern towns were not just racial. Mother exhorted me never to play with white boys from the "wrong part of town," where the poverty was deeper than ours and where there was more domestic violence, rough language, and fundamentalist religion. Because there were no private schools, all the white children in the area attended school together, no matter their economic standing. As town kids, we learned that country kids were different. Some were so poor that they frequently wore clothing made of flour sacks and brought lunches in paper bags containing nothing but greasy cornbread.

Mother preferred that we play with black children rather than "poor whites" who could infect us with the courser aspects of their culture. On one day, a black boy whom I knew from the store took me to his family's humble shack, where his mother earned the family's income by washing and ironing clothes for whites. He and I drank water from his well and helped light the kerosene lamps, the only source of light after dark. On another day, I visited the home of a rich white boy and was served lemonade and cookies on the veranda. We were poor, but nothing as poor as the country children. My family's lack of money never barred us from being accepted by genteel whites—landowners, merchants, doctors, lawyers, ministers of the mainline Protestant churches, and public officials—who formed the top layers of society. Manners were what defined the boundaries among the white families, and Mother was more than adequately endowed with those virtues.

One factor that unified the entire community was the Great Depression. Week by week, year by year, it smothered us and punished everyone we knew. It gnawed at virtually every aspect of life. When the banks suddenly closed, the price of cotton and other commodities plummeted. The public schools could not pay the teachers, who nevertheless continued teaching for near-worthless scrip. I would walk to the train station and see jobless men jumping from freight cars to beg for food at every house. I never saw one turned away. When these men moved on to unknown destinations, more would take their places. Most came from the cities and industrial areas, where the conditions were worse than in our towns because every household had a garden or knew a farmer who had livestock and grain at a decent price. I remember Mother crying in the kitchen after she fed a hungry seventeen-year-old lad at the back door of our house and heard how he'd left his home in the city to fruitlessly search for a job elsewhere.

Pop said we were more fortunate than many people during the Depression, but I think he was being overly optimistic. He did not have enough money in the bank to lose much, and he had a store stocked with merchandise all bought on credit. When customers could not pay their bills, he extended them credit, meaning less income for our family. Many times, we had to find cheaper housing. When we first arrived in Somerville, we lived in a modest house with indoor plumbing on a prominent street near the town square. But as the Depression tightened its grip in 1932, Pop found a cheaper house of edge of town with peeling paint built long before the Civil War.

The owner fixed it up enough to be inhabited, but he left so many open cracks that our wood stove could not keep the house warm on the coldest days. The owner also built a privy in the backyard and ran a water line one hundred feet short of our back door. The cost of running the water line to the house was prohibitive, and Pop never complained to the owner. It was our only source of water, and as the family's only boy, I carried buckets of water each day to the house and vegetable garden. Children clearly have different standards of comfort than adults, so I never really considered us to be poor. Although we called our home "the Shack," my memory of the place recalls beauty and enjoyment. There were enormous oaks shading a yard that extended into a countryside of fields, forests, swimming holes, and blackberry patches.

So scarce was my family's cash flow that our parents were forever inventing ways to make and save money. Pop had an overproductive cow, and Mother would make gallons of custard thickened with Junket tablets. On Saturday, we would buy a fifty-pound block of ice, chip it into a ten-gallon freezer, and take turns churning ice cream. Then we delivered it six blocks in my red wagon to the store, where we sold two small ice cream cones for a nickel. My wagon was put to many other economic uses, although not all with a profitable outcome. When Pop discovered that he could buy pancake syrup in little cans shaped like log cabins cheaper by the gross through the mail, my sister Sarah Frances and I scurried to the post office and stacked the cans high on my wagon and headed for home. As we sped around a corner, the cans toppled off into a ditch. So many of the cans ended up in the ditch—looking like a great storm had wrecked a miniature town—that we tossed the remaining cans down as well. Our friends showed up to join the game in peals of laughter, ignoring the astonished stares of adults.

It was a hard life for my parents, who were constantly overworked and never took a vacation until all the children were grown. But they always found a way to provide the necessities and love to sustain us. Mother endured it all with grace and good humor. Although we had little material wealth, we had an abundance of adventures. At a tender age, we children roamed the town and countryside at will, and there seemed to be no boundaries to our freedoms. We explored fields and forests for miles around without telling anyone where we were going. We staked out swimming holes, chopped Christmas trees, and picked blackberries and plums wherever we wanted and were never rebuked by property owners or our parents.

When there were barriers to our freedom, we relished in testing them. One cold Sunday afternoon my eldest sister Emily and I found a swimming hole covered with ice. Of course, we skated on it, and Emily, being heavier than I, fell through. I plunged into the icy water and helped her out. We ran a mile back home with teeth chattering and icicles forming on our clothes. But no pneumonia; no colds; no lectures. Only a roaring fire to warm us and a forgiving mother. Children were expected to do things like that.

In one small town, we lived beside a large field of clover with shade trees. In summer, when we never wore shoes, we would run through the field, where hundreds of bees feasted on the clover. Screams of pain would arise and we would flee home, where Mother administered wet baking soda. But I never remember being admonished or told not to go through that field barefooted. It was simply, "Watch for the bees," a warning soon forgotten.

One day, some of the boys in school invited me to play hooky and spend the day at a creek running through isolated woods a mile from town. It was early spring, and the willows were beginning to show the first signs of green. The creek was gurgling with clear water so cold we could not stay submerged for very long, so we played naked on the rocks and warmed our bodies dry in the sunshine. By the time we got home, everyone in town knew where we had been. The next day, we had our reckoning. Our teacher, the prettiest in the school, took us one by one into the hall and administered the usual corporal punishment. She ordered me to lean over and grasp my ankles. Then, with both hands, she gave me six or seven licks with a board, but not hard enough to really hurt. When I returned to the classroom, I could see the admiration on the faces of my classmates, even those of the bullies who had forced me to fight in the schoolyard. The custom was that if you got a spanking at school, you would get another at home, but my parents thought I had been punished enough. It was a glorious experience.

Another lesson taught at an early age was the benefit of work, and I was employed in Pop's store when I could barely see over the counter. At my lunch break on Saturday, Pop would give me fifteen cents to buy a bowl of soup, milk, and a piece of pie at the café. At the end of the day he would pay my wages: one dime. I also worked at a friend's farm on the edge of town, where his father raised sweet potatoes. During planting time, my friend and

I were hired to place the tender seedlings at one-foot intervals in rows of freshly plowed earth. The work required only a limber back and a tolerance for tedium. I earned seven and a half cents an hour. There was no explanation for the half cent except that it could put you over the threshold for a small purchase. Two hours of work meant fifteen cents: a dime for an *Our Gang* movie, which were the only films Mother would permit us to see until we were in our teens, and a nickel for a double popsicle. At the end of an eight-hour day, I would have sixty cents to squander on all kinds of pleasures.

My friend's father owned a dairy and, in the evening after a long day of work, we would load milk into an old Plymouth for delivery. We boys would stand on the running board and, at every stop, run the milk in quart glass bottles to the front doors and bring back empty bottles for the next day. I received no money for this. My pay was the privilege of standing on the running board at dusk and feeling the warm air blow in my hair as we zipped down gravel roads while the stars came out.

It was an innocent and simple world that many families today try to replicate by educating children at home or barring them from television and other access to the real world. But despite their efforts, they can never completely re-create the cocoon of our safe and insular society. Because ours was a sheltered world, we learned about independence and self-reliance as soon as we could walk. There was little pampering or handholding. I do not remember my parents or older sisters ever reading books to me. I went through twelve years in school without my parents ever questioning me about my mediocre grades because there was never any promise of education for us beyond public high school. For play, I was turned loose on the town as long as I did not become involved with the rowdies on the other side of the tracks. Nothing reined in my sense of freedom or curiosity for exploration.

CHAPTER 3

Spilled Seed

SUMMER WAS REVIVAL TIME, AND PEOPLE TURNED OUT IN LARGE NUM-
bers for the evening church services featuring traveling evangelists to excite
the crowds. Even to a twelve-year-old boy, the services were never dull. I
remember most vividly a swarthy preacher who illustrated his sermons with
magic, or chemistry, although I never knew which. He would place a bowl
piled high with a white substance on the altar, dowse it with a flammable
liquid, and light it. When the flames died, the bowl contained a black mound.
Then he would spray it with another liquid, and the mound again would
become as white as snow. The lesson was about sin and redemption. We boys
were more interested in how he did the trick with the bowl than his spiritual
message. But the visual image was so stark that the message remained with
me for years whenever temptations arose.

There were many things to tempt us, especially in a community where
people rigidly believed in sin and set up barriers intended to keep us from
approaching it. Unlike our cousins in Memphis, we were not allowed to
play with "spot cards," which were originally devised for gambling. Folk
and square dancing, especially one dance called "the Big Apple," a national
craze, was allowed. But "clinch dancing," as the name describes, was never
tolerated. Alcoholic beverages, including beer and wine, were considered a
path to destruction of the soul. My first awareness of liquor was when we
rented a house that had previously belonged to a bootlegger. We found a
trapdoor in the floor directly below my bed that led to a secret, yet empty,
cache. One night a man knocked at our front door looking to buy a bottle
of moonshine, and the neighbors talked about it excitedly for days. I learned
later in life that some young men in our towns would make occasional visits

to Memphis whorehouses, that some adults had drunken parties, and that some husbands and wives cheated on each other. But news of those indiscretions never leaked down to children.

As I grew older, real-world influences penetrated my small-town life, including popular songs we heard on a radio that Pop managed to acquire during the Depression. When he first turned it on, the entire neighborhood packed into our living room, eager to hear the voices and songs from distant places. But the only sound we heard was static. So Pop strung a long wire high in the oak trees of our yard and connected it to the radio. Music flowed in like magic from WMC in Memphis more than fifty miles away. The lyrics enticed me the most, suggesting a life far away that I hoped someday I might know. Paul Small, with the George Olsen Orchestra, crooned a sentimental fox-trot tune that was at the top of the charts. The words by Irving Berlin played over in my head for so long that some are still in my memory:

Say it isn't so.
Everywhere I go
Everyone I know
Whispers that you're growing tired of me.
Say it isn't so.

I envisioned some faraway smoky nightspot filled with mystery and awe. Why is he so sad? Who is the "you"? Why doesn't he just ask her if she loves him? The song conjured images of what delicious sadness in the world awaited me.

The arrival of adolescence changed my perception of our idyllic small towns. The uncompromising enforcement of Victorian mores that carried over into the twentieth century allowed no outlet for sexual passions other than sublimation: "Go out and play, get your mind on something else." I tried that by holding on to the adventures of childhood and crafting stories of fantasy and imagination. The mere act of walking home from school was ripe for creative adventure. Each day I passed a decaying, vine-covered mansion under giant oaks that I called the Cathouse because so many cats crept around the grounds. Everyone in town knew that the aged spinster who lived there alone was an artist who had studied and worked in New York, returning home in her later years with her paintings, which she never sold because her mother had forbidden such crass transactions. She was a recluse whom we feared, and it was a thrill to pass her fascinating house and speculate on the horrors that must certainly lurk inside.

The town cemetery was a little out of the way but worth the detour to visit the ancient dead. Several Confederate generals were reputed to be buried there, but it was difficult to confirm how many because the decayed tombstones were covered in moss and the dense overgrowth of crooked branches. But the stories I created about those resting there made a spooky scene that rivaled the Cathouse.

The next stop was my father's store, where I had easy access to the candy displayed behind glass that was sold loose by the pound. I am sure Pop never made a profit on his candy sales due to my consumption alone. But no one ever mentioned it, any more than they did my pimples and crooked teeth, which everyone considered something to be ignored or outlived and never something that could be prevented or fixed. My sugar intake ignited my energies, not for homework or reading but for more adventure.

Two blocks from home, there was an antebellum brick house with tall columns where a stooped old lady named Mrs. Washington lived alone except for her servants. Not much was known in town about her except that she owned an expensive black limousine driven by a black chauffeur in uniform. A heavy iron fence around her garden and orchard was a challenging obstacle to climb, but one day I scaled it to pick the jonquils that bloomed there in profusion. Mrs. Washington caught me and was not forgiving. She ordered her chauffeur to follow me in the limousine as I ran home clutching the flowers while she berated me from the back seat of the car. Fortunately, Mother was not at home, and I was soon safely inside free from Mrs. Washington's ire. As her car sped away, I went outside and began banging tennis balls against the clapboards of the house, burning my sugar and loosening nails and flakes of paint.

By age sixteen, I was ready to give up childish wanderings. I was exceedingly shy with no social life beyond Sunday school. There was a girl in my class who was very pretty, but she was the daughter of a mill worker who lived in a run-down part of town and therefore was not part of the class-conscious circle of our friends. She was a girl my mother would have forbidden. One day during class, I somehow found the courage to ask her to go with me to the high school dance. Without offering an excuse, she simply said, "No."

I could feel the blush on my cheeks and the familiar sense of humiliation. After school, I hurried straight to the last house on our street, surrounded only by fields of bitter weeds and eroded gullies. The sensation that washed over me in that scene of desolate nature is so vivid in my conscience that I feel compelled to tell it even though it is deeply personal. I was taught a verse in the Bible forbidding a man to spill his seed on the ground. Pop also instructed me not to spill any seed at all, that to do so would lead to mental illness, insanity, and other dire conditions. Yet these prohibitions from God, my father, and even the *Boy Scout Handbook* somehow stimulated me to do exactly the opposite. I seeded the gullies, the bitter weed fields, and the roots of the chinaberry tree. I seeded the dirt floor of the basement, the lawn, and the vegetable garden. Each act ended with a surge of shame. Yet each lecture only brought the desire for more seeding.

It was an act of rebellion and an experience in alienation sought by non-conformists who need places to hide, particularly when they are constantly subjected to scorn or rejection. This was especially true in rural towns, where admonitions were so strongly pronounced and enforced that misfits could not escape into anonymity as they could in a city. Shy outsiders, more than gregarious types, were reminded daily of the sins for which they should feel ashamed.

This may explain, at least in part, why so many southerners of my generation from tight little communities became journalists in later life. We tended to be social exiles as youths and found it difficult to blend into the popular circles. We were accustomed to being outside observers removed from the crowd. I believe that surges of shame and feelings of inferiority make one more sensitive to the hurts of others. Douglas Kneeland, a wise reporter and editor for the *New York Times* and the *Chicago Tribune*, was a product of small-town Maine who once said that most newspaper reporters are the kind of people who cry in movies, not the hard-boiled stereotype that many people envision. Combine that sensitivity with a distrust of conventional wisdom, a scrutiny bred by popular but outlandish fundamentalism teaching that every word of the Bible is literally true, and you have the prototype of a southerner like me drawn into journalism.

I didn't know as a teenager that I would become a journalist. But my upbringing bred self-reliance, individualism, and optimism—the very traits I would later rely upon professionally to question authoritarian standards and personally reject the same place that produced these character traits. Small-town culture taught me that there was little in life I could not accomplish or master no matter how large or complicated. That environment encouraged me to believe that life beyond the small town had more to offer than it could take away. I was not daunted by complexity or ambiguity. Sometimes my laid-back style hindered my ability to compete in a larger, fast-paced world, but I gained an extra advantage in always finding a silver lining even when there was none. Small-town America nurtured a keen sense of security and tranquility that would endure far into adulthood. I came to believe in the unexpected powers of fate and circumstance, and, in a strange twist, I learned that Anna's death was a blessing for me. If Pop had not been disinherited, I probably would have grown up in comfortable privilege in Memphis and much more likely to conform to the societal structures associated with being a businessman or merchant. I doubt I would have become a journalist, the outlier who is always asking why.

As a teenager, I found no cure for my constant desire to know more about the wider world beyond my town. In high school, I had the opportunity to attend a church youth conference in the big city of Memphis, where I stayed with my relatives and learned that they inhabited a completely different world. For instance, my uncle talked about taking his family on a vacation to California. Most families in our town never took vacations. I borrowed a tweed suit from my cousin and rode on the Memphis trolley to the church conference. When I arrived, I was shocked to learn that the other teenagers were using their parents' cars to skip the conference and cruise around the city to night spots and restaurants. This behavior was something beyond my imagination. In my town, we had no night spots or restaurants and very few cars.

One of those rebellious teens was a girl named Betty Wood, the daughter of a prominent engineer and city leader. I didn't know that girls like Betty existed in life. She was an extrovert who thought nothing of slipping into the fanciest downtown department store to buy a bangle of bracelets and charge the purchase to her father's credit account. She jangled them in my face as we returned to her father's car to join the other teens. I returned home smitten with Betty and determined to design a larger life for myself even though I had no plan how to achieve that. It wasn't long after my trip to Memphis that influences larger than I ever conceived would arrive to dictate my destiny.

CHAPTER 4

Lessons of War

IN EVERY WAR, THE VERY YOUNG ARE SENT TO FIGHT LONG BEFORE THEY
have reached maturity. If they survive, they either become wise at an early age
or physically and mentally impaired for life. In my case, war was the agent
that jarred me from my isolated existence.

The afternoon of December 7, 1941, was, at first, as boring and leisurely as
any Sunday. We lived in Brownsville, Tennessee, and Mother and my younger
sister, Mary Betty, had barely cleared the noontime dinner table when we
heard a radio broadcast about the attack on Pearl Harbor that forced the
United States to finally enter World War II. I was a senior in high school and
an easy mark for the draft that would ultimately be instated. We were all filled
with instant patriotism and anger at the Japanese. But I was also interested
in making the basketball team, so I spent my afternoons practicing goals at
the high school with no thought of going to war.

As the school year droned on, my teachers grew apprehensive about the
draft, but I was still unfazed. I made the basketball team and took typing and
history classes, the latter taught by an octogenarian lady with dyed frizzy hair
who led us through the glorious rise of the British Empire but never reached
the twentieth century. Only at my graduation in May did I sense that my life
was about to be changed forever.

In the summer of 1942, as many of my friends began leaving for war, I
became upset that I might not be accepted in the army because I was terribly
skinny. I wasn't eager to serve as a soldier, but I had no idea what I wanted
to do with my life. My high school grades were not exceptional, and I had
no desire to go to college even if my parents could have afforded to send me.
The worst future I could imagine was staying in Brownsville, so I volunteered

for enlistment and soon found myself in an induction station in Alabama. A military doctor in the examination room, seeking to cheer me up, looked at my naked, skinny body and said, "You are going to make a good soldier."

I was eventually assigned to a cannon company of a Mississippi National Guard unit that had been federalized early in the war. The noncommissioned officers were mostly Mississippians, but the ranks were filled with draftees from as far away as New York. It was my first time to meet a real Yankee.

We were scheduled to go to Europe, so they issued us winter clothes and sent us on maneuvers in the snow-covered West Virginia mountains to prepare for cold-weather fighting. Once we completed our training, however, the army changed its mind. They took back our woolens, issued us khakis, and shipped us to the South Pacific by a converted banana boat named the *Adabelle Lykes*. The boat was so slow it took us six weeks to get to New Guinea by way of the Panama Canal. This was the adventure I had longed for, and I absorbed all the new intoxicating sounds and smells.

At the same time, I was extremely homesick. I received a letter from Pop saying that he was writing from the store on a Sunday "in order to be with you." It was the first time he ever expressed a desire to be closer to me. In the letter, he recalled my job as his clerk and how he wanted me to join him to run the store when I returned home. I could never bear to tell him that the prospect of doing that filled me with dread.

Among the letters were many from Betty, whom I had stayed in touch with after our first meeting in Memphis. She was in college and wrote about her contributions to the war effort by attending soldier reception dances and working as a candy striper nursing assistant. I wrote back to her about my training and travels. I yearned to hear more from her even though it was difficult to relate to her life and experiences, which were so different from mine.

After settling in New Guinea, we moved from island to island securing airbases as the Allies under General Douglas MacArthur encroached on territory previously claimed by Japan. Because our 105-millimeter cannons were ill suited for jungle warfare, we were mostly a rifle company. It wasn't long before the reality of war's hardships settled in. The Japanese, who were in retreat as American forces moved in, seemed to be less of an enemy than the jungle rot, a chronic skin lesion on our hands and arms. Our skin also turned yellow from the Atabrine tablets we took to combat malaria. Our captain was a gung-ho, ramrod-straight Baptist preacher from Mississippi who, when there were no Japanese to fight, had us digging ditches or performing chores to keep us in fighting shape. We suffered casualties from airborne Japanese bombs and, sadly, from friendly fire, when one patrol mistook another for the enemy. But we were spared the kind of bloody battles that wiped out whole units of Americans in Europe and parts of the South Pacific.

In fact, our job was to show evidence that Americans were taking and occupying patches of land as part of a production staged by the war's most ingenious public relations manager, MacArthur, who showed up at our bases with great fanfare to demonstrate to the world that we were winning the war. One day, we were lined in formation as MacArthur arrived, standing erect in his jeep and chomping on his signature oversize corncob pipe. He drove by saluting to us with a clip of his hand from the trademark crush cap he had designed to his specifications. The military cap was enormous and adorned with two sets of gold appliqué leaves—one on the bill and the second on the cap's high peak. Above the appliqué was a giant gold eagle. The general was always followed by a gaggle of photographers, news reporters, and filmmakers.

On another occasion, MacArthur joined us as we took a series of islands from our Higgins landing crafts. He waded into the water with us, thrusting his rifle above his head and barking orders to advance. The islands were not heavily fortified, so the seizures were more of a stunt for the cameras and reporters than a bona fide advance of force. There were other times, however, when we advanced with MacArthur at our side on islands where the enemy lurked.

One of those islands was Morotai, part of what was then the Dutch East Indies between New Guinea and the Philippines. That was where, for the first time, I entered the adult world of mental maturity. I am appalled when I reflect on my ignorance at the time. I had no idea that Nazi Germany was slaughtering its own Jewish citizens. I also did not know what was happening with the war in other parts of the world or what was going on in the United States, except for occasional mail from home.

We landed on Morotai, under cover of heavy naval bombardment, led by MacArthur, and we soon took a beachhead from the Japanese, who moved their main forces to the mountains. Our forces were dispersed in encampments, but at nightfall a Japanese plane came overhead and dropped a scattering of bombs. Two of my friends were killed. With the Japanese forces undefeated, I realized that I, too, might die and thought long and hard about it, especially during those nights on Morotai when planes roared over and we retreated to bunkers. One night, while on guard staring into the dark jungle to detect any Japanese preparing to make a sneak attack, I had an epiphany. Drawing on my Presbyterian background and the doctrine that a person belongs to God forever in both life and death, I suddenly accepted the reality that I was prepared to die. I have never since feared death.

I also learned on that island about the dark side of humanity. The few Japanese on our island who fled to the mountains were no longer a threat, but, for reasons never explained to us, we were sent out in patrols to find and kill them. We had been thoroughly conditioned both as civilians and as soldiers to believe that all Japanese were subhuman and evil. It is now hard to believe how easily we were persuaded to accept that biased fallacy. But we were brainwashed to believe that the enemy was wicked.

Once we reached the mountains, we sat in scattered pairs and waited for the enemy to appear. I was with a soldier whose name I do not remember. We had been sitting quietly for a long time when suddenly we saw an emaciated Japanese soldier with a rifle slung over his shoulder idly walking through the bushes. We raised our carbines. My companion fired first but I followed immediately, and the soldier slumped dead to the ground. Our sergeant appeared, and we searched the body. A wallet and photos fell out of the Japanese soldier's pocket. One picture showed a smiling woman and happy children, obviously his family left behind, with an appealing rural scene in the background. We left the body as it was and returned to our outpost, where we received congratulations from the officers.

That scene haunted me for a long time. We had the means on that island to impound prisoners, but our superiors never told us to harbor the enemy, even when my comrade and I could have easily overtaken this enemy soldier. What was it about war that precluded any concern for the innocent relatives of our enemy? Was it a matter of racial hatred on our part? Was it necessary to indoctrinate us with hatred when our cause was just? These questions kept rolling through my head, and I was terrorized by the memory of my actions. This was not something I could talk about to my family, friends, or the chaplain, given the ferocity of feelings toward the Japanese. And many soldiers I knew simply didn't talk about the horrors of the war, especially when those in Europe had suffered much more harrowing experiences. We just wanted to move beyond it. So, I started reading, hoping to gain a general knowledge to help me in my quest even if there were no direct answers to my questions.

It was surprising how many books were available, although little demanded, to peripatetic infantry as the war was winding down. Someone in our armed forces believed that the millions of men and women in the military should not be sent back to civilian society without a modicum of learning. I found an abundance of classic novels and even textbooks. With increasing amounts of downtime as the war neared an end, I had lots of time to read, and I discovered the joy of learning. My incessant reading caused me, for the first time, to yearn to go to college with hopes that my meager army savings would pay the way. What I didn't know was that the GI Bill of Rights, a landmark piece of legislation, would pay my tuition and board at the university of my choice.

CHAPTER 5

The Mystery of Mississippi

AS I RETURNED HOME TO ATTEND EMORY UNIVERSITY IN ATLANTA, MY chief interest was studying contemporary novels and short stories. But my early attempts at fiction writing were not promising, so I turned to journalism as the poor cousin of the literary life, even though the thought of being a newspaperman as depicted in the movies frightened me: too much bravado and disorder for my introverted nature. I soon learned from first-class professors that journalism, even at small newspapers, could be a high calling of public service, and that was attractive to me. I majored in journalism and wrote on the university newspaper, where another student, Claude Sitton, was an editor. I graduated from Emory excited about my prospects as I headed to Mississippi, a destination I chose because my parents had retired there, and I needed to help support them.

But I was completely unprepared, despite my upbringing in southern orthodoxy, for what lay ahead as I rode a Greyhound bus into Mississippi in the summer of 1949. The state had the nation's highest percentage of blacks and the highest rates of poverty and illiteracy. It also possessed other features that made it unique. More than any other southern state, ultraconservative Mississippi bred a political philosophy that rewarded acid-tongued race baiters and tolerated naked oppression and lynchings.

It had not always been a bastion of racial suppression. In the early 1800s, Mississippi was a stronghold of Jacksonian democracy, which empowered the independent farmer, and a leader in extending the ballot to the general population. But that changed between 1830 and 1850, as vast new farmland was cultivated. Landowners relied so heavily on slaves for agricultural production that race became the dominant theme in all things southern. After the Civil War, a series of congressional Reconstruction acts nullified southern state governments and allowed all adult males, black or white, to vote. Mississippi had its first biracial election in 1867, and more blacks than whites registered to vote. The state elected at least 226 blacks to public office during Reconstruction, including two black US senators. However, this period lasted less than ten years with the rise of white supremacy and a constitutional convention in 1890 during which the state constitution was amended to require blacks to pay a poll tax and take a literacy test in order to "reduce the Negro majorities to a negligible political quantity." It worked so well that blacks, who made up 60 percent of the voters in Mississippi in 1890, had become less than 10 percent of the electorate by 1899. By the early 1900s, the state was electing leaders like Governor Theodore Bilbo, nicknamed "the Man" because he referred to himself in the third person, who was an outspoken white supremacist and a member of the Ku Klux Klan (KKK). He also ran as a candidate promoting a populist platform of tax reforms and compulsory school attendance; he went on to become a US senator.

Racism continued to have a firm foothold in the state. A year before I graduated from Emory, Mississippi governor Fielding Wright ran for US vice president with a new political party, the States' Rights Democratic Party (the Dixiecrats), which splintered from the national Democratic Party when it nominated Harry S. Truman for president and embraced a civil rights platform. Wright called racial segregation an "eternal truth" and told blacks to move to another state if they wanted the same treatment as whites.

The large populations of blacks in Mississippi, whose ancestors had been slaves, lived in a sealed, separate society from the stern white ruling class, and the academic teachings at Emory, one of the South's leading universities, had not prepared me for potential conflict. I remember only one fleeting occasion when a faculty member suggested that the deep South might be on a collision course due to its stubborn adherence to blanket discrimination against blacks. Certainly, the gathering storm clouds must have been known in academic circles. Gunnar Myrdal's *An American Dilemma*, a voluminous and prognostic study of racial intolerance in the South, had been in wide circulation since 1944. But there was no mention of this in my sociology and history classes. Emory had no courses on African American studies or literature. The one mention of what might lie ahead was made by Calvin Kytle, a liberal professor who wrote about Georgia's corrupt politics and segregationist stance in national magazines. In a journalism course, he challenged us to think about the South's oppression of "Negroes," as blacks were universally called then. But this was not on my mind as I headed toward Mississippi. I could have never anticipated that this place would drastically change my own sense of identity while becoming a springboard for my career.

I assumed I was returning to my roots of southern small towns, where life went on without disruption as it had since the previous century. I didn't know that in large urban centers such as Atlanta, black leaders cognizant of Myrdal's writings were beginning to question the South's blatant discrimination in both law and practice.

I arrived in Mississippi with five dollars in my pocket and no prospects for a job. I hitchhiked through the state, calling on daily papers in search of employment. The only reporter job I found was at the *Morning Star*, a new daily newspaper in Greenwood, a conservative town of eighteen thousand people in the heart of the rich Delta cotton farmland and 125 miles south of Memphis.

I was paid $42.50 a week to report local news, select national and foreign stories from the wire service, edit copy, write headlines, and correct proofs. When the printer showed up drunk, I laid out the lead type in the chase to be put on the press. Sometimes we "put the paper to bed" at 1:00 a.m., just in time to sleep and start all over again the next morning. For one Christmas edition of the paper, I worked as the only editor and city reporter.

Except for crime news, almost all my dispatches were about whites and distributed among white readers, even though most of the town's residents were black. I gave little thought to this lopsided representation. I was more offended by an occasional order from the publisher to censor the news. For example, when a prominent department store owner shot and killed himself in his home, I was instructed to write only that he died suddenly because everyone in town knew by word of mouth all the details of his suicide.

I quickly learned the power of the press. One day, several white women from a working-class white neighborhood came into our newspaper office to complain that the city school board was allocating more money to schools in wealthy neighborhoods than to theirs. I wrote a story about the unequal spending, and it created enough of an uproar that the school board eventually revised its funding policy. Yet it never occurred to me or any other white person in town to question that if the board was shortchanging schools for poor whites, it was most certainly giving even less to the all-black schools.

Everyone knew that was the way it had always been, and both rich and poor whites thought it entirely proper.

It took a while for me to acclimate to Mississippi. I both hated and adored the place. Its raw natural beauty was succinctly captured by the Mississippi author Eudora Welty in her novel *Delta Wedding* in which a nine-year-old girl arrives in the Mississippi Delta in 1923 aboard a train called the Yellow Dog:

> And then, as if a hand reached along the green ridge and all of a sudden pulled down the hill and every tree in the world and left cotton fields, the Delta began. . . . The land was perfectly flat and level but it shimmered like the wing of a lighted dragonfly.

I traveled along the same route as the Yellow Dog, noticing the stark contrast between this massive elliptical floodplain and the state's hill country in the north. Many years later, I wrote about the brooding Delta, originally part of the Cherokee nation, in my own richly romantic terms, trying to capture the eerie essence of halted time:

> April is a time of anticipation. The dark soil lies naked to the spring sky, awaiting the seed that in one growing season can make the owner rich or plunge him deeper into debt. The willows along the bayous are in full leaf. The vetches and other winter ground cover are dark green, as are the distant forests. The rivers run a deep gray. There are few pastels in the Delta; the dark shades signify a richness that makes the Delta's inhabitants reckless entrepreneurs while people in the hardscrabble hills pinch pennies and cling to puritanical ways.

But the Delta was richer in possessions and creeds than in its ageless dirt. Elizabeth Spencer wrote in her memoir:

> Behavior and manners came to us from an eighteenth-century code of life. People in Carrollton often seem to have stepped out of Jane Austen. Authorities from the past stood in austere ranks—the Bible, the Romans, the Greeks. Our finest houses looked like classical temples. Our lawyers quoted Cicero. Our ministers knew Hebrew.

In the 1950s, both the Delta and the adjacent hill country were trying to hold onto the eighteenth century. In Corinth, a barren town in the northeast corner of the state, I witnessed a young woman dressed like a pioneer in a gray bonnet and long dress of rustic cloth crossing a crowded street while nursing a baby, her white breast glistening in the sun. It was a scene that seemed an apparition from the past. The eroded hills, where generations of farmers tried to grow cotton and corn only to fall deeper into poverty, gave way to the deep forests and black creeks and rivers of the bottomlands, where even experienced woodsmen could wander lost for days.

I liked to travel along the Natchez Trace, formerly an overland trail running from Nashville, Tennessee, to Natchez, Mississippi, that had been converted into a 444-mile national parkway. I would divert from the parkway to examine sections of the original road, deeply rutted from horses' hoofs and wagon wheels, which everyone from dignitaries to robbers had traveled. Along the parkway were the homes of old Mississippi plantation families who never seemed to acknowledge their loss in the Civil War or their fall from opulent wealth once they no longer owned slaves. Even years later, ignoring the attrition of their fortunes and in what seemed a desperate grasp at the golden days, they would sometimes sell a plot of their land to throw a party on the scale that their peers expected of them.

In Jackson, the street design originated from a plan by Thomas Jefferson, and I adored the Old State Capitol (now housing the Mississippi State Historical Museum) where Andrew Jackson once spoke. A prime example of Greek revival architecture, its graceful lines were quite different from the harsh Victorian-era capitols in some other cities. I saw the old capitol as a symbol of a saner era in Mississippi when Jacksonian democracy was strong.

For me, being in Mississippi was to live in antebellum America, and it invoked a sense of raw history. It was the most authentic and visceral place I knew. The best aspects of the state were a fulfillment of the small-town culture I had known as a child, uncorrupted by urban centers and modern trends in society and politics.

After two years, I was ready to move on from the Greenwood paper, and I found a job at the larger, afternoon *Jackson Daily News*, whose front-page banner proclaimed, "Mississippi's Greatest Newspaper." The paper was run by Frederick Sullens, a fiery editor whose columns entertained and infuriated readers daily.

Sullens had no shortage of venom, but he also had a sense of humor, and attacking politicians was his favorite sport. He was a long-time enemy of Theodore Bilbo, partly because the two had engaged in a constant exchange of barbs, and Sullens was forever finding innovative ways to attack him. When Bilbo called Sullens a "degenerate by birth, a carpetbagger by inheritance, a liar by instinct, a slanderer and assassin of character by practice, and a coward by nature," Sullens retorted that if Bilbo were elected governor, the eagle on the Capitol dome should be replaced with a "puking buzzard." When a state senator from Yazoo City became embroiled in an argument with the five-foot-two-inch Bilbo and struck him with a walking cane, Sullens wrote the headline, "War Horse of Yazoo Broke Good Walking Stick over the Head of Poplarville Pervert."

Sullens had little contact with the reporting staff except when he could use them for his attacks on politicians. In 1951, shortly after I joined the paper as a reporter, he was waging an all-out war against Paul B. Johnson Jr., a leading gubernatorial candidate and the son of former governor Paul B. Johnson Sr. No one could remember exactly why Sullens hated Johnson Sr., but he wrote vicious columns about him. Their blood feud culminated when Johnson Sr. sought revenge in the lobby of the Walthall Hotel, a Jackson gathering place for politicians and journalists, and struck Sullens with his walking cane. Apparently, walking canes tended to be the preferred weapon of choice in those days. Sullens survived the attack to outlive Johnson Sr. but then directed his bile at Johnson Jr. when the latter became a prominent candidate.

Sullens figured he could sink Johnson Jr.'s candidacy once and for all if he could show that Johnson Jr. had support from the few blacks who could vote. The editor of Mississippi's oldest black-owned weekly newspaper, Percy Greene, endorsed Johnson Jr., who had previously campaigned as a New Deal Democrat and a champion for blacks and poor whites. There were not enough black voters in the state to have an impact on the outcome, but Sullens thought that if he could show an alliance between Greene and the Johnson Jr. campaign, it would alienate a substantial number of white voters. When Sullens's spies told him that Greene was scheduled to visit Johnson Jr. at his campaign headquarters, Sullens dispatched a photographer and me to stand outside to catch Greene entering or exiting. We waited all day, but Greene was apparently tipped off and never appeared. In my youthful naïveté, our stakeout seemed routinely normal, and I never thought to object to Sullens's use of staff to carry out his trickery.

Sullens reserved his greatest unbridled passion for the preservation of all things southern, including white supremacy. In 1951, Sullens wrote an editorial that filled half the front page warning of the impossible effects of twenty thousand potential black voters in Mississippi who could turn the gubernatorial election against Johnson Jr.'s opponent, aptly named Hugh White. "Practically all of them are followers of President Truman and want to see social equality rammed down the throats of the people of Mississippi," Sullens wrote. "They want anti-segregation, anti–poll tax, anti-lynching and FEPC [Fair Employment Practices Commission] laws enacted by Congress." There could be riots, he warned, and a vote against White would be a vote for outside groups like the National Association for the Advancement of Colored People (NAACP), the Congress of Industrial Organizations (CIO), the National Negro Congress, the Southern Conference on Racial Relations, and the Civil Rights Congress. Sullens failed to mention that these thousands of blacks could not register to vote or that Johnson Jr. was not a supporter of these groups. But the weight of Sullens's words became evident when White won the election. It was only after Sullens was long dead that Johnson Jr. finally was elected governor after four attempts and embracing a segregationist stance. After becoming governor, however, Johnson Jr. reverted to a more moderate position, saying he welcomed federal help to calm racial violence because he understood the costs to the state's reputation and economy.

During my first months at the *Daily News*, I wrote about floods, armed robberies, bootleggers, cattle thieves, and a 106-year-old Confederate veteran who showed me his scars from the Civil War battle at Vicksburg. I wrote one dispatch about a Sam Spade–like detective who had a thriving business because he owned the only lie detector in Mississippi and Louisiana. Soon I was assigned to the state capitol, the best reporting job on the paper, and wrote about the legislature and political corruption. I also reunited with Betty, who lived with her parents in Memphis, and we began courting long distance between the two cities. She still had all the vivacity and lust for life that impressed me when I first met her, and she filled my few nonworking hours with enjoyment. And she loved to read my articles and keep pace with the news.

Working at the *Daily News* was the first time I became aware that the issue of race was rising to a low boil in Mississippi. With the persistent urging of black leaders, the Jackson mayor was encouraging the city, where about one-third of the population was black, to hire its first group of black police officers to patrol in black neighborhoods. I wrote about successful opposition to the idea from the Jackson city council even though most of the thirty-seven southern cities that had hired black officers, including Dallas and Little Rock, reported favorable outcomes.

In 1951, Mississippi officials were also turning their attention to the stark disparity between black and white schools in the state. This was not because state leaders were interested in upgrading black schools but because they saw the federal government trying to integrate professional and graduate schools in neighboring southern states, and they thought they might be next. At the time, the federal legal doctrine of "separate but equal" public facilities did not violate the Constitution's Fourteenth Amendment, and state and local governments could segregate blacks and whites if each group's public facilities, including schools, were equal. Some Mississippi leaders suggested that spending more money on black schools would provide a leveling with white schools and prevent any future federal intervention.

The *Daily News* issued dire warnings about federal encroachment. "Will the State of Mississippi lose its race against time in equalizing Negro school facilities—or does the state's public school system face possible disintegration?" a front-page editorial opined. "That is a question that is deeply disturbing the state's public officials and a large segment of Mississippi citizenry." The *Daily News* was also worried about the cost of upgrading black schools to preserve racial segregation, and published articles stating that improvements would cost a total of at least $400 million in eleven southern states. Although black students made up one-third of elementary and secondary school enrollment in those states, the monetary value of the black schools was only 15 percent of the states' total school value. And in Mississippi, the disparity was even greater, as white schools were assessed to be four times more valuable than black schools. It was estimated that it would take a decade to bring black schools up to the same level as white schools in Mississippi, even if the white schools remained in the same condition over that time.

I watched as some of the state's most cunning minds devised crafty methods to retain a racially separated system. I didn't give a lot of thought to the greater implications of federal versus state control, but I did sense that Mississippi was digging in its heels over what might become a major confrontation.

CHAPTER 6

Death Bolted Swiftly through His Body

THE MOST PROMINENT RACE STORY TO BRING BANNER HEADLINES AND national attention to Mississippi in 1951 was the execution of a black grocery-truck driver named Willie McGee, who had been convicted of raping a white housewife name Willette Hawkins in Laurel, Mississippi, six years earlier. To this day, the definitive truth about what happened between McGee and Hawkins remains unclear. Hawkins said she was raped, but McGee claimed she seduced him and then changed her story when rumors of their consensual affair circulated in the small town. An all-white jury took less than three minutes to hand down a guilty verdict.

McGee's death sentence and his long appeals process received international attention, especially when luminaries like Albert Einstein, William Faulkner, Paul Robeson, and Norman Mailer rallied to McGee's defense. McGee's sympathizers protested around the world, including thousands of union packinghouse workers in Chicago and crowds outside a London movie theater carrying signs reading, "WILLIE MUST NOT DIE!" Other sympathizers picketed in front of the White House and chained themselves in a circle around the columns of the Lincoln Memorial. Bella Abzug, a young labor attorney in New York who later became a US congresswoman, was McGee's defense attorney.

When I was assigned to cover the story for the *Daily News* in 1951, McGee's appeals had run their course (the US Supreme Court on three occasions declined to intervene in the case), and demonstrators and reporters from New York were descending upon Jackson in the final days before the scheduled execution at midnight on Monday, May 7. John Popham, a southerner who was considered a dean of journalism and the first to cover the South on a regular basis for a northern newspaper, was there for the *New York Times*. *Life* magazine ran a two-page exposé.

I wrote a front-page story about demonstrations in Jackson, describing how highway patrolmen and police closed in on twenty-five stylishly dressed white women as they protested in front of the state capitol building on a Saturday morning. Some of the women had traveled from neighboring southern states, but most were from New York, and some represented the Greenwich Village chapter of the Civil Rights Commission, a group branded by the US Justice Department as a communist front.

The leader of these protesters was Anne Braden, a rather pretty but sallow-faced woman who had spearheaded a hospital desegregation campaign in Kentucky and later rose to national prominence as a civil rights activist. I quoted Braden in my article. "We are here because we are determined that no more innocent men shall die in the name of protecting Southern white womanhood," she said. "We have been made a party to this injustice too long." An elderly white bystander wearing a straw hat walked up to the protesters and told them, "They ought to beat the hell out of you. I don't care if you are ladies."

When the women ignored a police request to disperse, they were hauled into headquarters, booked, and jailed as part of a larger roundup of forty-three people arrested in Jackson that day, including some blacks and tourist bystanders caught up in the mass arrest. I noted in my article that some women spoke with northern accents and refused to eat the lunch that the jail provided. "I can't eat that slop," one woman told police. "Can we send out for something?"

A bevy of national reporters and photographers showed up at police headquarters to find a chaotic mix of arrested protesters, overwhelmed police officers, and hundreds of spectators who had arrived to watch the commotion. The police quickly took away the cameras of some news photographers until the chief of detectives ordered them returned. We could hear the women in the jail cells when they burst into song:

Hallelujah I'm a traveler,
Hallelujah ain't it fine.
That's why I'm traveling,
Down freedom's main line.

Oh, I hate Jim Crow,
And Jim Crow hates me.
That's why I'm fighting
For Willie McGee.

Then they sang "John Brown's Body," a tribute to the pre–Civil War slavery abolitionist, set to the "Glory Hallelujah" chorus of "The Battle Hymn of the Republic."

Some spectators sympathized with the protesters, but others told me, "They ought to put them in the cell with Willie McGee." Abzug, who was in Jackson to enter a clemency appeal, arranged for the protesters to be released under a bond agreement that they would leave the state immediately. Abzug was not pleased that she had to interrupt her clemency appeal to get protesters out of jail, but she realized that time was short, and the protesters would have no other opportunity to be heard if they remained in jail.

By Monday morning, Abzug was in a packed federal courtroom in Jackson pleading for a stay of McGee's execution, arguing that Mississippi officials had shown racial prejudice and conspired to violate McGee's civil rights. I was in the courtroom all afternoon watching spectators squirm with impatience as the lawyers argued the case. Finally, after six long hours, Judge Sidney Mize denied the stay, saying, "The petitioner is now a criminal and can now be called a criminal. He has been convicted in a fair trial and has had every opportunity." Mize noted that the defense counsel provided no new information to reverse the sentencing. The hearing ended at 7:00 p.m., but McGee's lawyers continued to appeal the decision to higher courts in the few remaining hours before the midnight execution.

Once the hearing in Jackson ended, I returned to my newsroom to quickly file my story and learned that both the US Court of Appeals in New Orleans and the US Supreme Court had turned down eleventh-hour requests for a stay. McGee had exhausted all his options and would die at midnight.

I jumped in my car and drove ninety miles southeast to the Jones County courthouse in Laurel, Mississippi, where McGee awaited his execution. In 1940, the Mississippi legislature voted to replace the gallows with the electric chair as a method of execution, but residents who lived near a state penitentiary in Sunflower County, where the executions were to be conducted, had protested against using that site. So, the state decided to haul a portable electric chair from county to county for each execution. The massive straight-backed oak electric chair was delivered by truck to Laurel and carried into the courtroom where McGee had previously been convicted. A power line was strung from a generator on the truck through a courtroom window to the wooden chair.

By 10:00 p.m., more than five hundred people had gathered outside the courthouse. Most were men, some sitting in lawn chairs, who mumbled and laughed as they waited. The weather was pleasant and the scene festive. Boys and young men climbed to the top limbs of tall trees around the courthouse for a better view through the open windows. I pushed my way forward to the front of the crowd. "Let's everybody be nice," a highway patrolman standing on the concrete courthouse steps said to calm the crowd. When he announced that McGee was going to die, everyone shouted a cheerful glee. "We want no demonstrations," the patrolman said. "You have been patient a long time."

Jimmy Ward, another reporter at the *Daily News*, was one of the few reporters allowed in the courtroom to witness the death. I was responsible for reporting on the activity outside the courthouse. In Ward's front-page story, he described how a black, bald barber, smelling like hair tonic, arrived at the courthouse accompanied by sheriff's deputies to shave McGee's head. The barber walked past Willette Hawkins's husband and his brother-in-law, who were waiting with a hundred other people to witness the execution. Willette Hawkins had been in the Jackson courthouse earlier in the day for the federal court hearing, but she was not in Laurel for the execution. Neither was Abzug, who stayed in Jackson to make a personal last-minute appeal to the Mississippi governor and attorney general at the governor's mansion. Neither official would grant McGee clemency.

Guards escorted McGee to the looming chair, which looked like a giant rocking chair except it was wired with electric cables. McGee showed little sign of emotion. Ward wrote about it in graphic detail. "Willie McGee still had a cocky air about him as he took his seat in the electric chair. But he died with a tear in his eye. . . . Death bolted swiftly through his body beginning at 12:06 a.m. as the chair rocked backward and the generator outside groaned with an extra load." After one long jolt, his body went limp.

Those of us outside knew the execution had begun when the generator loudly kicked into gear. A cheer went up among the crowd around me. I felt sick as blood washed from my face. The guards loaded McGee's listless body onto a gurney, and the crowd cheered again when black funeral home attendants carted the body, covered with a white sheet, to a black hearse outside the courthouse. The attendants appeared frightened, and law enforcement officers pushed the crowd back.

I looked around me and thought about how barbaric the scene was. There seemed to be an inordinate amount of cruelty in those times, perhaps because people had just come out of the brutality of World War II. But whatever the reason, the meanness was so immediate that it resonated deeply with me.

Once the hearse drove away, there wasn't much left to hold the crowd's attention at such a late hour, and people began meandering home. I did the same, feeling emotionally and physically drained and much older than my twenty-seven years.

CHAPTER 7

A Rare Work Environment

I STAYED AT THE *DAILY NEWS* FOR ABOUT ANOTHER YEAR, AND BY THAT time I was engaged to be married to Betty. I had never met, and never would meet again, someone like her. Her vivacious spirit and optimism were infectious, and she sincerely appreciated the scope of a larger world beyond our own. I never got down on my knee and asked, "Will you marry me?" It was not necessary. Love this deep needed no words. We both knew we would wed, so there was no call for a formal proposal. We would desperately need more money for the family we planned to start, but the *Daily News* refused to give me a raise. I was also eager to leave the paper because its tone was progressively degenerating into racist rant. Jimmy Ward soon after became the paper's editor and spewed forth race-baiting and hate-filled editorials. His poison earned the paper a reputation as one the worst in the nation.

In 1952, I married Betty and earned another five dollars a week by moving to United Press (UP), later called United Press International (UPI), whose three-man Jackson bureau covered state government and reported news throughout the state. In Mississippi, UP supplied local news through a telephone wire to twenty-eight radio stations, twelve newspapers, and a handful of television stations that subscribed to the wire service. I wrote stories about everything Mississippi: fires in the Delta, ghost towns along the Mississippi River, Civil War treasure seekers, and Democratic Party politics. In keeping with her adventurous spirit, Betty patiently tolerated my erratic and demanding work schedule. She loved to hear about my adventures at the end of each workday.

Working for UP required a facile mind and nimble fingers. Ordinarily we used typewriters, but on an important breaking story, we could save time by typing it directly on teletype machines, with one version for newspapers, another for broadcasters. Teletype keys punched a code on tape, which was subsequently fed into a machine that printed the words for whatever outlets were on the circuit. However, a mistake or a false start, once punched in, could not be corrected, and we engaged in all kinds of mental gymnastics to make the story come out right as the tape sped along at a rapid pace. The bureau sometimes turned down promising applicants simply because they could not type on the tape quickly enough and answer the telephone at the same time. I probably was the slowest worker in the bureau but still prided myself on being able to type faster than the machine could print it out.

We worked with budgetary constraints as well. The division headquarters in Atlanta always warned us in the direst terms that we were far over our skimpy budget. Each advisory was followed by a second admonition: under no circumstances, even with a limited budget, were we to fail in getting the news. Get it fast and get it first. We never met our budget, but no one was ever fired as a result.

Draconian methods of keeping costs down were the work of UP's business manager in New York, L. B. Mickel. He became known as "Save a Nickel Mickel" for his frequent memos ordering us to hold down expenses. We later held reunions under the name "the Downhold Club," and one club membership card signed by Mickel himself read: "Nothing is so cheap that it cannot be done cheaper." We were never given a good explanation for these stingy standards, but I learned later that our owner, the Scripps-Howard newspaper chain, a privately held company, was losing money.

Our competitor was the Associated Press (AP), an objective and competent wire service. Because UP sold its services cheaper than AP to be competitive, we always worked inexpensively and had to be creative. When we wrote daily roundups of the Cotton States baseball league, we were given only the batters' names, scores by innings, and the winning and losing pitchers. With this meager information and liberal amounts of imagination, we would create flamboyant descriptions of the games with little concern about legitimacy. It was an art that made Ronald Reagan famous as a sports broadcaster, and some wire reporters made big names for themselves bringing the Cotton States roundup to life. In addition, we doubled as clerks. If we did not produce an accurate weather report by 6:00 a.m., irate station managers would threaten to cancel their UP subscriptions. I had nightmares about arriving late to work to find radio station managers raising hell over a missing weather report.

Working close to the bone had its hazards. One morning, a reporter in our bureau wrote a story that a prominent game warden in north Mississippi had been indicted for a felony. The story came from the front page of the Jackson *Clarion-Ledger*, and the reporter simply lifted the information without checking to see if it were true, a frequent practice with our budget restrictions. A radio station in the warden's hometown broadcast our story, and we were soon faced with a lawsuit charging slander because there was no indictment against the game warden. My boss in Atlanta was not surprised by my explanation for the mistake but told me that under no circumstances was I to testify in court about how we got the story. But he gave me no advice on what to say instead. Determined not to lie under oath, I sought out a lawyer who advised me to wait and see if I was subpoenaed. Fortunately, the case was settled out of court after UP ran a correction and an apology. It was a hard lesson about the necessity of accuracy.

Despite these constraints, our UP staff was surprisingly happy, and in 1953 I was promoted to bureau manager. I have never known an organization where morale was higher, and our band of young men (women in wire service bureaus were extremely rare) was buoyed by the excitement of beating the larger and better-paid AP staff. UP's New York headquarters stoked our fire by sending out regular memos pitting us against AP and ranking how each news service got the most play on major stories. The small newspapers and broadcasters in the state could only afford to use one wire service, so we constantly sought to steal business from AP. Persuading a publisher to kick out AP brought kudos from all the top managers in the company. "Warmest congratulations on taking this north Mississippi bell cow away from the enemy," one Atlanta manager wrote in a congratulatory letter when we convinced the publisher of the West Point paper to replace AP with our service.

There were, of course, occasions when AP beat us despite our best efforts. Late one Saturday afternoon, a tornado struck a Vicksburg movie theater and killed thirty-eight children and adults. Our reporter H. L. Stevenson sped forty-five miles to Vicksburg while Bill Middlebrooks and I stayed in the bureau working the telephones and relaying the story to Atlanta, where Bill Tucker, one of the best rewrite persons of his day, polished and sent it along with new leads late into the night. Despite our best efforts, AP got most of the play on this story in the larger papers. Tucker's theory was that the local newspapers had second-team editors in charge on Saturday nights, and they didn't know which wire service to use. Disappointments like this only stimulated us to work harder because successes could be heady experiences.

Our UP bureau in Jackson became a rare work environment where talented young reporters were dedicated to the trade despite the long hours, little pay, pushback from ornery subscribers, and uncomfortable exposure to seismic pressures in society.

Scripps-Howard later absorbed the Hearst-owned International News Service in the late 1950s and rebranded UP as United Press International. UPI, which with its worldwide news gathering and distribution system, had wide prominence in America. Scripps-Howard eventually sold UPI because of sustained losses, and the service today is a mere shadow of its former self. But during my career as a journalist, it seemed that every person I met in the profession had at one time worked for UP or UPI. These included Walter Cronkite, Harrison Salisbury, and hundreds of other, lesser-known reporters. Most were young, bright, ambitious beginners who came to UPI when few other jobs were available on major newspapers. After a short stint with UPI, which paid notoriously low salaries with little prospect for raises, the young reporters were then better able to find jobs elsewhere with improved chances of advancement.

Wire service experience was considered essential training. For example, when Hedrick Smith graduated from Williams College and asked James Reston, then the Washington bureau chief for the *New York Times*, for a job, Reston was impressed but sent Smith to UPI to be broken in. After a couple of years in Memphis writing no-frills local news for UPI, Smith went back to Reston, who hired him to help cover the US State Department, the Vietnam War, and civil rights. Years later, Smith won a Pulitzer Prize for his reporting from the Soviet Union.

During my initial time at UP, I didn't write any stories about racial conflict. The McGee execution had come and gone, and for the most part the state settled back into its long-held traditions. Since Reconstruction, Mississippi, like other states in the Deep South, had enforced absolute segregation with local Jim Crow laws at hotels, restaurants, public buildings, schools, apartment buildings, churches, theaters, libraries, recreation facilities, trains, buses, and newspapers. Some counties had three sets of restrooms—one for whites, one

for "colored," and one for Native Americans. In the few places where segregation was not specifically stated in law, intimidation worked just as well.

By 1953, however, the issue of separate public schools was gaining momentum in the nation as the US Supreme Court was preparing to rule on
cases challenging the practice, and Mississippi's elected officials and public
leaders were preoccupied with finding any way possible to keep things just
as they were.

At UP, we reported in considerable detail the extensive strategy meetings
Mississippi legislators were holding to prepare for a court ruling. I reported
that Governor Hugh White admitted freely that he didn't know what he
would do if the Supreme Court abolished segregation rather than uphold
the "separate but equal" doctrine. White and the state education committee
found it inconceivable that the doctrine would be overruled, and so they
planned to devise the largest program of any southern state to equalize black
and white schools. Their elaborate plan called for consolidating white schools
and spending $40 million a year—including $13 million in new taxes—to
improve both black and white schools. It immediately faced opposition.

A consensus on the plan was difficult to reach, partly because the quality
of the black schools lagged so far behind that the state could not move fast
enough to satisfy a "separate but equal" status. My articles mostly included
quotations from white leaders, but I also interviewed J. D. Boyd, president of
the state Negro Teachers Association, which had worked toward equalizing
the salaries of black and white teachers. "Our schools are so far behind that
any slowing up of the program is working an undue hardship on Negroes,"
he told me. I visited some black schools around the state and found the scene
untenable. The facilities were run down, classrooms were overcrowded, and
teachers struggled in a chaotic climate of dysfunction. It seemed impossible
that these schools could be brought up to par with the white schools. Pro-
crastination was the white leaders' only response to stave off what they called
this "terrible disaster" of desegregation, as they became anxious spectators
waiting for the court to rule.

A year later, on May 17, 1954, when the court eventually ruled unani-
mously in *Brown v. Board of Education* that separate but equal schools were
unconstitutional, the reaction in Mississippi was immediate and inflamed.
Fred Sullens and others predicted that the inevitable bloodletting would not
stain the conscience of segregationists but instead "the white marble steps of
the Supreme Court."

All UP reporters in Jackson spent the entire day on the telephone calling anyone in Mississippi who would say something about the ruling. Our stories quoted top state officials saying they hoped the Supreme Court ruling would not destroy the system of separated schools for at least another half century. Mississippi's Democratic US senator James O. Eastland assured segregationists, "You are not required to obey any court which passes out such a ruling. In fact, you are obligated to defy it." Governor White, confined to his mansion with a kidney ailment, referred the matter to a special committee formed by the legislature to find ways to maintain separated schools. The speaker of the state's House of Representatives recommended abolishing the public school system and turning it over to private local officials. The front page of one Mississippi newspaper that carried our stories featured the headline, "Mississippi Seeks Sidestepping Way, Slow and Cautious." In all our calls that day, it was impossible to find white leaders willing to speak publicly in favor of the ruling. There was a solid wall of defiance that was to grow in the months and years ahead.

One group to react quickly to the *Brown* decision was the white business establishment, who feared that a disruption of the caste system could hurt the state's economy. Mississippi didn't have much wealth to lose, but the little it had was a cherished commodity. I began writing about vigilante preservers gathering around the state in reaction to the court ruling. A small band of prominent and influential businessmen met in Indianola to form a group called the White Citizens' Council, which opposed integration mainly for economic reasons. They believed in conformity, economic stability, and the practicality of law and order over radical change. In their view, the rest of the nation could desegregate their schools, but Mississippi could not sustain such disruption in the social order.

At first, the White Citizens' Council was not taken seriously. Yet, over subsequent years, the council gained footing and influence, and the Indianola chapter was the first of many that formed in multiple southern states. The White Citizens' Council epitomized the complexities of race in the South. Some council members were educated, enlightened, and considered liberal by their peers, and later came to promote peaceful integration. Other members saw their purpose as nothing more than maintaining the status quo and preserving economic order when the business interests of the community were at stake. In their eyes, they were not bigoted racists but a temperate voice of established traditions.

The Supreme Court ruling also galvanized blacks in Mississippi. Before the *Brown* decision, black organizations had no traceable foothold in the state except in the black community and were not part of the white consciousness or lexicon. One reason was because news organizations in Mississippi were as segregated as other parts of society. Small, marginal black newspapers and even the larger established black newspapers in Memphis, Chicago, and New York reported on blacks, but these publications circulated only in the black community. White leaders quickly rejected the information in these publications as false and unreliable. Most white newspapers across the country did not report news about blacks unless they were involved in some heinous crime. Likewise, in Mississippi, the newspapers, wire services, and broadcast stations—with rare exceptions such as the Greenville *Delta Democrat-Times* and the New Orleans *Times-Picayune*—simply did not report about blacks.

The *Brown* decision suddenly awakened a long-suppressed black voice in Mississippi, which, while still faint, was growing louder about not only school discrimination but the whole gamut of wrongs that had been inflicted for generations. This was when our challenges as a news organization began. AP's structure and tradition of distribution and income made it heavily dependent on local media subscribers who routinely ignored black concerns or staunchly opposed any change in race relations. For instance, AP was housed in the offices of the Jackson *Clarion-Ledger* and the *Daily News,* the two biggest papers in the state and the leading voices for the perpetuation of second-class citizenship for blacks. So it was difficult for AP to break its association with those newspapers and other publishers in the state to pursue an independent reporting of racial news.

UP, on the other hand, sold its wire services without formal connections to local newspapers and broadcasters, so we had some autonomy within the local news community over our coverage. My editors in Atlanta never told me what kind of news we should or should not cover. We were told to pursue anything of interest to our clients and to get it quickly. For the first time in my budding career, I did not have anyone above me in daily control of my work. In early 1955, I wrote an article about how thousands of voters in Mississippi had been deleted from the rolls when the legislature reinforced the state constitution with even stricter literacy tests that even a constitutional lawyer would flunk. Some local clients tried to dictate our discretion by not using dispatches we produced about the black community. H. L. Stevenson, a reporter in our bureau who was a liberal and a pragmatist, knew this better than I when in 1955 he instructed our new reporter, Lewis Lord. Stevenson sat down in front of a typewriter and produced this fictional lead: "A freight train crashed into a stalled bus at a crossing here today, killing 10 people. However, all of them were Negroes."

He ripped the item from the typewriter, handed it to Lord, and said sarcastically, "The lesson is don't spend money reporting a story like this. Our clients don't want it." It was one of many lessons Lord learned at UP. A few weeks later, after a Friday evening roundup of high school football results, Stevenson took Lord to an all-night diner for grits and eggs. The two Mississippians—a twenty-five-year-old former infantry sergeant from Picayune and an eighteen-year-old Millsaps College freshman from Natchez—engaged in small talk. Then Stevenson said, "What do you think about segregation?"

Lord, who had never ventured outside the Jim Crow South, poked at his eggs and confessed, "I haven't thought much about that."

"Well, you better think about it," Stevenson ordered.

Lord later described this encounter, which he said "messed with him," as the most valuable advice for critical thinking he had ever received.

But in 1955, there was one story in Mississippi that could not be ignored, which brought national attention to our doorstep to change my career and life forever.

CHAPTER 8

"Sumner: A Good Place to Raise a Boy"

IN THE HOT SUMMER OF 1955, A FOURTEEN-YEAR-OLD BLACK TEENAGER named Emmett Till was visiting relatives in the misnamed hamlet of Money, Mississippi, a barren spot in rural Leflore County where two highways, neither leading to much of anywhere, intersected. One highway ran across the flat Mississippi Delta with its dark, alluvial soil rich with nutrients for growing thousands of acres of cotton; the other highway led fifteen miles to Greenwood, where I had worked my first newspaper job.

In late August, Till was leaving Bryant General Store in Money with his cousins when he allegedly wolf-whistled at the attractive twenty-one-year-old white wife of the store's owner. Four days later, two white men abducted Till from his great-uncle's home in the middle of the night.

I first heard about his disappearance a few days later from sources in Greenwood, and I understood the dangers faced by a black boy making any untoward advances to a white woman. It surprised me that he would make any suggestive comments or gestures, because everyone knew the dire consequences. Yet Till was visiting from Chicago, and, even though his mother had warned him to watch his behavior while visiting the Deep South, he may not have understood the insular and archaic nature of backwater towns like Money, with their Jim Crow laws. Whites, unable to accept the history and reality of miscegenation, feared and denied even the slightest social interaction between the races. If he had done what townspeople said, I was certain that the missing Till was dead.

When I arrived in Money, not only was everyone in town talking about Till's disappearance, they also knew exactly who was responsible. Townspeople were bragging about how the store owner and his half brother had roused Till from sleep and spirited him away in the depth of night. Locals were saying that if they had not acted, they would not have vindicated the reputation of the store owner's wife and would have suffered humiliation among their white peers.

Within a short time, the two men were arrested. One publisher saw my story on the UP newswire and printed it on the front page of his small-town paper:

Greenwood (UP)—Two white men charged with kidnapping a 14-year-old Chicago Negro because they claimed he insulted the wife of one of the men, claimed today they released the missing boy unharmed. Sheriff George Smith said Roy Bryant, a storekeeper in nearby Money community and his half-brother, J. W. Milam, were held on kidnap charges in the mysterious disappearance of Emmett Till of Chicago. They were arrested yesterday.

The sheriff suspected foul play and began an extensive search for Till's body. I went to Money and the surrounding area to cover the investigation. I remember standing in the withering heat on the banks of the Tallahatchie River as boats dragged logs and wires to scour the river bottom. Within days, they dredged up a body so badly shot, bludgeoned, and decomposed that it barely resembled a human. A seventy-five-pound cotton gin fan was tied with barbed wire around the neck and body. The only remaining trace of Till's identity was an initialed ring that Till was wearing that belonged to his father, who had died ten years earlier.

Once the body was recovered, Bryant and Milam were charged with murder, and I interviewed their mother, who had six other sons and three daughters. As she sat gazing at her children's photographs in her home in nearby Sharkey, she said none of her sons harbored racial hostility, adding that Bryant and Milam had served honorably in the military.

The body was returned to Till's thirty-two-year-old mother, Mamie Bradley (she later changed her name to Mamie Till Mobley), in Chicago, where she insisted that there be an open-coffin funeral so the world could see what had happened to her son in Mississippi. UP in Chicago quoted her as saying, "Down there it's like walking into a den of snakes. They will do these things without hardly any provocation—they don't even need provocation." She said she would "fight to the end to see justice done and the State of Mississippi will pay for this."

Bradley's decision to publicize her son's death, at first through the black press, brought national attention. Horrific photographs of Till in his open casket, his face bloated, discolored, and disfigured, appeared in the September issue of *Jet* magazine, a national black publication. The magazine also published photos of tens of thousands of people lining Chicago streets to view Till's body and attend the funeral. The northern white press responded soon after, and the story finally reached white readers. Bradley and Chicago's mayor, a white man named Richard J. Daley, called unsuccessfully on Republican president Dwight Eisenhower to respond to the murder.

The white Illinois attorney general wrote a letter to Mississippi officials urging them to conduct a complete murder investigation. At first, Governor Fielding Wright claimed that the crime was being overplayed. But then, as the killing attracted greater media attention and Wright became more concerned about Mississippi's national image, he denied that Mississippians condoned the killing and said, "The people of Mississippi are anxious to see justice done in this case." Pro-segregation leaders in Mississippi expressed regret over Till's death, and law enforcement officials promised a strong prosecution.

On September 17, I temporarily moved to Money to interview townspeople and prepare for what was dubbed the "wolf-whistle trial." It was the same day as my third wedding anniversary, but this story had become a national sensation and the biggest story I had ever covered. Betty understood the significance and said we would celebrate in Jackson after the trial. Bryant and Milam were held in the Clarksdale jail, fifty miles from Money, and Sheriff George Smith stationed a battalion of thirty Mississippi national guardsmen—armed with M-1 rifles and riot gear—to guard the defendants. Smith said he had received two anonymous threats from blacks seeking retaliation, and he had heard rumors that carloads of blacks from Illinois would stage protests.

As with most racially charged scenarios in the South, the reaction in Money was complicated. Parochialism bred an intolerance to foreign influences, and most whites felt absolute scorn that these men had been arrested and charged. The locals' cynicism and crude jokes were sickening. One quip I heard around town was: "Isn't that just like a nigger to swim across the Tallahatchie River with a gin fan around his neck?"

An extremely small minority of whites, however, were indignant and ashamed over the killing. One letter to the editor in a newspaper stated, "Now is the time for every citizen who loves the state of Mississippi to 'Stand up and be counted' before hoodlum white trash brings us to destruction." The letter said that segregationists, generally dubbed "segs," were the ones responsible for the downfall of the state and its reputation.

The primary reason for these disparate reactions among whites was mainly economic, because there were two distinct white cultures—the aristocratic rich and the working-class poor. The aristocrats, mainly plantation owners, were cultured, many having been educated in some of the nation's best schools before returning to Mississippi. They were in control of the black labor market, in which workers toiled on thousands of acres of farmland. The landholders were wealthy, drove around the Delta in large Cadillacs, and decorated their spacious homes with European antiques brought home from their world travels. Generally speaking, they could be humane on a one-on-one basis with the blacks who worked for them, and some of them objected to Till's murder in a well-mannered fashion by simply not joining the chorus of ugly racism. Abstaining from the racist excesses of white society in Mississippi may seem like a mere default position, but the culture of white superiority was so strong that even the smallest deviation was considered an act of disobedience.

At the other end of the spectrum were poor whites, who either relied on the wealthy landowners for their living or attempted to cultivate the gravelly soil of the hill country, where they, and their crops, struggled for survival. Either way, their poverty was rampant, and there were far more poor whites than there were aristocratic landowners. They harbored a seething resentment toward both the rich and the blacks, the latter with whom they competed for jobs.

With the Till murder, however, a third voice echoed in Mississippi that I had not heard since the *Brown* decision. Black leaders from the North were calling for action. US congressman Charles Diggs, a Democrat from Detroit, was putting pressure on the US Justice Department to examine the Till case. Roy Wilkins, national NAACP executive secretary, called the crime a "lynching" carried out by whites to prove themselves superior. "It's in the virus, it's in the blood of the Mississippian," he said. "He can't help it." In Chicago, Henry Huff, chairman of the NAACP's Legal Redress Committee, called on Mississippi politicians and legal authorities to act.

The press quoted not only these national black leaders but local ones as well. T. R. M. Howard—a black surgeon, president of the National Medical Association representing black doctors, an activist, and a prominent landowner and businessman in the all-black town of Mound Bayou near Money—joined the chorus of outrage over Till's death and declared that if "the slaughtering of Negroes is allowed to continue, Mississippi will have a civil war. Negroes are only going to take so much."

A considerable number of blacks showed up when the one-week trial opened at the small courthouse in Sumner, Mississippi, thirty miles north of Money in Tallahatchie County, where the body had been found. Sumner was as backward thinking as Money, with no progressive influences such as a local college or cultural events. Yet a sign at the entrance to town read, "Sumner: A Good Place to Raise a Boy," and the village of five hundred people was much like the southern towns where I'd grown up.

It was in this quiet farming hamlet that armies of journalists, national civil rights leaders, and members of Congress descended, quickly transforming the trial into a cause célèbre in the United States and abroad. The usual courthouse loiterers of retired farmers, checkers players, and elected officials were miffed and surprised by the fuss and media attention. They stared in amazement as scores of reporters and dozens of cameramen set up their equipment on the courthouse lawn. It took a new growing season to restore the grass that was trampled by trial officers, spectators, and the press. The spectators considered even those of us from Mississippi to be outside agitators. "The NAACP is really making you work," one resident told me.

Although television was relatively new, some people owned one, including the Chinese grocer who had a store near the courthouse. I remember how remarkable it was that when I went into the store to buy a soda, I saw on the TV that news of the trial was being broadcast all the way from New York City. I had no idea how influential television would become in advancing the civil rights movement. This was one of the first signs that the atrocities of the Jim Crow laws would be broadcast to homes across America from Mississippi and eventually throughout the South.

Whites across the nation were learning through the media that the South was not a distant colony but, instead, very much a part of their own country. It was not easy for the television reporters who arrived in Sumner to get their footage back to their editors. Some networks put reels of film on a bus to Memphis, where they were then flown to New York. Others loaded the reels each day onto private planes at a small airfield seven miles outside Sumner.

The trial also marked the advent of live radio newscasts by many small stations in Mississippi and Louisiana. The stations received more calls from listeners than ever before, thanking them for having a person on the scene to report the proceedings. Radio news reporters would rush to phones to call in developments, and their reports were recorded and aired immediately. Announcers would promote the coverage, telling listeners to "stay tuned to hear the latest from Sumner on the trial."

Although I was still a novice, UP sent me to cover the trial alone. I soon discovered that I was competing against three AP reporters and some of the best reporters in the nation—both black and white—from Chicago, Detroit, New Orleans, and New York. Journalists included Bill Minor for the *Times-Picayune*, John Chancellor for NBC television, and James L. Kilgallen for International News Service. Kilgallen had covered the Charles Lindbergh kidnapping trial and was considered the world's best trial reporter. John Popham, who had an aversion to airplanes and so drove his green Buick fifty thousand miles a year to cover the South, was there for the *New York Times*, as he had been for the McGee execution. For the first time, I worked with black reporters who came from out of state including Moses Newsom for the Memphis *Tri-State Defender* and Simeon Booker for Chicago's *Jet* Magazine. Western Union set up temporary quarters in the courthouse and transmitted twenty-two thousand words of copy each day to the editors of the various news organizations.

Till's murder was so gruesome and heinous that it raised hackles far beyond American borders. Our little UP office in Jackson got requests from Tokyo and Paris for reports on the trial. Not even the McGee execution generated as much press coverage as this trial, and I couldn't recall a case this big in the history of the state. A young reporter there from New York named David Halberstam later said that the trial was "the first great media event of the civil rights movement." Blacks had been publicly lynched in Mississippi for years, but this was the first time I could recall that white men were being tried for murdering a black person, much less a black boy. The public reaction to photographs of Till's beaten and bloated body was so visceral that Till may as well have been dangling from a tree on the courthouse lawn.

Mississippi newspapers, radio stations, and television stations that relied on UP could not reject our coverage when outlets across the world were demanding information about the trial. That did not, however, stop some local outlets from exercising their own control over the story. I received daily complaints from unhappy Mississippi subscribers that UP was covering the trial. And WLBT-TV, the NBC affiliate in Jackson, posted a "Cable Difficulty" banner across the television screen when the *Today* show interviewed NAACP lawyer Thurgood Marshall about the trial.

Suddenly my byline, which until then had only circulated in Mississippi and neighboring states, was showing up on the front pages of newspapers in distant places I had never seen like Pennsylvania, Illinois, Wisconsin, Nevada, Japan, and France. I understood what a big break this story was for me professionally, but I was unaware of how large the story would become in the annals of civil rights history and in my own personal perception of the South.

The best fiction writer could not have conjured up a story as juicy as this real-life drama. It possessed all the elements of pathos in a Greek tragedy: murder, sex, and vengeance among characters straight out of central casting.

One of the most prominent characters was Tallahatchie County's sheriff, H. Clarence Strider, a wealthy plantation owner who fit the stereotypical profile of a Mississippi redneck. Weighing in at 270 pounds, he threw his holster-belted potbelly around like a cured ham. His hair, beginning to whiten at the temples, was slicked back, and thick glasses framed the wide temples above his oversized jowls. He wore the standard dress of the day—a short-sleeved, buttoned-down white shirt tucked into high-waisted khaki pants. Even in the courtroom, he didn't wear a sheriff's uniform so that he could deliberately convey the message, "I do not reign over the people. I am the people. I am the law of the people."

He wanted order in his county, and he didn't appreciate the presence of the press or the NAACP. "We never have any trouble until some of our southern niggers go up North and the NAACP talks to 'em and they come back home," he told me. "If they would keep their nose and mouths out of our business, we would be able to do more when enforcing the laws of Tallahatchie County and Mississippi." At the same time, he vowed to give the defendants a fair trial.

CHAPTER 9

"Thar He"

THE TRIAL BEGAN ON SEPTEMBER 19, AND THE COURTROOM WAS TENSE AND crowded as about 250 people crammed inside with standing room only. They arrived early every morning to claim seats, but those who couldn't fit into the courtroom, both black and white, were wedged tightly together in the courthouse corridors. A lot of teenage girls showed up to watch the excitement.

The scene was complete chaos, especially during recesses when a young boy peddled sandwiches and Coca-Cola in the courtroom as if it were a ballgame. One courtroom window shattered when spectators jammed against it, window shades were dislodged and dangled from their rollers, and dirty smudges marred the newly painted green walls. The sheriff's deputies were busy cleaning up debris in the courtroom during breaks.

When new witnesses were ushered in, verbal clashes broke out between the civil rights advocates and the locals. The judge could barely keep order, and Sheriff Strider barked commands at the crowd. He was particularly adamant about keeping the courtroom segregated. About fifty black spectators were relegated to the back of the room. Strider forbade a dozen black reporters representing national and international publications—including Clotye Murdock Larsson, a woman reporter from *Ebony*—from entering the courtroom until he was overruled by the judge. "Hello, niggers," Strider finally greeted the black reporters as he then cordoned them to a corner of the courtroom at a card table away from the other press. "We haven't mixed so far down here and we don't intend to," he explained.

When Congressman Diggs showed up at the trial, Strider refused to let him in, and a black journalist tried to intervene on his behalf. "A nigger congressman?" Strider's deputy exclaimed in disbelief. Once Diggs was finally allowed to enter, he was told to join the black press, where Till's mother was also seated. They could barely fit around the tiny table.

Although it was mid-September, the stale heat of summer lingered. There was no air conditioning, and two paddle fans suspended from the high ceiling barely stirred a whiff of air. The naked lightbulbs dangling overhead contributed to the sweltering temperature. Everyone fanned themselves with scraps of paper in nonrhythmic disorder. Milam's mother wiped sweat from her son's face during the breaks. *New York Times* reporter Popham, maintaining his dignified fashion, wore his suit jacket the entire first day of the trial. The defendants, dressed in short-sleeved white cotton shirts and khaki pants, had no handcuffs or shackles.

Both Milam and Bryant displayed self-assured cockiness even though the penalty for their charges was death in the electric chair. Their attorneys said they were "in very good spirits." Both men were accompanied by their wives, wearing trim gray dresses, and a total of four sons, who were scrubbed and dressed in their Sunday best. The children swung from the courtroom railings, played Cowboys and Indians, and squealed until relatives plied them with chewing gum, candy, water, and soda pop. Eventually, the boys shed their shirts as they sat perched on their fathers' laps and roamed the courtroom bare chested. More than once, their parents had to leave their seats to retrieve one of the boys from some mischief.

The courtroom was on the second floor, accessible only by narrow stairs. One room on the first floor had been converted into a makeshift press room with typewriters and teletype machines, and UP installed a telephone so I could call in frequent updates to my editors in Atlanta. I updated the lead to my story at least ten times a day and added inserts with the latest new development in the trial. UP had an insatiable demand for as many details as often as I could provide them. The more sensational the details, the better my editors liked it.

With each new development, I would dash from the courtroom and run downstairs to call my editors. Whites who could not find seats in the courtroom crowded around me and listened to my dispatches to get the latest developments. I had to speak loud to be heard over the crowds, and that was frightening because the locals did not want the story getting out to the rest of the nation and the world. They were verbally hostile to the press, but there were so many of us that there was not much they could do other than raise a ruckus.

After calling in my updates, I would race back up the stairs to the courtroom, squeeze my way back to the press table—sometimes past the oversize
stomachs of Strider and his deputies—and ask other reporters who didn't
have the same deadline pressures to fill me in on what I'd missed. I was a
thin and lanky thirty-one-year-old, and by the end of the one-week trial, the
muscles in my legs had grown about half an inch thicker from running the
stairs.

The judge delayed the start of the trial on its first day so that photographers could take pictures. Twelve white males were selected for the jury
from a list of registered voters—nine farmers, an insurance agent, and two
carpenters. Two-thirds of Tallahatchie County's population was black, but
because of the required poll tax and literacy test, not one black person was
registered to vote and, therefore, not included in the jury pool. Three jurors
were excused because they had connections with a fund created among
townspeople to raise money to pay the local defense attorneys. One prospective juror had contributed one dollar to the fund, enough conflict of interest
that he was not seated on the jury.

On the second day, the small card table for the black reporters was replaced with a larger one. The defendants' children were again brought to
the courtroom, but they became restless and were ushered out. The bailiff
twice ordered spectators to clear the aisles as a fire precaution. Finally, the
judge recessed the trial early because the courtroom was overcrowded, and
the prosecution said it needed more time to produce witnesses. Everyone in
town knew that several people saw Till's abduction and overheard him being
beaten in the barn of a plantation managed by one of Milam's brothers, but
the witnesses understandably feared for their lives and had not come forth.
The local activist T. R. M. Howard said that he could produce witnesses if
given time. That evening, groups of reporters, state officials, and NAACP
members fanned out to find new witnesses. The black reporters were much
better at this than white reporters, because they had access and credibility
in the black community.

Some colleagues and I heard rumors that James Hicks, a reporter for
the Afro-American News Service, had been arrested during the search. We
chased this lead and learned that Hicks had been picked up for an alleged
minor traffic violation, warned, and released. While other reporters were
looking for new witnesses, I heard another rumor that I felt was worth chasing. Despite the droves of reporters in Sumner, one incident went unnoticed

during the early morning hours. Someone set fire to an eight-foot-tall cross wrapped in fuel-soaked cloth near the town's railroad depot, and I spoke with a man who said he found the cross ablaze and extinguished it. I was the only journalist to file a story about the burning cross, and I wrote that although the town was the scene of a trial that had "stirred indignation around the world," the burning cross, a symbol of vile racism, had gone virtually unnoticed. "There was little talk about the incident," I wrote. That night, it seemed I would never reach my resting place. There was no place to stay in Sumner, so all the white reporters drove twenty miles each evening to our motel in Clarksdale.

When the trial resumed on the third day, Howard was true to his word and produced a new witness named Willie Reed, an eighteen-year-old sharecropper who testified how he had heard beatings and screams from the plantation barn.

Not only was Reed's testimony sensational, but it was significant for the prosecution because it turned the evidence from circumstantial to direct. In addition, I had never heard of or seen a black man testify against a white defendant in Mississippi. A murmur of excitement swept through the crowded courtroom when Reed took the stand. In a soft, low voice, he recounted how early Sunday morning he saw Till riding in the back of a Chevy truck with four white men. Then, as Reed took a shortcut through the plantation to buy cigarettes, he heard hollering and "a whole lot of licks" coming from the barn where the same Chevy truck was parked outside. When Milam came out of the barn carrying a .45 pistol to get a drink from the well, he asked Reed if he had heard anything. Reed quickly told him no and hurried on. The defense tried unsuccessfully to have the testimony thrown out, saying Reed's account was not related to Till's disappearance or the ultimate location of the body.

Yet perhaps the most dramatic testimony came from Till's great-uncle, Mose Wright, a sixty-four-year-old tall, lanky cotton picker with wrinkles chiseled into his weather-worn face. Known among locals as Old Man Mose, Wright told a hushed courtroom how one of the defendants came to his house for Till in the middle of the night with "a pistol in one hand and a flashlight in the other." Sitting on a cane-bottom chair in the witness box next to the judge, Wright gestured dramatically as he described the events that night at his home three miles from Money.

Some people in the courtroom believed in enforcing the law and were trying to serve justice, or at least go through the motions, including the young white prosecutor questioning Wright. "Uncle Mose, what time did you and your family go to bed?" the district attorney asked him.

"About 1:00 a.m.," Wright answered. An hour later, there came a knock at the door. Wright relayed to the jury what this nighttime caller told him from behind the door: "Preacher, preacher, this is Mr. Bryant and I want to talk to you and the boy." Wright then said, "I got up and opened the door."

"Who was at the door?" the district attorney asked.

It was Bryant and Milam, Wright said, and Milam told him, "I want the boy that did that talk at Money."

Wright said that the men woke Till, told him to get dressed, and drove him toward Money in a car with no headlights.

When asked if he could identify anyone in the courtroom who came to his house that night, Wright rose from his chair, pointed his boney toil-worn finger at Milam, and said, "Thar he." The courtroom was perfectly silent in disbelief, knowing how rare it was for a black man to confront a white defendant. I didn't know if it was outrage or indignation that prompted Wright to face down two white men before the eyes of everyone in town, but I thought he must be crazy. Both Wright and Reed had received death threats and remained in protective hiding provided by the NAACP throughout the trial.

"When was the last time you saw Emmett Till or his body?" the district attorney continued.

"When they took it out of the river," Wright said solemnly.

Till's mother, who was staying at Howard's house during the trial and was protected by Howard's bodyguards, also testified. Bradley was an attractive and articulate woman with a soft but steady voice. Attired immaculately in a black dress with a jeweled hat, earrings, and a necklace, she appeared much more refined and cosmopolitan than the country wives of the defendants, who looked sullen sitting next to their husbands. Bradley was composed as she recalled how she was in bed one morning in Chicago when she received word of her son's death. When prosecutors showed her a photograph of the body pulled from the Tallahatchie River, she bowed her head and removed her glasses to wipe her eyes.

"Is that the picture of your son?" the prosecutor asked Bradley.

"Yes sir," she said in a voice drained of emotion. She also identified her late husband's ring that was found on the body and said her son left Chicago wearing it.

She recalled how she warned her son that Mississippi was different and reminded him to humble himself before whites. "I told him he would have to adopt a new way of life when he went to the South and to say 'yes sir' and 'no ma'am' at all times and that if an incident should ever arise to make it necessary for him to get to his knees and beg forgiveness he should do so," she said. "I told him never to get in fights with any white boys."

The district attorney questioned other witnesses who made what I thought was an iron-clad case of murder in the first degree. In a statement to the jury, the district attorney called the crime "a court martial with a death penalty imposed." He added, "I was born and bred in the South. The very worst punishment that should have occurred was to take a razor strap, turn him over a barrel and give him a little beating. . . . A man deals with a child accordingly as a child, not as man to man."

When the state rested its case, I ran to the telephone to update my lead. I beat both the Associated Press and the International News Service and received lots of kudos from my editors in Atlanta.

The defense brought out a string of character witnesses, but the defendants did not take the stand and they had no alibis. Bryant's wife, Carolyn, testified without the jury present because the judge ruled that her account was not positively linked to Till. But we published her testimony in the newspapers, and some local papers ran a front-page photograph of her resting her head on her husband's shoulder. In her testimony, she recounted how a young black man with a northern brogue came into the store, grabbed her hand and waist, and used vile language she could not repeat. He bought two cents' worth of bubble gum and whistled at her, she said. She could not identify Till as the perpetrator. (Carolyn Bryant recanted her story in 2008 when she told a historian gathering information for a book published in 2017 that she had lied about Till menacing her. "Nothing that boy did could ever justify what happened to him," she told the historian.)

Strider, in an unusual move, testified for the defense, saying there was doubt that the dredged body was Till's because it was bloated beyond recognition. He also agreed with the defense's claim that Till was alive and well, living with his grandfather in Detroit. A physician and an undertaker also questioned the identity of the body, saying it was not Till's because the body had decomposed longer than the three days he had been missing.

In his closing statement, the defense attorney told the jury he was sure "every last Anglo-Saxon one of you has the courage to free these men." He also warned that if they rendered a guilty verdict, "your forefathers will turn over in their graves."

My most lucid memory of the trial was the delivery of the verdict. The facts hinted at a possible just reward, and the defendants looked worried as they sat waiting with their wives. The jury took only sixty-seven minutes to reach a verdict, and one juror told reporters that it would have been sooner had they not taken a break to quench their throats with soda pop. "Not guilty," they proclaimed. The jury foreman said the strongest consideration in their decision was that Till's identity had not been proven beyond a reasonable doubt.

There was a muted response, and no outburst from the civil rights supporters or blacks in the courtroom. Bradley, anticipating the worst, had left the courtroom before the verdict was handed down and was waiting at Howard's home. But cheers rose from the defendants and their supporters, who patted Milam's and Bryant's heads and backs as though they were children who had won a Little League game. Strider reached forward to congratulate them. Milam sat back and chewed a cigar as his wife peered into the cameras. Balding and paunchy, Milam said the verdict was "what I was hoping for," and hugged his smiling wife. Bryant gave his wife a long and impassioned open-mouthed kiss, suggesting that no black man should dare tread upon the consecrated status of a southern white woman. The cameras ate it up. Asked later in a press conference how he felt, Bryant said, "I'm just glad it's over."

In her own press conference after the trial, Bradley expressed no surprise at the verdict. She expected an acquittal and added, "lynching is now in order." The next day, she, Diggs, and Reed drove to Memphis to catch a plane to Chicago. Once Reed arrived in Chicago, he said he felt safe but he missed his cotton patch in Mississippi and his twenty-five-year-old girlfriend. "I feel kinda lonely for Ella Mae," he told a UP reporter in Chicago. Wright moved away from his farm forever, saying, "I'm through with Mississippi."

It was not completely over for Milam and Bryant. They still faced possible kidnapping charges but returned to Money, where Bryant reopened his store and Milam oversaw the harvest of a bumper cotton crop.

Like Bradley, I knew to expect the unjust verdict, given the history of Tallahatchie County, where it was considered a right for whites to kill any black. Milam and Bryant could not have continued living in Mississippi with any respect if they had not resorted to murder. No one expected anything other than acquittal. In fact, days before the verdict was reached, I stopped in to visit a local newspaperman. He said he thought too much consideration was given during the trial to Till's age. "He may have only been fourteen, but I'm told he had a dong on him like this," he said, gesturing with his forearm. He dismissed any claim that Till's lynching was wrong.

After sitting in that courtroom for five days and hearing evidence beyond a doubt that the defendants were guilty, the verdict still shocked me. Tired and angry, I drank a beer and got in my car to drive home to Jackson. How would I explain to Betty and my two young daughters that something like this happened in America, much less in a state we called home?

A few miles outside of Sumner, I felt a nagging tug in the pit of my stomach. I was mentally and physically exhausted. And I was also beginning to see that my long indifference to southern suppression of blacks was as displaced as the motives of those who enforced the suppression. I hunched over the steering wheel and cried. I couldn't stop crying for many miles. I wanted to cry Mississippi out of my very core.

CHAPTER 10

Living with Political Insanity

SIX WEEKS AFTER THE TRIAL, I JOINED A FEW OTHER REPORTERS AND photographers at a courthouse near Sumner to hear the judge report that a twenty-man, all-white grand jury voted not to indict Bryant and Milam on kidnapping charges. The announcement attracted little attention from local residents or the media. After the judge's announcement, Milam stopped by a nearby filling station to sip a celebratory beer and told me, "I'm happy about the whole thing." I quoted a black leader in my story who said the lack of indictments was not surprising "to anyone acquainted with the administration of justice in Mississippi." I also cited an editorial in the Greenwood *Morning Star* that defended the jurors' decision. "Where is there a husband worthy of the name who would not protect his wife . . . ?" the paper's editorial proclaimed. "Had Bryant been present and slain Till on the spot, there would not be a grand jury in the South who would have indicted him, and not many in the nation."

The case was officially closed even though months later both men confessed to the murder in a paid interview with *Look* magazine. Black customers began to boycott Bryant's store, and it closed within fifteen months. The half brothers became social outcasts in their own white community because residents said they would feel safer if the duo lived somewhere else. Bryant and his family eventually moved to Texas, where he was joined by Milam, who was arrested for bootlegging but not prosecuted. Decades later, both men eventually moved back to Mississippi and divorced their wives. Neither man was brought to justice, and both died before the Justice Department reopened the case in 2004 to investigate other possible accomplices. A grand jury in 2007 voted to not issue indictments against additional individuals.

When I returned to Sumner in 1955, I found the residents of Tallahatchie and Leflore Counties glad to be rid of the trial and the national attention. The case had created a big stir that, once settled, was forgotten. The only outcome of the trial in those counties was a deepening and steadfast resistance to change and a reinforcement of white racism. In fact, Mississippi was not receiving national attention on the race issue for the first time since 1954 and was having one of its best years for business activity. Racially motivated killings had eased temporarily, and the state was carrying out its program to retain segregated schools, despite the Supreme Court ruling, by upgrading both black and white schools. Of $9 million in state spending to improve schools, $6 million was used at black schools.

I reported that some black educators supported separate but equal schools, partly because they feared losing state funding, and they joined with white leaders to stave off desegregation. These black leaders felt that pushing integration too quickly was detrimental to black progress and that white Mississippians were not ready for drastic change. It seemed that segregation, a statewide standard of almost universal acceptance, was here to stay. Two black newspaper editors, in what they described as an effort to promote race relations and progress for blacks, broke ranks with the NAACP to support separate but equal conditions for blacks. They also worked with the Mississippi State Sovereignty Commission, a secret police unit created by the legislature in 1956 in reaction to the *Brown* decision to maintain segregation and stymie federal intervention. It took a while for the commission to find its footing mainly because it had no specific tasks until the NAACP filed lawsuits in Mississippi to force integration. During the commission's first year, its only function was to study sickle cell anemia as a reason to prohibit interracial marriage. It had an unused $250,000 budget, lacked personnel, and had not conducted any investigations or used its subpoena power. These resources would all be used extensively in later years when the commission gave aid and comfort to the KKK and damaged the reputations of innocent citizens.

What I didn't know after the Till trial—primarily because I was white and reporting predominantly in the white community—is that black activists in Mississippi were organizing supporters. Clarksdale harbored one hub of this activity because the town's economy was based on cotton farming and sharecropping, so the large black community was tight knit. In addition, a black pharmacist and prominent leader named Aaron Henry had a vision for change. At the time, Henry was little known among whites outside Clarksdale, although he later became president of the Mississippi NAACP. He called me at UP one day and invited me to attend one of his organizing rallies. I was taken aback. It was unusual to receive any tips on stories with a racial angle, and even more irregular to hear from someone in the black community. But Henry was a shrewd strategist who understood the possible effect of inviting the white press to his Sunday rally. Perhaps he had read Gunnar Myrdal's analysis emphasizing the importance of blacks getting the dominant all-white media to write about race often and candidly, such that "Americans outside the South could no longer look the other way."

Because Sunday was my only day off and I was planning to spend time with my family, I asked him if I could bring them along. "Of course," he said without hesitation. "They are welcome." It was a warm, clear day as Betty and I loaded our three daughters into the family car and headed 140 miles north of Jackson to Clarksdale. I had no idea what to expect that afternoon, but when my family and I stepped into a large church sanctuary, we were treated like royalty. Henry introduced us from the pulpit, and hundreds of congregants turned and smiled at our blonde, blue-eyed girls. The congregation clapped, cheered, and greeted us with handshakes and hugs. Being a small-town southerner served me well at times like this. We were the only white people in that Clarksdale church, but I felt at home.

Although the rally felt like a church service, with gospel singing, long sermons, and testimonials to the power and hope of Jesus, its chief objective was to garner support to earn voting rights for blacks. Henry and others realized that enfranchisement meant power, even though they had no idea that it would be almost another decade—with passage of the Voting Rights Act of 1965—before blacks in the South would finally be permitted to vote in large numbers.

The unity and determination of those gathered in the church were overwhelming. Few things are more powerful than harnessed passion. I was astounded by the eloquent oration of speaker after speaker as they illuminated the logic of their cause without bitterness or hatred. They spoke with a hopefulness that their day would indeed come, if not in this life then at least in another. Their songs, magnifying their message, poured out from the bottom of their souls.

As I sat through hours of music and preaching, I began to analyze my own identity and heritage. I felt ashamed about the injustices and cruelty my people had inflicted on blacks even though we shared a common religion. I had not previously doubted my loving parents and friends, who readily accepted the state of racial affairs. I was taught that black people were innately inferior to whites and were prosperous and happy when confined to a separate society. This belief was rarely challenged by parents, schools, universities, or the church. I realized it was absurd that generation after generation lived and died believing this to be true.

I recalled the small brick Presbyterian church in Somerville, Tennessee, where I was required as a boy to attend Sunday school every week without fail. My teacher was the wife of a local doctor who gave us the gospel expurgated from the King James Version, believing it was an article of her faith. Yet I later learned that, outside the church, she was a right-wing conservative who railed against President Franklin D. Roosevelt's New Deal no matter how humane or generous it might be for the poor. She fully supported preserving a system that suppressed people of color. In the context of the Clarksdale sanctuary, her lessons of hope, faith, and charity seemed rooted in a foolish myth of white superiority.

After the rally, I wrote a brief article, making sure it followed the dispassionate style required of wire service copy, and telephoned it to the Jackson bureau to be relayed to newspapers and broadcast stations in the region. I would like to have a copy of it today, although I have no idea if it was ever printed. Most of the owners of local radio and television stations and newspapers were still opposed to using stories about the black community and left news like Henry's rally on the editing room floor. What I witnessed that Sunday afternoon in Clarksdale was the first stirrings of a black movement generating from within Mississippi. I thought the story was newsworthy, and the deeds and actions of blacks, who made up 45 percent of the state's population, could not remain invisible forever.

As bureau chief, I had the authority to cover whatever stories I deemed newsworthy. Although I knew that coverage about race relations would not be well received by our local clientele, I began focusing on these stories and was pleased that my bosses in Atlanta and New York did not object. I knew that the wire service could not adopt an opinion or a one-sided point of view about race relations, but it should report the truth and keep a vigilant watch for violations of individual or group freedoms of every citizen. I wrote a story from Tchula, Mississippi, where two-thirds of the residents were black, about two white men who had been asked by their white neighbors to move because there were rumors that blacks and whites had swum together at their 2,700-acre cooperative farm set up to provide farming assistance and social services to poor white and black agricultural workers. The farm sponsored a day camp for black children to swim during the summer, but the only "mixed swimming" was when the black nursemaid swam with the farm owners' children. About seven hundred whites jammed into a high school gymnasium for a meeting organized by the White Citizens' Council to adopt a resolution asking the men to disband the farm and move from the county to avoid another Emmett Till wolf-whistle case. "We don't want a Sumner here," a meeting organizer said. The two men initially defied the "invitation" to move from Tchula but later left the state when they received death threats.

I wrote another dispatch about a prominent white Mississippi attorney charged with statutory rape of his seventeen-year-old black babysitter. I found an affidavit brought by the girl's parents buried deep in the criminal docket, and although I couldn't convince the prosecutors or judges to discuss the charges, a grand jury eventually indicted the attorney, and he was found guilty with a suspended sentence. The state supreme court affirmed the verdict on appeal.

These stories did little to endear UP to most of our Mississippi clients and we were often caught between meeting their demands and reporting on events that challenged the controlling interests. One topic that satisfied both concerns was the political arena, because it was one passion in the Mississippi trifecta of God, football, and politics. The national Democratic Party was beginning to endorse more progressive race relations, causing some die-hard southern Democrats to do the unthinkable and reject the party. For generations, party lines had been drawn by the Civil War, which southerners still called "the recent unpleasantness." Every white Mississippi student had been taught to grow up to be a Democrat to rebuke Abraham Lincoln and his Republican Party, which had freed the slaves and imposed reforms. As a result, the South was solid territory for a highly conservative, all-white Democratic Party. I wrote about the wholesale intimidation of blacks at the polls when twenty-six blacks voted in the all-black community of Mound Bayou, only to be told by the county Democratic Committee that their ballots would not be counted. The Democratic Party in Mississippi was for whites only, the committee insisted.

In response to the national Democratic Party's focus on race relations, conservative southern Democrats and midwestern Republicans in the US Congress formed a block that controlled most seats in both chambers. "I'm for anyone for president who is a states' righter, even if he's a Republican," said one Democratic Mississippi senator. In 1952, I reported that "dissatisfied Democrats" in Mississippi were defecting to form a Democrats-for-Eisenhower coalition, and that "political flip-flops are heard from all wings of the rambling and divided Democratic organization."

The Democratic Party in Mississippi was challenged even further in 1957 when John F. Kennedy, a Democratic senator from Massachusetts with presidential ambitions, came to Jackson to speak to an overflow crowd of two thousand people at the statewide gathering of the Mississippi Young Democrats. Kennedy, a liberal candidate, sensed a remote possibility of upsetting the long-standing southern Democratic coalition. I covered his speech, describing him as a "young New Englander," and quoted him saying that although Democrats will always have differences, "what unites us is greater than what divides us." He said he supported school desegregation in the South just as he did in his home city of Boston. "I think most of us agree on the necessity to uphold law and order in every part of the land," he said. The reception was muted. He was skinny and had an oversize head. He wasn't a very good speaker, and his delivery was rather homely compared to the silver-tongued politicians of the South. His funny-sounding northern accent blared like a honking goose.

Then he lambasted the Eisenhower administration for adopting a foreign policy of "retreat and retrenchment" and for not being frank with the public about America's position with Russia in the arms race. That brought a standing ovation. Despite his accent and choppy delivery, his good looks and broad smile appealed to some in the young audience. I had never heard of Kennedy before that evening. And I didn't know that a new, liberal Democratic Party would eventually take hold in America with civil rights as a major rallying point. That seemed impossible, especially when I was reporting how the all-white Mississippi legislature was enacting bizarre measures to counteract a national agenda for equal rights.

One of my dispatches began, "It isn't hard to start an argument in the Mississippi legislature—unless you've got a bill bearing a segregation label. Then it's not considered proper to raise a voice in protest even when established principles of government are involved." For example, one bill to finance local chapters of the White Citizens' Council breezed through the Senate with two dissenting votes after being pushed ahead of two hundred pending bills.

Supporters said the bill allowed state financing because the White Citizens' Council perpetuated and preserved the constitutional state government. The NAACP said if that were the case, then it should also receive state money. Segregationists were livid, saying the bill was specifically designed for the White Citizens' Council chapters only. The governor, J. P. Coleman, who was considered moderate and was called "a segregationist but not a wild man," opposed the bill, and it was defeated.

The Mississippi legislature also proposed creating a blacklist for public officials to use when hiring staff. The NAACP, of course, ranked first on the list, but a host of other organizations such as churches opposing segregation and black college fraternities donating money to the NAACP were listed as well. Another proposed bill sought to require public school teachers to disclose their memberships in and contributions to organizations, and be fired if they were affiliated with an organization on the blacklist.

Inclusion on the blacklist could have greater consequences than a job loss. I wrote about the twelve-year-old daughter of a blacklisted civil rights activist who was whipped by a city marshal and a variety store owner in Batesville, Mississippi, for allegedly shoplifting a candy bar. Aaron Henry and a local NAACP representative named Medgar Evers reported the beating to the Mississippi governor and the FBI. The governor declined to pursue the matter because he said there were conflicting accounts about what had happened and he believed it should be handled by the local authorities. The city marshal and store owner denied they had beaten the girl and blamed the NAACP for fabricating the story. The FBI investigated the incident without taking any further action. Steve Allen, a comedian and the host of the *Tonight Show*, saw the UPI article in a Hollywood paper and wrote to the city marshal, asking him to explain what happened. In the letter, Allen also said that the incident had harmed America's international reputation, reminding the marshal that one-fourth of the world's population was black. The city marshal said he had no intention of responding to the letter. The girl's father eventually moved his family to Gary, Indiana, because they continued to get harassed in Mississippi.

Covering the Mississippi legislature during this time was like reporting on a three-ring circus. At every turn, the legislators attempted to undermine all federal actions and court edicts that interfered with Mississippi's right to segregate and disenfranchise. As they had with the Supreme Court's *Brown* decision, white officials latched their arguments to John C. Calhoun's nineteenth-century doctrine of nullification and interposition, by which states declared federal laws null and void if they deemed them unconstitutional. Calhoun was the nation's seventh vice president and a southerner who had inspired secessionists before the Civil War. Most educated observers considered his doctrine repudiated once and for all by the outcome of the Civil War, but the Mississippi legislature sought novel ways to defy federal authority. The following commentary, which I wrote in 1958, described the political climate of the day:

JACKSON, Miss., Nov. 23 (UPI)—A word is playing an important part in Mississippi politics.

It is on the tongue of every politician, and those with aspiration for office are trying to keep it from being pinned on them as a label. The word is "moderate," which according to *Webster's International Dictionary*, means "kept within due bounds, observing reasonable limits, not excessive, limited in degree of activity or excitement, not violent, etc."

Its application today is on the integration issue. At least three politicians last week said in speeches there is no place for moderates in Mississippi politics. Jackson attorney Ross Barnett, who is running for governor, said in Vicksburg, "I don't know the meaning of the word moderate."

Shortly after, Barnett won his gubernatorial election, and his victory opened the door for the White Citizens' Council to work more actively with the state government to brand moderates as the enemy. One of the more influential moderates was Hodding Carter Sr., publisher of the Greenville *Delta Democrat-Times*, a small yet sound newspaper. Carter was reared in the typical southern racist tradition, but he adopted a strong progressive voice and eventually won a Pulitzer Prize for an editorial condemning racial bigotry. Whenever I felt I was going crazy in the macabre world of Mississippi, I'd look to Carter for a reality check. He gave me hope, and if not for him, I think I would have fled Mississippi right then and there.

In February 1959, Carter called me about a black sharecropper and his wife who had been arrested under suspicious circumstances for the murder of their white landlord. Carter said he did not have an extra reporter available and asked if we could track down the story. The law enforcement authorities were uncooperative by telephone, so I drove one hundred miles to a cotton farm near Rosedale, where the alleged crime had occurred, and filed an exclusive story. The landlord was Joseph S. Decker, who twenty years earlier had served three years in federal prison for practicing slavery when he chained a black woman to a bedpost for several days and forced her husband to work in the fields. Now Decker was accusing a black sharecropper, L. D. Patterson, of owing him $107. Decker, armed with a pistol, furiously stormed into the Patterson shack late at night demanding payment. Patterson fatally shot Decker and fled with his wife through the fields with bloodhounds fast on their trail. The couple was captured and jailed. The law and evidence supported Patterson's claim that he was defending himself and his wife from a hostile, armed intruder. The couple was eventually released, but the outcome could have been different had the authorities succeeded in keeping the story under wraps, as they so often did in these cases.

We also had more news tips coming from blacks as well. An NAACP leader in Jackson called our bureau to report that his relative in Chicago heard that a farm worker in rural Mississippi had been lynched by his landlord and the local sheriff. Our reporter made some calls, but the sheriff dismissed the incident and told him that he had seen the worker hanging around town that very morning. When our reporter arrived at the scene, he found the worker imprisoned and charged with assault on his landlord. The defendant's mother said her son had been beaten by the landlord and the sheriff and then questioned by the FBI. By this time, people in town were grumbling that UPI was "stirring up trouble," and our reporter left town under threat. The FBI said it found no grounds for intervening in the case and would not disclose its findings. We wrote a long story with details, but it received no more than two paragraphs on the national wires. Our staff was spent and frustrated, but in other instances our stories were getting bigger national headlines.

One story widely circulated outside the South was during the spring of 1959, when we reported on the lynching of Mack Charles Parker, a twenty-three-year-old black truck driver from Poplarville, Mississippi, who was accused of kidnapping and raping a pregnant white woman. Three days before his trial, a vigilante posse of white men dragged him screaming from the county jail, beat and shot him, wrapped his corpse in logging chains, and dumped it into the Pearl River. The mob was led by a former deputy sheriff, and a jailer allowed the men to abscond with Parker. Because this was not just murder but also kidnapping and breaking into a prison, the FBI was sent to investigate. I assigned Cliff Sessions, a reporter in our bureau from Bolton, Mississippi, and a graduate of Mississippi Southern College, to the scene, where he remained for several weeks filing copy on what seemed a fruitless investigation despite a large number of FBI agents assigned to the case. Sessions successfully obtained a copy of a secret FBI report, but he didn't use his byline on the story to protect the source who had leaked the report.

Back in Washington, FBI director J. Edgar Hoover was criticized in the press for a lack of diligence in the Parker investigation. Although the FBI assigned sixty agents to the case, the local judge and prosecutor refused to share information with federal officials. The FBI also faced resistance from the townspeople of Poplarville, who referred to the FBI presence as "the occupation" and wanted the investigation handled by local and state officers. The FBI compiled enough information, however, to turn over a handful of suspects to the Mississippi governor's office, including one man who made no secret of his involvement. James "Preacher" Lee, a local Baptist minister, bragged openly around town about his role in the abduction, saying, "God's word set forth that the Negro is a servant."

Despite the evidence and two grand juries investigating the crime, no indictments or arrests were forthcoming. A federal grand jury failed to issue an indictment after receiving incorrect instructions from Judge Sidney Mize, the same judge who had denied Willie McGee's last-minute appeal to stay his execution.

Sessions's chilling news accounts of vigilante justice and unobfuscated conspiracy riled Hoover. One day I was shocked to see a column on the wire service by Lyle Wilson, UPI's Washington bureau chief and a UPI vice president, praising the quality of the FBI's Poplarville investigation but also asserting that a UPI reporter was interfering with the investigation. That could only be Sessions, who became the focus of contempt in Poplarville. I complained to Wilson, asking why he would publish such an accusation against our own reporter without even consulting Sessions or me. "I'm sorry, John," Wilson said, "I didn't want to write it but I owed the Director one." That was not unusual in the days of the Hoover reign. He would talk only to those writers who would polish his image in return for exclusive information. In fairness to UPI, however, this was the only incident during my decade-long tenure with the wire service in which I was aware that an editor or manager attempted to influence our reporting.

I learned many years after the Parker case that some FBI agents—not all but some—were sympathetic to local whites at the time of the crime and, therefore, far less diligent in investigating civil rights cases. In addition, the US Justice Department maintained an official list of subversive organizations it had kept since the 1940s to track Soviet-controlled groups. By the mid-1950s, the list was expanded to ninety national organizations, some as innocuous as the League of American Writers and the Congress of African Women. In 2009, the FBI reopened the Parker case, one of more than a hundred cases involving black victims that were scheduled to be revisited under the Emmett Till Unsolved Civil Rights Crime Act of 2007.

CHAPTER 11

Overcoming Pressures

LIVING AND WORKING IN MISSISSIPPI WAS A DAILY STRUGGLE, BUT I WAS in a unique position to write vivid stories that would have otherwise gone untold. Living in a stifling environment was uncomfortable but also stimulating. There were rumblings of societal change, and some people were more prescient than I in foreseeing the future. William Faulkner, for instance, wrote: "We speak now against the day when our Southern people who will resist to the last these inevitable changes in social relations, will, when they have been forced to accept what they at one time might have accepted with dignity and goodwill, will say, 'Why didn't someone tell us this before? Tell us this in time?'"

It was difficult to imagine that the standards of American twentieth-century life would ever reach the strange, rural outpost of Mississippi. Other southern states with larger stakes in national commerce were slowly conforming to calls for racial progress. But not Mississippi. The state had no major cities or nationally prominent universities, and the wealthy plantation elite set the policies and controlled the legislature. Per capita, the state ranked the most abysmal in all economic indicators—with the highest rates of illiteracy, poverty, teen pregnancy, starvation, and infant mortality. The motto in Arkansas and Alabama was "Thank God for Mississippi," because the state was always the worst on ranking lists. It was the poorest state in the nation and had the largest percentage of blacks.

Despite the dim prospects for change, a few of us in law, journalism, business, pulpits, and grassroots politics saw the stirrings of discontent, and we wanted to be part of a transformation. I had witnessed enough senseless thinking and brutal acts toward minorities to know, as hard as it was to accept, that the practices of my family and people in our small towns were fallacies. I had fantasies of starting a weekly newspaper to report on what was happening in Mississippi and why. I confided my desire to Frank E. Smith, a moderate member of the US Congress later defeated for reelection in 1962 because he was too closely aligned with President Kennedy. "Oh, everybody wants to start a statewide news weekly," he said, and reminded me that without access to power and wealth, there was little success for such an endeavor.

So I remained content at UPI, knowing it was the only news organization in the state to take a new approach to describe the nuances of how people thought about the past and the future. The state needed competent, skeptical reporters who could, if nothing else, keep the record straight. We sparked the ire of many white leaders when we wrote race-related stories for UPI national distribution. One day, a state assistant attorney general buttonholed me in a corridor of the capitol and said with an indignant oily-nice tone so common in the South, "You wouldn't want your children going to school with those of your yard man, would you?"

I quietly told him I didn't take sides and I was simply reporting the news. Conviviality, a pervasive manner of the South, was a necessary skill to survive. Most of the media owners and managers we dealt with across the state were, like me, from small southern towns. I spoke their language and could engage them in storytelling over drinks, which could turn arguments into laughter. Mannerisms, speech, and skin color made me tolerable. I may have been an eccentric gone astray, but they still considered me one of them. If I had come from the North—or even from Memphis—I probably would have been run out of the state.

Luckily, we at UPI were not central in the social network and not as vulnerable to threats as others who owned small-town newspapers such as Hodding Carter Sr.; Ira Harkey, publisher of the Pascagoula *Chronicle-Star*; or Hazel Brannon Smith, the owner and editor of four weekly newspapers. Carter received so many threats for his paper's support of fair treatment of blacks that he kept a loaded pistol in his desk drawer. Harkey, who won a Pulitzer Prize for antisegregation editorials, had crosses burned on his front lawn and shots fired at his newspaper office. Smith, who won a Pulitzer Prize for editorials about the White Citizens' Council, was eventually run out of business for her courageous stance denouncing inhumane treatment of blacks. Bill Minor, who harbored a strange affliction to stay in Mississippi to "change the state from within," later bought one of Smith's papers. For years, he wrote courageous weekly columns, with the motto "once a week, but never weakly," challenging the Mississippi establishment.

At UPI, we did not write opinion pieces or display an ideology. But, when it came to race relations, objectivity was irrelevant to our subscribers, who were growing increasingly upset with our coverage, and I became worried about our bureau's financial safety. Suddenly, everyone seemed to be an expert on how the delicate subject should be handled and had a gripe about our coverage. One day, a radio station manager in Hattiesburg walked into my office carrying one of our articles. "It's tainted," he said, although it was a straight, unbiased account of blacks integrating a Memphis elementary school under court order. "What is your objection?" I asked. "It glorifies the Nigra," the manager replied. "Can't you report the facts without romancing the Negro race?"

I felt additional pressure from our subscribers when I foolishly agreed in 1959 to take on an additional role as UPI state sales representative to bump my low salary up to $155 a week to provide for my growing family. My new role entailed running both the news and business sides of the bureau. I spent two or three days a week spinning around the state in a little green Rambler explaining to clients and prospective subscribers why we had superior service to our rival, AP. In my usual naïveté, I underestimated the extent to which our subscribers did not want news about emerging black issues. This was especially true among broadcasters, the constant and steady bulk of our client base, who were among the most ideologically conservative. Most were native to the state and had gotten into broadcasting mainly for the money it promised. They believed that they, not the public, owned the airwaves, and they railed constantly against Washington for regulating their business.

I spent time listening to their tirades against UPI and "liberals" as they threatened, either directly or implicitly, to cancel our service. One four-hour session with a station owner named Phillip Brady in Brookhaven left me depressed for days, not so much from the fear of economic loss as from the disoriented feeling I had when I crossed purposes with the kind of people I had grown up with. Brady tried to persuade me that the state's resistance to integration was absolute. He didn't cancel his contract with UPI, but he made my life miserable by always criticizing our coverage.

Mississippi was a very parochial place. Although it had more than two million people, it was in many ways like a small town. Everyone in the state knew each other. They had gone to college together or were related within vast, extended families. At times, it seemed that the entire state was racist and that everyone around me believed something different from what I did. Their beliefs and actions were reinforced by tradition, religion, and, most importantly, the law. I would rise every morning and ask myself, "Is there something wrong with me?"

One person who made me feel that way almost every day was Fred Beard, a prominent and respected member of an old land-prosperous Mississippi family and the manager of one of the state's pioneering radio stations, WJDX, and its companion television station, WLBT. Beard had studied at a large out-of-state business school and seemed progressive about business matters. He was a pillar of Jackson's First Presbyterian Church and moved in the top civic circles. When it came to politics and race, his anger knew no bounds, and his main target was the federal government. Unfortunately, I heard from Beard a lot, because his radio and television stations were among our big subscribers. One day, when an important story was moving on the wires from Washington, Beard stuck his head in our door and shouted, "A story from Washington? Someone should drop a bomb on that place and blow it up." Another day, he piled a stack of conspiratorial brochures and right-wing books in my lap and made me promise to read every page or he would not renew his contract with UPI. When he left, I read the titles, including George Crocker's *Roosevelt's Road to Russia*, and dumped them in the trash can. Negotiating a subscription contract with Beard was not easy. There was his usual ranting and raving, not just about our prices but about the type of stories we offered. Fortunately, he had an able and professional news director, Richard Sanders, who understood that our service was vital to their operations and convinced Beard to renew the contract.

It was Cliff Sessions, however, who bore the worst of Beard's intemperance. As Sessions began writing more often about protests, demonstrations, and sit-ins in Jackson, Beard cornered him at city hall and gratuitously berated him in front a crowd of people, including other reporters. "You are an integrationist, I know you are," Beard shouted at Sessions. "Go crawl back under your rock. You've been exposed." WLBT eventually had its license revoked by the Federal Communications Commission, not for Beard's personal behavior but for the racially inflammatory broadcasts that he inspired.

Despite these daily aggravations, there were some promising prospects in Mississippi journalism and the state's business community. When we published an article that two towns would comply with a federal order to desegregate bus and train stations, the reaction was quick and frantic. The mayor of Grenada, who had not anticipated opposition from the White Citizens' Council, told a local newspaper that he had been misquoted and a victim of false news reports. I wrote a letter to the newspaper's publisher saying, "It was perfectly clear that when the Citizens' Council people put the screws on your mayor, then came the statements of denial. It doesn't matter to us what they do about the bus stations in Grenada, but it is news that has to be covered. And I sure resent being used as a scapegoat for a public official who is forced to back down from his prearranged plan." The publisher agreed with me and printed my letter on the front page of his paper. I never heard from the mayor.

A new daily newspaper, the *Jackson State Times*, was launched with $1 million from investors including Dumas Milner, a millionaire manufacturer and local Chevrolet dealer. The *State Times* became an opposing voice to the monopolistic practices of the *Daily News* and the *Clarion-Ledger*, the two Jackson papers owned by Thomas and Robert Hederman that carried more blatantly racist copy than any other daily newspaper in the South. When the *State Times* subscribed to our service, the Hederman family was forced to also subscribe to ward off any competition from the new paper.

The Hedermans had a reputation for using bare-knuckle pressure to gain whatever they wanted, and I soon felt their wrath. During the 1960 gubernatorial election, I received a call from Robert Hederman, the patriarch of the family, summoning me to his office. He was a tall, imposing man with blue eyes that turned piercingly cold when he felt someone had crossed him. He was waiting behind his desk holding an article I had written on election night describing the victory of conservative Dixiecrat Ross Barnett.

The Hedermans had endorsed Barnett and contributed heavily to his campaign. Robert Hederman complained that my description of Barnett as "an aging segregationist" was biased. "I am aging, you are aging," he said. Technically, he was correct. I should not have used "aging" as an identifier of someone being old. But my purpose, which I dared not convey to Hederman, was that I was trying, in a clumsy way, to signal to out-of-state readers that Barnett was an old buffoon. He figuratively and literally stumbled his way into and through his one term in office. At a campaign stop, he stepped off his plane and walked blithely into the propeller. For the rest of the campaign he appeared with a bandaged arm in a sling, attracting the sympathy vote that gave him a small margin in his victory. Robert Hederman had called me to his office to put me on notice that the Hedermans, who wielded even more political and economic power now that Barnett had been elected, were watching for any infraction of reporting that might damage Barnett or their defiance of civil rights.

Barnett, a personal-injury trial lawyer, knew little about government and nothing about the role of the press. Shortly after he was inaugurated, he began calling me at home on Saturday evenings to complain about something I had written. A workaholic, he read my Sunday analysis pieces the day before in early-released editions. I can't recall all the details of his complaints, but they involved my repeated renditions, which I thought were fair and impartial, of his mishandling of state government.

One evening, just as I settled into a steaming hot bath, Barnett called. There was no putting him off, and I finally asked Betty to bring me the phone. She rolled her eyes as she handed me the receiver. For almost two hours, as the water turned cold, he rambled on with assertions that made no sense to me. And I am sure my answers went past him by just as wide a mark. Finally, and mercifully, the conversation ended, but with no connection formed between us.

As long as UPI provided good news content, we could stay ahead of AP and the controversy and survive in Mississippi. We became, in effect, a "paper of record," reporting every traffic death, every crime worthy of notice, every state supreme court decision, and all the economic and political news we could pull together. We also reported on virtually every bill of any importance introduced in the legislature and its daily actions. Political campaigns and elections allowed us to get ahead in state coverage because people turned out en masse for campaign rallies, and on election night virtually every adult ear was tuned to the returns.

Beating our competition during a gubernatorial election gained us a secure advantage over AP. Because no independent election service tabulated votes on election night, each individual news organization gathered unofficial returns, and tallying the votes was not easy. UPI had a crude method. We hired a correspondent in each of the state's eighty-two counties to telephone us with any changes in the count. We set up charts listing the counties, the total precincts, and the votes for each candidate. We wrote the votes from each county on a strip of cardboard, which we then attached with a clothespin to a cord strung across the office. Each new strip covered an old strip as votes accumulated; by the end of the evening, a county might have as many as ten or twelve overlying strips. We hired adding-machine operators to periodically compute the number of precincts reported and the total for each candidate. Reporters could then read the bottom line and put the latest results on the wire. As cumbersome as this was, it provided a quicker and often more accurate account than AP, which got its numbers from its various member papers and processed the tallies through its New Orleans bureau.

We also beat AP in declaring a candidate the winner. The TV networks do that now with exit polls, but we relied on our clunky yet reliable method. Because we knew that the outcome in rural, remote counties could accurately predict the result for the whole state, we also hired people who knew local politics like the back of their hands and could figure out final tallies from incomplete returns. Our declaration of a winner was never wrong, and I took delight in preparing promotional materials a few days later touting our performance.

In 1960, I attended my first presidential nominating convention to report on how conservative southern delegates created havoc within the national Democratic Party when Hubert Humphrey, a young, newly elected US senator from Minnesota, successfully added a civil rights plank to the platform. The entire Mississippi delegation and half the Alabama delegates walked out of the convention in protest. "We think it's obnoxious," one southern delegate told me. For the first time in history, Mississippi delegates put forth two separate slates—one for delegates pledged to Kennedy, the Democratic nominee, and the other for unpledged delegates. Republicans watched this splintering with glee, hoping it would give their nominee, Vice President Richard M. Nixon, a better chance of carrying Mississippi in the upcoming presidential election.

Yet, the split afforded neither Nixon nor Kennedy a victory in Mississippi. In the general election, Mississippi delegates voted for US senator Harry Flood Byrd, a conservative segregationist from Virginia, for president and Strom Thurmond, a US senator from South Carolina, as vice president. On election day, Mississippi and Alabama were the only two states in the nation to throw their support to Byrd, and Kennedy barely squeaked out a national victory over Nixon.

By 1960, we had increased our full-time staff from three to five reporters, and we served twelve of the state's nineteen daily newspapers. Of those twelve, we served nine newspapers exclusively. And we never yielded once to demands that we scale back our coverage of the emerging civil rights issues. Some days, more than half the stories on our wire pertained either directly or indirectly to race. In fact, I became concerned that this type of news was dominating our daily reports to the extent that I was blocking out other key events and putting too much burden on our limited staff. And I didn't want to be preoccupied with imbalanced coverage on a single issue. But I couldn't ignore how important the story of race relations was becoming to Mississippi and the nation.

Other reporters at UPI understood the significance as well, although I am not sure we all realized then how race relations in Mississippi would change our world view and ultimately our careers. H. L. Stevenson went on to become UPI's editor in chief and vice president in New York, Cliff Sessions rose to chief spokesman for the Justice Department in Washington, and Lewis Lord became a senior writer for *U.S. News and World Report* magazine in Washington.

My professional decisions at UPI took a toll on my personal life. I didn't feel I was in physical danger, but Betty and I were ostracized by people in our neighborhood, who accused us of being communists. Betty was subjected to snide remarks from women with whom she worked in church and civic affairs. We were reminded that "upsetting the apple cart" was not a dignified southern style. We didn't discuss politics or my work with our extended families, who were not "segs" but were conservative and didn't understand why we were willing to risk our reputation and status. They wondered why would we disturb a system that worked well for us.

Every morning Betty and I would awake further removed from the mind-set of most people in the state, including religious leaders. I wrote an article with the lead: "The racial integration issue has become such a disturbing element among Southern Protestants that many clergymen see it as a threat to unity among denominations." It described how southern churches were rebelling against their national organizations when the national body recommended accepting all people as congregants, regardless of their color. When the governing body of an influential branch of the national Presbyterian Church adopted a pro-integration report, a powerful and wealthy church in Jackson voted to cut off its financial ties, contending that freedom of fellowship did not mean "an unnatural association of people." In another Jackson church, members withheld their financial pledges until they were assured that no blacks would join the church.

Our social life was confined to a few friends in journalism and to a moderate church where we found others who were concerned about the state's myopic views on race and defiance. While we alienated many white people, we gained new friendships among blacks, including an interesting newcomer to Jackson. Medgar Evers, a young Mississippi native who became state field secretary of the NAACP, was gaining a leadership role by organizing boycotts, challenging the University of Mississippi's whites-only admissions policy, and setting up new NAACP chapters. He and his older brother, Charles, were among the first black World War II veterans to try to vote in Mississippi in 1946. Medgar Evers was by far the most exemplary and dignified of all the major figures I met during the civil rights movement, and I considered him among the most reliable of sources for news stories. He was almost saintly and angelic, totally without guile, and never displayed hatred in my presence toward his white opponents. But he was strongly determined to free blacks from the oppression he had known in rural Newton County, where he had grown up.

Cliff Sessions, who was younger and more daring than I, invited Evers and his wife, Myrlie, for cocktails at the Sessions's home on North State Street in Jackson and asked Betty and me to join them. Cliff and his wife, Shirley, lived in a large, exclusively white apartment building in an all-white neighborhood. Blacks and whites rarely mingled socially, and Evers had been depicted in the white community as a dangerous, rabble-rousing agitator. Betty and I immediately accepted the invitation, but there was a real sense of tension and risk when we gathered. Knowing he was being watched by white vigilante groups, Sessions kept the drapes drawn tight. Despite the threat of danger, that evening was one of the most relaxing and enjoyable occasions I can remember, as the conversation flowed from movies to baseball to politics and, inevitably, to the strife within Mississippi. Evers was driven by a strong streak of justice, as if it were impossible for him to rest without sacrifice for a greater good. Fortunately, the evening passed without incident.

Some years later, when Evers was shot and killed in his driveway on a June evening in 1963 by a fanatic racist, the first person Myrlie called was Sessions. Evers had explicitly instructed Myrlie: "If anything happens to me, call Cliff first, not the police." When I learned of his death, I remembered with pained sorrow the evening we had enjoyed and tried futilely to understand how a beacon of humanity could be extinguished in a senseless act of violence.

CHAPTER 12

Out of Mississippi

BY 1960, I FELT I HAD BEEN IN MISSISSIPPI TOO LONG. I WAS DRAINED BY the tensions and demands of the wire service. I needed a larger salary for my family, and UPI provided no advancement except the drudgery work of being an editor or a manager in other locales. No other jobs in the state promised a future that would enable me to participate in national journalism.

I applied for a Nieman Fellowship at Harvard University, a prestigious one-year study program that boasted a lengthy list of distinguished alumni, including Greenville publisher Hodding Carter Sr., who had been a Nieman fellow before World War II. With a strong recommendation from Carter, I was accepted for the 1960–1961 academic year. Betty and I packed up our four daughters, including a newborn, into our two-tone Chevrolet and pulled a U-Haul trailer to Boston. With Mississippi in our rearview mirror, we coached the girls in their new vernacular. "Repeat after me," I told them: "Pahk the cah in Hahvahd Yahd."

It was inevitable that moving out of Mississippi would leave me with feelings of guilt for abandoning a small band of journalists and activists who remained behind on the front lines. But I had lofty ambitions to become a national journalist, and now, in my mid-thirties, I was a bit behind on my career path after three years in the army and a decade in Mississippi. I was competing against the brightest students just graduating from the eastern colleges. It was time for me to move on.

Eighteen journalists, almost all white men, were selected for the program, and my year at Harvard was one of the most academically enlightening and exhilarating experiences of my life. Louis Lyons, curator of the Nieman Foundation, introduced us to the university's leading faculty members and visiting dignitaries. The campus was infused with an intellectual excitement, and we could sit in on any classes and lectures we chose, ranging from theology and art to science and engineering, with virtually no requirement to make grades. I took advantage of every available avenue. It was a year of expansive growth and insight into a world of enlightenment. My time there shaped my future life and work almost as much as my small-town upbringing and my reporting experiences in Mississippi.

I felt akin to the southern protagonist Quentin Compson in *Absalom, Absalom!*, Faulkner's Gothic 1936 novel about fictional Yoknapatawpha County, Mississippi. Compson arrived at Harvard only to be questioned by his Canadian roommates and others: "Tell about the South. What's it like there. Why do they live there. Why do they live at all." Like Compson, I found it difficult to answer those questions, not just to my schoolmates but to myself as well. The only answers I had were family, heritage, and familiarity.

The Harvard fellowship lasted one year, and we were required under the rules to return to our previous jobs for at least a year. I went back to UPI in Jackson, finding much of the state unchanged but noticing small inroads on the race issue. One of my first articles after returning described a federal court hearing in Jackson about whether James H. Meredith, a twenty-eight-year-old Mississippi-born World War II air force veteran, should be the first black student admitted to the University of Mississippi. Other states such as North Carolina and Virginia were reluctantly, yet peacefully, admitting their first black students to state universities. Meredith, with the backing of the NAACP Legal Defense and Education Fund, filed a lawsuit against Ole Miss for rejecting him twice because of his race.

The judge hearing the case was Sidney Mize, the same judge as in the Willie McGee and Mack Charles Parker cases. It felt like déjà vu. During the hearing, the state questioned Meredith for hours about his personal life and medical history, particularly as it pertained to the issue of his race.

Meredith said he had suffered in the past from nervous tension over racial incidents and had sought treatment from an air force doctor. The state's assistant attorney general brought forth military medical records showing that Meredith felt a "need to fight" over racial problems, but because his anger was expressed in a nonaggressive fashion, no treatment had been recommended.

During the day's questioning, Meredith denied being paid to file the lawsuit but confirmed that he had sought help from the NAACP legal team because he knew they helped people whose civil rights had been denied. The assistant attorney general immediately objected to this statement, saying, "That is the heart of this matter. We deny there has been a denial of civil rights." Mize upheld the objection, and the hearing lasted for days. Four months later, Mize denied Meredith's request for a preliminary injunction, saying that Meredith had not been denied admission based on race. Meredith's lawyer immediately filed an appeal with the US Court of Appeals, and the case eventually went to the US Supreme Court.

Despite permanent fixtures like Judge Mize, there were visible signs that outside organized opposition to segregation was finally penetrating Mississippi. In September 1961, one of the first lunchroom sit-ins in the state was staged at the Trailways bus terminal in Jackson. Fifteen Episcopal priests, including three who were black and one who was the son-in-law of New York governor Nelson Rockefeller, were arrested and charged with breach of peace after they tried to eat at the bus terminal's whites-only restaurant. The clergymen were part of a group of ministers touring the nation on an antisegregation "prayer pilgrimage."

It was the first time I had covered a sit-in, and I delicately described it in a short article as an "incident." I contacted Rockefeller in Rochester, New York, who did not seem surprised by the news. He said that his daughter's husband was interested in this cause and added that he admired the courage and dedication of those upholding the basic precepts of the country's founding.

After one year in Jackson, I again became restless to leave Mississippi and persuaded UPI to send me to the Washington bureau. Working in the nation's capital was the height of domestic journalism, and it would be a good place for me to make contacts for another job. We packed up our family and once again left Mississippi behind. I was given several important assignments, including reporting on the Justice and Labor Departments, the US Senate, and the White House.

Some assignments allowed me to meet sources who would be invaluable in the future, including Robert F. Kennedy Jr., who was not just the president's brother but also the US attorney general. I arrived in Washington a year after the Bay of Pigs Invasion, and the US government was still trying to win the release of 1,113 prisoners in Cuba. They were finally freed on Christmas Eve of 1962, and I wrote a story about how President Kennedy and his brother had engineered a deal to meet Cuban leader Fidel Castro's demand for $53 million in food, medicine, and humanitarian aid in exchange for the prisoners' release. The Justice Department revealed behind-the-scenes negotiations to the press only after the prisoners had arrived home safely. Those negotiations, which I wrote about, showed how the Kennedys were masters of backroom strategy and how Robert Kennedy used a hands-on approach to get things done.

When Congress failed to approve the use of taxpayer money as ransom, Robert Kennedy made personal pleas to pharmaceutical companies and baby-food manufacturers to make tax-deductible donations to Cuba. The administration also raised an additional $2.9 million in cash from private donations that Castro demanded in the final hours before the release. Robert Kennedy himself rang up one unnamed friend, who kicked in $1 million. My lead read: "'Sure,' the friend told Att. Gen. Robert Kennedy, 'write me down for a million.'" The Justice Department insisted on keeping the identity of the donor anonymous.

I realized then how creative and resourceful the wealthy Kennedys and their cohorts were in gaining and using influence. They possessed a sense of inevitability about getting their way. Writing this story was my first introduction to Robert Kennedy, and I found him to be smart and precocious. At the same time, he was also shy and bookish. He was more understated than his brother and didn't consider himself a major player in politics and government, although he was a primary operator in carrying out his brother's desires.

Both Kennedys understood the advantages of working closely with the press. Unlike today's media climate, in which access to high-level officials is carefully limited, the Kennedys, especially Robert, made themselves readily available to us. There were regular White House press conferences, and journalists followed the Kennedys around to get quotations or updates. I would stop by Robert Kennedy's office for an interview or see him on the street and ask him questions. On many occasions, he would give me information for a story and say, "I don't want you to quote me on this, but . . ." Then I would follow up with someone in the Justice Department who would confirm the information.

After several months of working in Washington, I discovered that my "dream job" was not what I had envisioned. After being in the thick of the news in Mississippi, the Washington job seemed routine because the well-oiled news was orchestrated by political spin doctors. I learned what the term "media circus" meant, and I was simply a paddle in the communication churn, given that news was routinely fed to us through press releases, committee hearings, and sources who sometimes planted stories. UPI and AP reporters roamed together, and we shared notes to provide news updates as a foundation for larger stories and analyses written by big newspapers and broadcasters. As wire reporters, we were not given much leeway for writing lengthy explanatory or in-depth articles.

I regretted leaving Mississippi despite its faults. I was frustrated to be in Washington while the race story continued to develop in the South. This became even more evident when James Meredith, finally armed with a US Supreme Court ruling in his favor, showed up to enroll at the University of Mississippi. It forced President Kennedy to carry through on his inaugural address pledge to ensure equal rights in America.

I watched from Washington as this historic event unfolded and wrote about how John and Robert Kennedy were "prepared for the painful decision of when and how much federal force to use" in order to usher Meredith through the doors of the university. Governor Ross Barnett, ready to seize the political advantage of a showdown with Meredith, vowed to block his entrance. My article described how President Kennedy wanted to avoid violence but kept hundreds of infantry soldiers on standby in Georgia in case Meredith could not get past Barnett's barricade of five hundred Mississippi state troopers. I described how the White House made no effort to conceal President Kennedy's concern about the situation, consulting five times in one day with his brother.

Although other southern governors had faced unhappy dilemmas and uncertain political futures when forced to choose between allowing integration or resisting federal mandates, the political gains with demonstrating opposition could be enormous. Arkansas governor Orval Faubus won a third term by a landslide because of his open defiance of the federal government when Little Rock Central High School was integrated in 1957. Barnett remained steadfast in his determination to bar Meredith's entry. He accused both Kennedys of "sowing the seeds of hate and violence" in a field that would produce a "bloody harvest," and he claimed that the civil rights movement was inspired by communists.

US Defense Secretary Robert S. McNamara flew back to Washington from West Germany in the middle of the night in case it became necessary to use military troops at the campus. Robert Kennedy had a long series of telephone conversations with Barnett, but the two came to no agreement. I felt some sympathy for Robert Kennedy, recalling my own frustrating telephone calls two years earlier with an intractable Barnett.

But I knew that Barnett had met his match. Robert Kennedy filed a contempt of court order against Barnett that was upheld by a federal appeals judge in New Orleans. Meredith was eventually admitted but not without violence as white students and segregationists rioted on the campus for days. President Kennedy called in US Marshals and army troops. Two people were killed and two hundred law enforcement personnel were injured. My reporting from distant Washington seemed pale in comparison to UPI dispatches from reporters like Cliff Sessions who were on the ground in Mississippi. I could see that I had left the South too early.

I was also missing another large story about race relations in the South. Reverend Martin Luther King Jr., of Atlanta, the civil rights movement's most formidable and prominent leader, was gaining strength with a message of nonviolent resistance, a tactic borrowed from India's independence leader, Mahatma Gandhi, that was a novel approach in the United States. King had been working toward a national agenda of civil rights since shortly after the Till trial, when he staged a boycott in Montgomery, Alabama, after a black woman named Rosa Parks refused to give up her seat to a white person on a city bus. In 1957, he founded the Southern Christian Leadership Conference (SCLC) to galvanize support, and he led an unsuccessful struggle for equal rights in 1962 in Albany, Georgia. By the spring of 1963, he had turned his sights to Birmingham, Alabama, one of the most racially divided cities in America.

The Birmingham campaign was marked by business boycotts, protests, and sit-ins, which culminated in confrontations between black demonstrators and white law enforcement. When hundreds of peaceful protesters marched in the streets of Birmingham to demand integrated facilities downtown, the police used high-pressure water hoses, billy clubs, and attack dogs to disperse the crowds from a park next to the Sixteenth Street Baptist Church. The protesters, some as young as eight years old, abided by King's nonviolent strategy and showed no resistance as the police overpowered them. In two days, the police arrested and detained more than seven hundred protesters including King in the Birmingham jail. The conflict was so violent that it attracted high-profile media attention, and President Kennedy addressed the nation, saying, "The events in Birmingham and elsewhere have so increased cries for equality that no city or state or legislative body can prudently choose to ignore them." The riots transferred the call for equal rights from the streets to the corridors of power and compelled the Kennedy administration to accelerate its efforts to draft comprehensive civil rights legislation. Robert Kennedy warned from Washington that Birmingham's refusal to grant equal rights to blacks could bring turmoil, although he questioned whether children should have participated in the protests.

My Mississippi experience helped me when the Kennedys began to shepherd a civil rights bill through Congress in June 1963. Opposition to the bill was spearheaded by arch-segregationist senators including James Eastland, chairman of the powerful Judiciary Committee, and Strom Thurmond. Both these Democratic senators repeatedly called Robert Kennedy and other Justice Department officials to appear at committee hearings about the bill, which included equal voting rights, equal public accommodations, and continued school desegregation. I covered the hearings, in which Thurmond issued a pointed line of questioning and invoked arcane committee rules to cut off the proceedings early. One reason he opposed the bill was because he said its accommodations portion would turn private businesses into public utilities. One witness, assistant attorney general Burke Marshall, reminded Thurmond that businesses were already regulated on wages, hours of operation, labeling, and packaging. "We've gone a long way toward a welfare state. Do you believe the government should have done all these things?" Thurmond asked. "Yes, Senator," Marshall replied.

In another hearing, Robert Kennedy urged members of Eastland's committee "to bring to law what we have always known in our hearts to be justice." I sat at the press table looking directly at Robert Kennedy as he argued that states' rights advocates corrupted the concept of justice. "States' rights as our forefathers conceived it was a protection of the right of the individual citizen," Robert Kennedy said. "Those who preach most frequently about states' rights today are not seeking the protection of the individual citizen, but his exploitation." He said the proposed bill was not a cure-all for racism in America but the first step to right past wrongs. "[O]ur responsibility as a nation is most plain. We must remove the injustices."

He even made a pragmatic pitch by appealing to the nation's self-interest. "Everywhere we look, we find irrefutable evidence that the Negroes in

America have yet to be given full citizenship and we find increasing evidence too that they are no longer willing to tolerate the burdens we have imposed on them," Robert Kennedy said. He cited racial unrest in Cambridge, Maryland, and Savannah, Georgia. "This is what happens when long-standing legitimate grievances are not remedied under law."

The Kennedys tapped into influences beyond the political world, bringing in popular sports figures to testify about the success of integrating sports teams. Baseball commissioner Ford Frick told Congress that integrating the Brooklyn Dodgers in the mid-1940s resulted in the loss of several minor-league teams in the South, but that the predictions of tragic consequences by signing Jackie Robinson never materialized. National Football League commissioner Pete Rozelle told a Senate committee that stadium seating and player facilities were already integrated, and he threatened that any city with racial segregation laws would not be approved for a new NFL franchise. "It is the color of the player's uniform, not his skin, that is important to the fans," said Joe Foss, American Football League commissioner.

The Kennedys also gained the public backing of the powerful unions and a commitment that union members would join the two hundred thousand integration activists who were planning a march on Washington in August. But even the Kennedys' sway could not stave off opposition from the large contingent of southern Democrats in Congress. Senator Sam J. Ervin, a North Carolina Democrat, said that civil rights legislation would give the Kennedys power that "no good public official would want and no bad official ought to have."

Covering the proposed civil rights legislation gave me some connection to the bigger story in the South, but I still felt like I was sitting on the sidelines of history, watching the best domestic news events of the century unfold from the safe and insular confines of Washington.

One day in the summer of 1963, ten months after arriving in Washington, I received a call at my desk in the Senate press gallery from Harrison Salisbury, the national editor of the *New York Times*, asking if I would be interested in reporting for the paper from the South. The region stretching from the Virginia Tidewater to eastern Texas was exploding with protests and conflicts. It was evident to everyone that the civil rights movement was here to stay and garnering more national attention each day. Salisbury told me the *Times* needed a reporter based in Atlanta to join Claude Sitton, who had succeeded John Popham. Sitton, my former college newspaper editor and an astute student of the South, was doing a masterful job of reporting the story, but he needed reinforcements.

I was eager to work for an esteemed paper where reporting jobs seemed accessible only to a talented few, and I could report on major national stories from the trenches. I wanted to be in the middle of this challenging story, but I had second thoughts about the offer. Living in the South was not an easy choice once I was confronted with the actual possibility. The impenetrable attitudes about race relations had caused my family constant strife and alienation, and the demands of the job certainly would not allow me to go home each evening after work to see them. This would be the fourth time moving my family in three years. But Betty, always up for a challenge, encouraged me, knowing it was a rare opportunity in a singular time in American history.

Although Sitton and others had considered several men for the job, I knew why I was chosen. I spoke Southern and had the right complexion to navigate my way through the white establishment of the South. My year at Harvard made me more attractive in the eyes of northern editors, and it also helped that the *Times'* executive editor, Turner Catledge, had grown up in Philadelphia, Mississippi.

After a series of interviews with editors in New York, I was hired, and Betty and I moved our family to Atlanta. Betty preferred Atlanta to other southern cities because it was more progressive, and it was a good central location for me to hopscotch from state to state. As we left Washington, King was preparing his now famous "I Have a Dream" speech for the March on Washington on August 28, 1963. That march was a kickoff to his national campaign, which would return to the South.

The *Times* was giving the civil rights movement priority coverage, and its commitment inspired other national news organizations to do the same. I felt I'd been given a rare opportunity to inform the public from a southern perspective about the untenable institution of racism. This was the land of my heritage, and I possessed an advantage in understanding the complexities and strangeness of the place and an ability to explain it in a balanced and nonsensational manner. I knew what many northerners did not know: not all integrationists were wild-eyed radicals; many were deeply religious and conservative. And not all segregationists were ignorant racists; some believed they were protecting their traditions and a cherished way of life. Chalking up racial strife simply to blind prejudice was shortsighted and dismissive.

As much as I understood the South, however, it was impossible for me as a white man to put myself in the place of a black person. No whites should even try. But I could be an objective observer dedicated to report all sides and both races. It would have been better to have had a black *Times* reporter, but the *Times* and many other national news organizations had not yet broken down their own racial barriers to hire black reporters.

My first article for the *Times*, published on August 21, 1963, covered a mass demonstration in Plaquemine, Louisiana, where seventy-five blacks were arrested for violating the town's ban on picketing. State troopers carrying cattle prods dispersed black protesters as three hundred whites looked on. Days earlier, hundreds of blacks had been repelled by tear gas as they marched to city hall.

This was the first mass street protest by blacks I'd covered, and it was a new and different sight. I had spent a decade writing about the brutal suppression of blacks in Mississippi, but I had not witnessed the organized opposition to that suppression that spilled into the streets. I also had not seen the white resistance to these protests, which I compared to dragging an angry tomcat by his tail across a thick carpet. If the white segregationists had been savvy, they would have ignored the protests. Instead, they provided the media with horrific and graphic scenes that rocked the nation.

CHAPTER 13

Bombingham

IN SEPTEMBER 1963, I TRAVELED TO ALABAMA, THE ONLY STATE WITH no integrated public schools, to write about several cities including Birmingham under federal court order to desegregate their classrooms. The state was still reeling from the Birmingham riots three months earlier and another more recent incident involving forced integration at the University of Alabama in Tuscaloosa. Two black students—Vivian Malone and James Hood—wanted to follow James Meredith's lead by breaking the color barrier at the all-white university. But Alabama governor George C. Wallace, who proclaimed in his inaugural speech, "Segregation now; segregation tomorrow; segregation forever," ordered state troopers to physically block Malone and Hood from registering for classes. Robert Kennedy took the upper hand by federalizing the Alabama National Guard under the command of President John Kennedy. When Malone and Hood arrived at the university, they were met by a defiant Wallace, who stood at the door to block their entrance. But the prospective students, accompanied by federal agents including US Assistant Attorney General John Doar, successfully entered through a back door and registered. President Kennedy addressed the nation on television and radio and pledged his commitment to comprehensive and long-reaching civil rights legislation.

Wallace was still smarting from the university showdown as primary and secondary public schools in Birmingham were preparing to open with court orders to desegregate. He launched a public relations campaign hoping to do two things: avoid using police to block black students from attending all-white public schools while also satisfying his segregationist supporters. Preeminent in Wallace's consideration was his political ambition. He was running for president in the Democratic primary, and although his chance of winning was slim, he wanted to show President Kennedy that he was not backing down from segregation or his resistance to federal control. "I am still determined to resist the efforts to take over our schools," he said. "I realize we are against powerful forces. We will win regardless of how long the fight takes. The American people are going to rise up and strike down those who have destroyed the rights of the individual and the states."

As the first day of school approached, Wallace and his staff hunkered down at the governor's mansion to devise a strategy of tough resistance. His first action was to issue an executive order barring blacks from white schools because white students would have their civil rights violated by the "disruptive" presence of black students.

Wallace, a short and intense man, looked drawn and tired as he met us for questions. He possessed a fiery defiance and announced that state troopers would turn away black students from white schools. "Society is coming apart at the seams," he said. "What good is it doing to force these situations when white people nowhere in the South want integration? What this country needs is a few first-class funerals, and a few political funerals too."

President Kennedy immediately denounced Wallace's decision, but Wallace said if the federal government stayed away, he would let local jurisdictions guide their own integration efforts. "[I]f they stay out, so will I," he said. "What is more democratic than this?"

The schools did not open without some disruption. Some parents in Birmingham withdrew their children when two black students showed up at an elementary school, and twelve whites were arrested in a two-hour demonstration at the city's all-white high school.

I stayed in Birmingham over the weekend to transmit my articles to New York and decided to fly home to Atlanta on Sunday, September 15, to celebrate my eleventh wedding anniversary with Betty. I had been chasing stories all over the South and hadn't been home for almost a month. I wanted badly to see my wife and four daughters. As I was driving my rental car toward the airport, I heard on the radio that a bomb had exploded at the Sixteenth Street Baptist Church and killed four children in their Sunday school class. I pulled a sharp U-turn and headed back downtown.

When I arrived at the church, I was aghast. The wreckage resembled postwar Berlin. One corner of the building exposed a gaping cavity of scattered yellow bricks. The stained-glass windows were blown out of their frames except for one showing an image of Jesus leading little children down a rosy path. A broken marble plaque commemorating the founding of the church in 1878 lay amid the rubble of broken glass and splintered debris.

The explosion occurred while a Sunday school teacher was finishing a morning lesson on "the Love that Forgives." Her message was now consumed in a scene of terror and death. Torn hymnals, splattered with blood, lay on the classroom floor. Scores of young blacks poured out of the church, bleeding, screaming, and moaning. Bystanders sobbed and prayed as the bodies of the four girls were brought forth from the wreckage.

"Oh God," a boy cried. "It's my sister. She's dead."

A teenage boy knelt in the street and recited the Lord's Prayer. Black residents from nearby neighborhoods rushed to the scene in anger. A crowd of black youths gathered across the street and rushed past the police to the church where they gazed in horror at the bodies. More crowds gathered in the park, where months earlier the police had clashed with protesters. Black leaders, including Reverend Charles Pillups, attempted to calm the crowds and pleaded with them not to march through the city. "This is exactly what they want you to do," Pillups told them. "Don't do it." The crowd broke up, but the leaders could not contain the outrage that continued throughout the day. I described it in my dispatch: "Tonight, this was a city of terror. Sporadic gunfire was heard in the Negro area and there were reports of scattered racial outbreaks." I quoted one man as saying, "My grandbaby was killed. You know how that makes me feel? I feel like blowing up the whole town."

While violence was contained near the church, there were outbursts in other parts of the city. Across town, the National States' Rights Party, a militant white supremacy group headquartered in Birmingham, hosted a rally in defiance of court-ordered integration. Two white sixteen-year-old youths were on their way home from the rally on a red motor scooter when they passed a black boy of the same age riding his bike with his thirteen-year-old brother, Virgil Ware, perched on the handlebars. One of the white boys pulled out a white-handled pistol and shot Virgil, killing him almost instantly.

In North Birmingham, a white police officer shot into a crowd of black boys throwing rocks at white teens and killed a sixteen-year-old black youth. A twenty-year-old black man set off a gasoline explosion that destroyed a grocery store in a black neighborhood because he was mad at the white owners. Crowds of blacks poured into the street, thinking the explosion was another racially targeted bomb, and were held back by police armed with shotguns, rifles, and submachine guns.

Unfortunately, bombings in this city were not unusual, and the city had earned the dubious moniker of "Bombingham." More than fifty bombings, all against blacks, had been recorded in the two decades. One bomb blew out the front half of a home owned by Martin Luther King Jr.'s younger brother, also a minister, while his wife and five children were sleeping.

What I witnessed at the Birmingham church was worse than anything I had ever seen at war. The testimonies of personal trauma continued when I visited the families of the victims the same night of the church bombing. I first went to the modest yet comfortable home of Claude and Gertrude Wesley in a black neighborhood where other bombs had exploded throughout the summer. Their only daughter, Cynthia, fourteen, was one of the four girls killed at the church. As I knocked on their door, I thought about my own children and how I would have reacted if they had been tragically and unjustly robbed from me. I felt awkward and intrusive standing on the front stoop when Wesley answered the door and invited me into their living room.

Wesley, a small, white-haired man of fifty-four, said adjusting to the loss of their daughter would not be easy for him and his wife, a second-grade teacher in the school where he was the principal. He said the family dog, a cocker spaniel named Toots, would take food only from Cynthia and that Toots would need to learn to eat without her. Then he described the bombing:

> I drove Cynthia to Sunday school and went to get some gasoline in my car. I was just a few blocks away when I heard the explosion. I knew it was our church. I rushed back but I could not find Cynthia. I wanted to think she had left the church, but someone told me I better go to the hospital. There they asked me what she was wearing. I told them a little class ring. They pulled out her hand and I saw the ring. Then I saw her black patent leather shoes and white socks. And I said, "That's her." I didn't want to see how she looked.

Wesley's next words stunned me. "This is how I feel," he said. "This thing that engulfed our child and others is worldwide. Many are involved in this social change. I have not asked why it happened to us. I don't feel bitter about it. I'm just hurt because our daughter was plucked from us." As I visited family after family of the victims, I was amazed that each showed similar grief and sadness—but no bitterness. I couldn't believe how brave they were.

Another mother, Maxine McNair, told me she was attending a women's Bible class when the bomb exploded and killed her only child, eleven-year-old Denise. "We were just finishing the class when I heard the explosion in the basement," she told me. "I put my hands to my ears and screamed, 'My baby, my baby.' I wanted to go where she was but someone led me outside." That was where she saw a ten-year-old girl she knew, bloody and injured, screaming and holding out her hands. McNair frantically searched for her daughter, and when rescue workers finally dug out some bodies, she saw Denise partly concealed by a sheet.

McNair, overcome by grief, could not continue her story, so her mother recounted how McNair had fallen on Denise and tried to erase the damage done to her body. "I just don't know how I feel today," McNair said once she regained her composure. "I'm so unhappy. I don't feel any bitterness." Her husband, Chris "Chick" McNair, who owned a photography studio, reached beyond his own personal suffering. "Even in war we do not bomb hospitals and churches," he said. "But I cannot help but believe that some good will come of this. If not, her death will have been in vain." That was a very philosophical, far-reaching view to embrace after their only child had been killed by someone who hated her for the color of her skin.

The third family I visited was Mr. and Mrs. Alvin C. Robertson, both teachers whose fourteen-year-old daughter, Carol, the youngest of their three children, died in the bombing. They lived a few blocks from the Wesleys. Carol and Cynthia were good friends and were together when they were killed. Alvin Robertson, his eyes cloudy from crying, said the church, which had served as an organizing place for the summer protesters, had received bomb threats. "I guess we should have been uneasy about leaving the children there," he said. "But it never occurred to me anyone would bomb a church with anybody in it." He said that after driving Carol to Sunday school, he returned home to join his wife, who was preparing for the 11:00 a.m. service. When someone called to tell them about the bombing, they rushed to the local university hospital and found Carol's body near the emergency room entrance marked "Colored Only." I asked the Robertsons if they shared the belief of many blacks that local authorities had not been diligent in investigating earlier racial bombings around the city. "I think they're doing the best they can," Alvin Robertson said. "I couldn't believe anything else."

The Robertsons, Wesleys, and McNairs were among the more affluent of Birmingham's blacks. But the family of the fourth victim was a divorced mother trying to rear her large family on a meager income. Alice Collins lived in a small, four-room house in a poor neighborhood, and her five children were in the church when the bomb exploded. One daughter, Addie Mae, fourteen, was killed, and another, Sarah, who was ten, was critically injured when she was hit by flying glass. I found Collins at the hospital sitting beside Sarah. "I feel mighty bad over it," she said. "But it could have been worse if all five had been killed." She said she was too numb to feel any hatred.

The next day, I attended the funeral of three bombing victims at a nearby Baptist church. King and Roy Wilkins, of the NAACP, spoke to an orderly crowd of several thousand people, who could not all fit into the church so they poured into the street. Virtually everyone was black, except for about fifty white ministers who sat in the rear of the sanctuary. King told the crowd in a riveting eulogy that the young victims did not die in vain. "Good still has a way of growing out of evil," he said in a booming cadence. "The blood of these girls must serve as a revitalizing force to bring light to this dark city." And then, knowing that his message reached beyond Birmingham, King targeted his words directly at the national psyche. "These deaths have something to say to each of us and to the federal government that has compromised on civil rights with a bloc of Southern Dixiecrats and Right-wing Republicans." It was the first time I had heard the phrase "right-wing Republicans."

I stayed in Birmingham for three weeks to report on the aftermath. I wrote about the reactions of twenty-five white fourth-graders attending a lower-middle-class public school, and missed my own daughters with each word I typed. I quoted a student's simple yet profound essay: "It [the bombings] would stop if people would quit waving Confederate flags and other things like that." The teacher fearfully asked not to be identified, and I used the children's essays because their simple words told the story best. Some children said things like, "I think the Negroes have a right to fight back" and "I think [the Negroes] should be free like the white people. . . . They should have a right to go to our school." I wanted their innocent words to show northern readers that not all whites in the South were racist. I ended with a quotation that could have been my own words at that age because it described my experiences growing up: "There is a colored man and women that works for my grandmother. They help her in the garden every summer.

My grandmother gives them vegetables out of the garden for helping her. They are very nice."

Reporting on the schoolchildren was a brief respite from the other, more substantial reactions I was covering. A federal grand jury indicted eight white men associated with the National States' Rights Party on charges of interfering with school integration weeks before the bombing. Four of the eight men arrived at federal court with broad smiles, and one carried a Confederate flag. The federal district judge said attempts had been made to intimidate and influence the grand jury and himself. He didn't provide further details but asked the FBI to investigate.

There were other court proceedings as well. I attended a preliminary hearing for the two white boys charged with the first-degree murder of Virgil Ware. Both boys arrived in court neatly dressed; one wore a Sunday school attendance button and an Eagle Scout pin on his lapel. The boys admitted shooting Ware but said they didn't mean to kill him. A detective said the boys' actions were "inspired" by the pro-segregation rally they had attended.

James Ware, Virgil's older brother, was also in the courtroom. He wore a bright red T-shirt and told the judge that the driver of the scooter raised a pistol and shot his brother. "[Virgil] fell off the wheel and I stopped and went to him," he recounted. "I said, 'Virgil, get up' and he said, 'I can't, I'm shot.' I said, 'No you're not, you're going to have a heart attack like that.'" He said he saw blood on Virgil's teeth, and Virgil said nothing. "He was dead," James Ware said. The white boys' mothers broke into tears when the judge announced they would be held without bond. They were eventually convicted of second-degree murder and given a seven-month suspension, but a judge replaced it with two years' probation.

Arrests in connection with the church bombing were not as immediate, and one week after the Sixteenth Street tragedy, two shrapnel bombs exploded in black neighborhoods, spraying the streets with nails and scrap metal. Eight homes and an automobile were damaged. No one was injured, but the bombs were a direct message to President Kennedy, because they occurred just hours before his two military arbitrators arrived.

The president's emissaries were scheduled to meet with the mayor, who had little support in the black community, and with black leaders selected by the mayor. But when President Kennedy's men arrived, they were greeted by an all-white delegation and spent most of the day with white officials. Their itinerary was a major tactical error and showed how President Kennedy and his representatives overlooked the growing significance of black voices. I wrote that black leaders felt the president's representatives were "pawns" of the Birmingham mayor. The representatives stayed two weeks, eventually met with a group of black leaders including two whose homes had been bombed, and recommended the formation of a biracial panel to establish better communications between the white and black communities. But it was obvious that the city was a long way from coming to grips with its race problem. It was unrealistic to think that two federal officials, whose role was merely advisory, could find a formula to solve the city's problems.

While these representatives were in Birmingham, troopers under the command of the state's public safety director, Colonel Albert Lingo, unexpectedly arrested two men in connection with bombings throughout the city but would not say whether they were involved in the church bombing. Governor Wallace, eager to stay ahead of the federal authorities, had orchestrated the surprise arrests, which were highly irregular because the arrested men were already under FBI surveillance for the church bombing and the arrests hampered the FBI's investigation. The FBI believed that Lingo's move was a charade, and black leaders said the arrests were an affront to the black community because the men were simply charged with misdemeanors for possessing dynamite without a permit and released under $300 bonds.

The suspects were Robert E. Chambliss, a fifty-eight-year-old Birmingham truck driver and former city employee, and twenty-two-year-old Charles Cagle. Both had been arrested previously for their KKK activities. A third suspect, thirty-six-year-old John W. Hall, was also arrested the next day. I went to their trials, where Chambliss and Hall were each convicted of illegally possessing and transporting dynamite, fined $100, and sentenced to short jail terms. No federal charges were filed. Cagle was sentenced to the maximum penalty—six months of hard labor and a $100 fine.

There was a constant uneasiness, and I felt that violence could break out with the slightest provocation. One of my articles contained images capturing that tension:

BIRMINGHAM, Ala., Oct. 5—Policemen armed with shotguns . . . A church packed with Negroes swaying to the rhythm of freedom songs . . . Gov. George C. Wallace's state troopers riding the streets under Confederate flags . . . A Ku Klux Klan wizard making bond for two men charged with possessing dynamite . . . A Negro leader warning of renewed demonstrations. These were the symbols this week of a city in a mood of suspended unrest.

The black community, making up 40 percent of the city's population, served notice that they were ready for change, and, surprisingly, they were supported by prominent members of the white community, who worried about the city's reputation. Fifty-three white Birmingham lawyers issued a public statement calling for citizens to abide by the *Brown* decision, even if they disagreed with it, to end the racial violence. Some of the attorneys were older conservative members of the Birmingham Bar Association, but most were young.

Charles Morgan, a thirty-two-year-old white lawyer, stood before the Young Men's Business Club the day after the bombings and blamed everyone from white ministers and parents to politicians and judges for being complicit, even if unintentionally, in the bombings:

> Who did it? The answer should be we all did it. . . . The "who" is every little individual who talks about the "niggers" and spreads the seeds of his hate to his neighbor and his son. The jokester, the crude oaf whose racial jokes rock the party with laughter. The "who" is every Governor who ever shouted for lawlessness and became a law violator.

He blamed the slow-moving courts, newspapers that defended laws of segregation, and ministers who barred blacks at the church door. "Every person in this community who has, in any way, contributed during the past several years to the popularity of hatred is at least as guilty, or more so, than the demented fool who threw that bomb," he declared.

With this reprimand from the white community, King returned in October to announce that demonstrations would resume unless the city council hired blacks in city jobs. "We demand that twenty-five Negro policemen be hired within two weeks and a face-to-face meeting be held with the city council to begin negotiations for the hiring of Negro firemen, clerks, and other civil employees," according to a joint statement issued at a press conference held by King and a prominent local black leader, Reverend Fred L. Shuttlesworth, president of the Alabama Christian Movement for Human Rights.

They threatened a nationwide March on Birmingham similar to the March on Washington and promised that the Birmingham demonstrations would be larger than those in the spring, when 2,500 people were arrested. "We are determined to see justice emerge," King and Shuttlesworth said. The mood was somewhat tempered when the city council said it would consider hiring black policemen, and eighty-eight local civic leaders and businessmen, including the president of a division of the United States Steel Corporation, published a full-page ad in the *Birmingham News* calling for the hiring of black police for duty in black neighborhoods. The council voted to overturn many segregation ordinances to integrate lunch counters, city parks, and golf courses, and the mayor appointed a biracial committee to address changes, but the council ultimately refused to hire black policemen or other black city employees.

Black leaders knew that change, although incremental, would come only with persistent swells of pressure. King's movement had found its footing in Birmingham and now, with the nation's eyes open, black leaders in other cities were inspired to organize and coalesce.

CHAPTER 14

A Brewing Storm

A BREWING STORM ON THE DELTA POSSESSES AN ETHEREAL QUALITY. First comes an eerie calm laying to rest the hard harvest. Then suddenly, vicious winds deliver pelting rain, and lightning pierces the horizon. Because the land is perfectly flat leading in every direction to worlds far beyond, the storm moves quickly, often leaving death and destruction in a random swath. The rain, no matter how overpowering, is a welcome relief to the days of summer drought. I believe that human nature is a by-product of surroundings. The English have their soft, subtle, and steady drizzle on bucolic green hills. The Delta has turbulent storms that drench the gullies with alluvial mud.

After Birmingham, the South's response to an unwelcome change in the social order was less than congenial, especially when measured by proper southern standards. I spent the next month traveling frantically from one hot spot to another to write about racial skirmishes, voter registration efforts, and black boycotts of white-owned stores. I returned to Plaquemine, Louisiana, where demonstrators were still fighting the city's ban on protesting. In one instance, when one thousand blacks had gathered in a church, a state policeman armed with a cattle prod rode his horse down the church's center aisle to clear out the crowd. Blacks retaliated by throwing bricks at the police. When I arrived, another civil rights meeting at a Baptist church was called off after three carloads of police threatened to break it up with tear gas.

Another day I drove to Tuscaloosa, Alabama, after receiving a tip that local law enforcement officials had refused to investigate the abduction and beating of three Ghanaian students and their two white companions who were on an educational tour of the South. The students stopped at a service station owned by Detroit Tigers pitcher Frank Lary to photograph a restroom

designated for "colored." Twenty hooded men abducted the students at gunpoint on a highway near Tuscaloosa and beat them with sticks, belts, and
fists. After the lashing, the students, eager to get out of Alabama, drove 230
miles to Nashville to receive medical treatment and report the incident to
the FBI.

The State Department in Washington was forced to apologize to the Ghanaian government, and the FBI investigated the matter. I wrote about the
beatings in the *Times*, but the incident aroused little concern or attention
in Alabama. The local police chief said that although the beatings probably
occurred because there had been similar incidents in the past, his department
would not follow up because no complaint was filed.

Reaching these remote corners of the South was not easy. I would board
small commercial prop planes that seldom flew directly from one small city
to another but instead connected through Atlanta, the hub for Delta Airlines,
which was the only major carrier serving the South. Changing planes in Atlanta gave me the opportunity to see my family at the airport, and we would
have picnic dinners with home-cooked food outside the terminal during my
layovers. Sometimes those quick glimpses were harder than not seeing them
at all because it made me realize how I much I was neglecting them. Betty
was always supportive, but at one airport reunion, I was pained to see my
three-year-old daughter run to another man she mistook for me, hug him
around the knees, and cry, "Daddy, Daddy." Once I boarded my connecting
flight with Betty's car keys in my pocket, and she had to maneuver a ride
home with four daughters and then return the next day with an extra set of
keys to retrieve the car.

One place I made repeated trips to in 1963 was Selma, Alabama, which
had no easy access by air, so I flew to Montgomery, rented a car, and drove
an hour south. I went there to report how several organizations were mobi-
lizing forces to gain voting rights. Selma had a population of twenty-eight
thousand and sat on the bluffs of the Alabama River in Dallas County. Blacks
easily outnumbered whites, yet only 250 of the 15,000 eligible black voters
were registered. National groups deliberately targeted Selma for a voting
rights campaign because, like Mississippi, the city exemplified the worst of
the South's voting abuses; all varieties of white resistance flourished here. Its
history and geography partly explained why.

Selma was the trading center and "queen city" of Alabama's Black Belt, a
strip of dark fertile prairie land extending like a waistband across the middle

girth of the state. The name reflected the color of the soil as well as most of
the people. Early settlers at first thought the dirt to be too sticky for crops and
moved on to the sandy loam in the nearby hills. But then it was discovered
that the belt had perfect soil for growing high cotton, and planters arrived
in droves with their slaves. Whites lived with a concentration of the wealth,
all gained through the toil of slaves.

The city imposed twenty-seven ordinances and laws governing slaves'
behavior. For instance, all slaves found on the streets after 8:00 p.m. without
written permission from their owners could be arrested, imprisoned, and,
without producing an excuse or bail, receive up to one hundred strikes or
thirty-nine lashes. They were also prohibited from smoking a pipe or cigar
or carrying a cane on city streets.

During the Civil War, the Black Belt was one of the first regions of the
South to call for secession, and Selma had an arsenal and naval foundry that
were sacked and burned by Union troops in 1865. Nathan Bedford Forrest,
the general who led my great grandfather, was defeated at the Battle of
Selma and escaped before Confederate soldiers surrendered to the Union
side. The Black Belt was ravaged by the Civil War and left embittered by
Reconstruction.

Advancement for blacks in the South during Reconstruction lasted only
briefly. Without an economic or educational base in which blacks could
thrive, the North aborted its efforts to achieve racial justice for freed slaves,
and elite southern whites emerged with unyielding conservatism. Except
for outright ownership of slaves, state laws and habits reverted to prewar
status, especially in the Black Belt. Selma, like much of the South, harbored a
lingering resentment toward the North and President Lincoln's carpetbagging
Republicans. In 1901, a Selma representative to the state legislature advocated
a poll tax on blacks to fund white schools. "When you pay $1.50 for a poll
tax, in Dallas County, I believe you disfranchise ten Negros," the legislator
said to promote his bill. "Give us this $1.50 for educational purposes and for
the disfranchisement of a vicious and useless class."

Between 1950 and 1960, one-tenth of the black population in the Black
Belt migrated north. Despite the exodus, blacks still outnumbered whites
three to one in some Black Belt counties, and whites had a deep fear of being
overrun by blacks if they gained power. One tactic to suppress blacks was
to deprive them of education, and the practice was reinforced by a belief
that blacks were innately inferior, a beneficent order of nature. One circuit

court judge in the Black Belt in the 1960s said, "Your Negro is a mixture of African types like the Congolite who has a long heel and the blue-gummed Ebo whose I.Q. is about fifty or fifty-fifty." I was amazed that few people found this thinking abhorrent.

Alabama's first White Citizens' Council formed in Dallas County, and, by 1963, Selma had the state's largest chapter with three thousand members. Whites viewed the civil rights movement as a sinister and foreign force—a residue of northern control dating to the Civil War—that would overturn their social structure.

White Selma was an anachronism of ancient grandeur. It had spacious streets, antebellum mansions, and a hundred-year-old hotel built to resemble a Venetian palace. It was also home to an air force base and twenty industrial facilities. Almost every public space was segregated, except the bus station, which had been integrated by federal order. The town's Carnegie Library removed its chairs to eliminate the risk of integrated seating. On the highway leading into Selma, a large sign bearing a hooded man on a white horse read, "Realm National Alabama, U.S. Klans in K.K.K., Inc. Units 47–110 welcomes you." A group of black leaders organized the Dallas County Improvement Association to establish an interracial committee to open dialogue between blacks and whites, but the white community refused to accept any recommendations. The city's inscribed traditions and history were as resistant to change as the devastating boll weevil was to early pesticides.

Selma was considered the perfect staging ground to gain voting rights by four national civil rights groups—Student Nonviolent Coordinating Committee (SNCC, pronounced "snick"), the NAACP, the Congress of Racial Equality (CORE), and King's SCLC. The Kennedy administration's first voter discrimination lawsuit was filed in 1961 in Selma, and the city had an attractive feature that civil rights groups deemed essential to its campaign. His name was James G. Clark, and he was just the kind of hotheaded and impulsive county sheriff who organizers knew would overreact to protests and, therefore, bring national attention to advance their cause. Clark, a forty-three-year-old cattle rancher and friend of Governor Wallace, was an air force veteran who wore an Eisenhower-style military uniform with a leaf-shaped "scrambled eggs" emblem on his cap visor. He had enthusiastically joined state troopers to suppress protesters in Birmingham.

Most importantly, Clark controlled the county's voter registration process. He opened the registration office in the county courthouse only two days a month, and only thirty people, although usually fewer, could register each day. When blacks arrived, they were given—unlike whites—a literacy test, which most of them failed, and they were thus denied registration. By the time I arrived in Selma in October 1963, civil rights organizers had already recruited blacks in Dallas County with the message that if they could vote, they could get rid of elected officials like Clark and Wallace. Their plan was to flood the courthouse with requests to register. The US Justice Department joined the organizers with a court injunction ordering an end to the dissuasive registration practices.

"We are not going to give in," a spokesman for the White Citizens' Council told me about the efforts to organize. "If we let them have one inch, they would want to go all the way." Clark also scoffed at the organizers and federal authorities as he began preparing his defenses. His deputized 150 white volunteer citizens, who formed an ad hoc posse that we reporters privately called "squirrel shooters" because they resembled a hunting party. He also called on Wallace, who dispatched as many state troopers as could be spared.

When blacks showed up at the three-story courthouse, Clark displayed an intimidating strength of force with a bumper-to-bumper wall of fifty state trooper cars and armed policemen stationed in upstairs windows. The citizen posse and police, carrying cattle prods and guns, patrolled the sidewalks while two hundred blacks waited to register. When two black SNCC workers took sandwiches and drinks to the waiting crowd, Clark, a 220-pound beefy man with thinning hair and a stern look, falsely accused the workers, "I won't have the crowd molested in any way." I watched as the aggression escalated quickly. Several officers pushed the two SNCC workers, and a dozen troopers prodded them with nightsticks. "Let me at 'em," one trooper said. The troopers carried the SNCC workers around the corner and loaded them into a bus headed for jail. I ran after them to see what happened next. When one worker stood up from his bus seat, a trooper knocked him down in the aisle. Then the officer moved aside while a small, middle-aged white man wearing dark horn-rimmed spectacles and a white shirt boarded the bus.

"Where are you niggers from?" the man asked the workers.

"I'm from Illinois," answered one worker.

"You better get back there then," the white man responded. "If I see you on the street at night then I'm going to kill you." Then he left the bus. He refused to give me his name, but said he was not a law enforcement officer.

I returned to the front of the courthouse and was standing in the street, not far off the curb, when a car raced toward me. The driver looked right at me, and I remember thinking that I had never seen such hatred in a man's eyes. A television reporter grabbed me by the collar and pulled me to the sidewalk just in time to avoid the car.

Like my colleagues, I tried to dress inconspicuously so as to avoid the anger and suspicion of white agitators. Some reporters opted for khaki pants, a white T-shirt, and a cap from the corner garage. But this was the dress of a Harvard student or civil rights worker. Other, more daring types tried a well-pressed suit and hat on the theory that they would be mistaken for an observer from Washington or the president of a Rotary Club. I preferred the middle road: a pair of wash-and-wear pants and a short-sleeved, button-down shirt, with or without a tie, depending on the occasion. This style usually attracted the least attention. No matter what we wore, we all learned to pare down our stenographer's notebook so that it fit in our pockets, where it would not tag us as reporters. In practice, however, notes were seldom needed other than a few names and dates, because what we saw was etched in our memory forever.

The protests continued day after day. In one month, Clark and his posse arrested more than three hundred people, including SNCC chairman John Lewis, a twenty-three-year-old up-and-coming presence in the movement. Lewis was the son of Alabama sharecroppers and grew up in a house with no electricity, no plumbing, and a dirt yard. He and his family worked in the fields every day except Sunday, when they rode a mule-pulled wagon to church for sermons, singing, and socializing.

When Lewis was fifteen years old, he heard a young black pastor in Atlanta named Martin Luther King Jr. give a sermon on the radio criticizing complacent Christians who ignored the call for racial justice. Lewis was so inspired that he decided he wanted to go to college to become a preacher like King and direct his religious teachings to social issues. Lewis applied to Troy State College in his hometown but never heard back. There was a good reason: no black had ever attended that college. But he wanted to break the color barrier and wrote to King asking for his help. King met with Lewis and said he would help him file a lawsuit against Troy if the seventeen-year-old got permission from his parents. But they were understandably afraid and refused to consent.

Instead, Lewis attended American Baptist Theological Seminary in Nashville and graduated from another Nashville school, Fisk University, where he met James Forman, a born revolutionary. Lewis's ambition to become a preacher was diverted by social activism. He and Forman, who had a caustic sense of humor but also suffered from recurring stomach ulcers, organized sit-ins and joined the Freedom Rides, which challenged segregated bus terminals across the South. Lewis gave a keynote speech alongside King at the March on Washington. Lewis and Forman formed SNCC, and Lewis was elected chairman shortly before the Selma demonstrations.

SNCC held mass meetings in Selma, usually in churches, with an open-door policy for all to join. Some meetings featured rousing speeches from Forman, who wore denims and sported an Afro haircut before the look became popular. "Sheriff Clark was disturbed," Forman said at one meeting after a day of demonstrations. "He scratched his head, rubbed his belly, and shuffled his feet. He never thought we could get that many people to the courthouse to register. Well, the white man has been shuffling us for three hundred years. We're going to catch up to him and he knows it."

High-profile, nationally recognized sympathizers also joined the demonstrations, including the comedian and writer Dick Gregory and his wife, who was arrested in the protests. When the black novelist James Baldwin witnessed the arrest of SNCC workers and the clubbing of a CBS photographer, he said Selma was "one of the worst places I ever saw."

Selma, like many communities in the South, also had some local whites who supported the civil rights cause. Sometimes, southern white women joined the marches and, on some occasions, successfully persuaded their husbands not to carry out violence. In one instance, a woman in a small southern town convinced her husband to stop vigilantes from storming a jail to seize an imprisoned black man. In Selma, a local white Catholic priest named Maurice F. Ouellet headed a mission, established in 1937, that operated schools, a hospital, and a children's club in black neighborhoods. He welcomed SNCC and chastised the city's other religious leaders for failing to take a stand against racism. "Will they allow a crime such as the one recently seen in Birmingham to come to Selma and then belatedly utter pious prayers for the deceased to salve their own consciences?" Reverend Ouellet wrote in the local newspaper. He received a quick and unequivocal reply—the white leaders blamed him for the demonstrations and asked him to leave the city. When he refused, they asked the archbishop to remove him, which happened two years later. Ouellet was also threatened with arrest for contributing to the delinquency of minors by encouraging students to protest, but a warrant was never issued.

The Selma campaign was relatively short lived. Clark effectively suppressed the voter drive by sheer force, and the number of adult protesters declined. National black leaders withdrew their support and turned their attention to other strongholds of white resistance. Not surprisingly, one of those places was Jackson, Mississippi, where a young and fledgling drive was growing under the leadership of Charles Evers, who succeeded his brother Medgar as the NAACP's Mississippi field secretary. Jackson had made some progress by hiring five black policemen, but they were not allowed to arrest whites. Some white storekeepers in black neighborhoods hired black clerks and stock boys, and some federal agencies hired blacks for jobs formerly open only to whites. But Jackson and Mississippi had a long way to go.

When I arrived in Jackson in November 1963, civil rights leaders were announcing their intention to register one hundred thousand blacks in Mississippi to vote. Only 2 percent of the state's black population was registered because the state had imposed additional registration requirements for blacks in the 1950s and 1960s such as requiring "good moral character" and instituting stricter writing tests. In Panola County, south of Jackson, only two blacks had been permitted to register since 1890. Civil rights leaders staged a "mock election" to show how blacks could vote if they were registered, featuring Aaron Henry as a write-in candidate, the same Clarksdale pharmacist who had hosted me and my family at a voter registration drive at his church. Norman Thomas, a seventy-nine-year-old former Socialist Party candidate who ran six times for president, arrived in Jackson to support Henry. "You almost have to have a passport to get into Mississippi," Thomas said after hearing that a Yale student assisting in the mock election had been arrested in Natchez for loitering and later released on condition that he leave town. About fifty students from Yale and Stanford arrived in Mississippi to help with Henry's campaign and the mock election.

The civil rights movement was not contained to a few isolated spots. I was traveling all over the South, jumping to South Carolina, Alabama, Louisiana, Mississippi, North Carolina, and Georgia in a single month to report on bombings, voter registration drives, and city integration efforts. I reported how in Atlanta, despite some advances, blacks were still barred from most movie theaters, required to eat at designated times in some downtown white restaurants, and denied hotel rooms once the "quota" for blacks was met. President Kennedy had issued an executive order mandating an end to discrimination in all federally funded housing agencies, but the Atlanta Housing Authority still operated segregated federal housing projects and had no blacks on its staff. All of this prompted blacks in Atlanta, who made up 40 percent of the city's population, to call for complete desegregation of public facilities and private accommodations. I also traveled to Tuscaloosa in late November because three bombs—encased in sacks rigged with fifteen-foot-long fuses—exploded near the University of Alabama dormitory where Vivian Malone had lived for five months after she and James Hood enrolled as the first black students. The bombs devastated nearby homes and businesses, but luckily there were no injuries.

President Kennedy watched the developments in Tuscaloosa and the fate of his civil rights bill in Congress as conservative southern Democrats threatened to stall its passage. But his primary focus was on his reelection campaign, and he was busy giving speeches in Miami and Texas.

CHAPTER 15

Dallas

Dark Night of the Soul

ON NOVEMBER 22, 1963, A FEW DAYS AFTER THE UNIVERSITY OF ALABAMA explosions, I drove my rental car deep into the Mississippi heartland to another assignment with a trunkful of week-old dirty laundry. I didn't mind the long, lonely drives on two-lane country roads. It gave me time to collect my thoughts between stories and think about how much I missed Betty, who was back in Atlanta rearing four girls by herself. My respect for her was boundless, and I could not have produced my work without her.

It was shortly after noon, after passing through the small town of New Albany, Mississippi—birthplace of William Faulkner—when I heard on my car radio that President Kennedy had been shot. My heart welled up into my throat. The violence I witnessed across the South had suddenly reached a new dimension. I hit the gas and sped eighty-five miles an hour through barren clay hill country to the next town, Tupelo. There, I found a desolate phone booth perched outside a general store surrounded by cotton fields and called the *Times*. "Get to Dallas," my editor barked.

I remember standing there with the phone lodged against my ear, dumbfounded and stunned by the news of the shooting. It was eerily quiet all around me. Nothing moved. All the crops had been harvested. The wind had nothing to stir. This felt like a calm before another storm.

Before getting back in the car, I made another call—this one to Betty in Atlanta, who had also heard the news. She was grateful I had called because she had no way to reach me. We were both frustrated as we tried to soothe each other's sorrow over a long-distance telephone line, and I was running out of quarters to feed the phone for extra time. Our daughters were on their way home from school, and she was dreading how to explain the inexplicable. I ached to get home to her and our children. She jokingly commented that Dallas would be safer than some of the towns where I had been recently traveling. I promised to call her as soon as I arrived in Dallas.

The nearest airport was in Memphis, a hundred miles away; by the time I boarded my plane, I had learned that the president had died. The flight to Dallas was nerve wracking. Everyone around me was sullen and in shock. I was worried about the future of the country and anxious over what to expect once I arrived. I had joined the *Times* only three months earlier, and I had never covered a story this big. Reporting the assassination of any president—much less a young and hallowed one with celebrity status—was more than I was prepared for. I remembered the first time I wrote about Kennedy during his speech in Jackson, and how he had risen to prominence since then.

I arrived in Dallas at 7:00 p.m., and Tom Wicker, my colleague at the *Times* who had been traveling with the president, had already filed a story about the assassination. The city was in a state of confusion and chaos. I quickly filed a story describing how the Secret Service had taken painstaking efforts to ensure President Kennedy's safety against any threats by making repeated scans along the parade route; they even taste-tested his steak lunch. They had gone so far as to inspect five thousand yellow roses arranged at the Dallas Trade Mart, a huge modern building that was to have been the president's final destination after a six-mile parade from the airport.

Wicker and I were soon joined by eight other *Times* reporters and editors. I filed another story reporting that Texas governor John B. Connally Jr. had been sitting in front of President Kennedy in the open-topped convertible and was shot in the back by one of the bullets. I quoted Connally's doctors as saying that the governor had suffered a "tangential wound" and that he most likely would have been shot through the heart if he had not turned to his right to see what had happened to the president. The sniper's bullet broke Connally's fifth rib and struck his right wrist before lodging in his left thigh. A fragment from his rib also punctured his lung.

A copy of that article with the headline, "CONNALLY GAINS, DOC-TORS REPORT; Turn May Have Saved Life—Full Recovery Likely," today hangs just feet away from a sixth-floor corner window of the former Texas School Book Depository where the assassin, Lee Harvey Oswald, fired his rifle. The building now houses the Sixth Floor Museum at Dealey Plaza, which showcases an extensive collection chronicling President Kennedy's life and death.

I also wrote about forensic reports from the president's doctors, who said three shots were fired. Two hit the president—one at the necktie knot of his throat and another at the right rear of his head. The second shot was "the fatal wound, we feel," one of the doctors said, "although it is possible that either one could have been fatal." The third bullet was presumed to have hit Connally. The article was significant because it provided an official assessment of how many shots were fired and where they struck the victims. The city was rife with ill-founded rumors and speculations about how many shots had been fired and from which direction. I also wrote about a Dallas clothing manufacturer with an eight-millimeter camera who caught about fifteen seconds of the shooting on a movie camera that supported the sequence of events reported by police.

I was assigned to find out as much as possible about Oswald, a task that quickly escalated when Jack Ruby, a local nightclub owner, shot and killed Oswald in the basement of the Dallas Police Department during Oswald's transfer to another jail. Little was known publicly about Oswald when he was shot, so I scrambled to piece together a profile of him. I spoke with Oswald's brother by telephone at a brick factory in Denton, Texas, where he worked. He expressed no bitterness toward his brother, or toward some of his Denton neighbors who had treated him and his family with hostility and indifference after the assassination. But Oswald's mother, Marguerite, whom I also interviewed, had a different reaction, saying "some Christians have not acted in a Christian way." She said one woman whom she considered a friend refused to help her collect the plethora of newspaper articles published about Oswald. She felt others were holding her responsible for her son's actions.

I also wrote about a gunsmith from Irving, Texas, who said he mounted a telescopic sight on a gun for a man named Oswald about a month before the shooting. Although he didn't specifically remember Oswald, the gunsmith found a receipt showing that Oswald had paid $4.50 for drilling and $1.50 for bore sighting a 6.5-millimeter Italian carbine. I reported that Oswald's proximity to the parade route was sheer happenstance. Oswald had taken a job as a stock clerk at the book depository months before the parade without knowing it would provide such a prime vantage point for an assassination. The parade route was determined two days before and announced only one day before President Kennedy arrived. I also interviewed a woman with whom Oswald and his wife had lived in Dallas. She told me how she had helped Oswald secure his clerk job after he returned to Dallas from a trip to Mexico.

Oswald's death fueled conspiracy theories that he had not acted alone, especially given the reports that Oswald was a defector to the Soviet Union and a self-proclaimed Marxist. I described my interview with a stenographer who said she had transcribed notes for Oswald as he wrote a book on the hardships of life in Russia, where he had lived for three years. The stenographer described Oswald as worried, scared, and fidgety when she typed the copious notes. She never finished the job because Oswald stopped her about a third of the way through. "Ten dollars is all I've got," he told her. She told him he could pay her later when he had more money. "No," Oswald said, handing her a ten-dollar bill and walking out. The stenographer said that she saw him twice after that on the street but that he ignored her.

I also reported how papers and books found in Oswald's home included letters from the Communist Party of America that gave Oswald advice on how to avoid "nosey neighbors" and set up a chapter of the Fair Play for Cuba Committee, which provided support for the Cuban revolution against attacks by the United States. I spoke with a representative of the Communist Party of America who said that its communications with Oswald did not mean he was a member of the party. The Fair Play for Cuba Committee's director also denied that Oswald represented the group. Oswald subscribed to the *Militant*, a weekly newspaper reflecting the views of the Socialist Workers Party, and he applied to become a member of the American Civil Liberties Union (ACLU), which for its part disavowed any association with Oswald.

To this day, I have never accepted so-called conspiracy theories to explain Oswald's motives for the assassination. Based on my reporting, I believe that the assassination was the work of one man with warped ideas.

The assassination inflicted deep scars on Dallas and its people. My editors thought that understanding this foreign place, neither purely southern nor western, might help explain the tragedy. "What is Dallas? Tell us what this place is all about," my editors said. The answer was not simple. It was a multifaceted city with a conflicting personality formed by both parochialism and ambition. The first place I went looking for an answer was the First Presbyterian Church just blocks from where President Kennedy was shot, hoping to find some semblance of sanity.

"We are proud of our heritage and our image," Dr. Thomas A. Fry told his congregation from the pulpit. "But something has happened like a cancer you cannot quite put your finger on. We have allowed the apostles of religious bigotry and the purveyors of political pornography to stir up the weak-minded." The pastor also denounced the literature branding President Kennedy a communist that had been distributed by extremists throughout the city before his arrival. I spoke to the minister's wife after the service, and she had a much simpler, and more direct, explanation: "We think it's the western tradition. They are used to shooting at everything they don't like."

Other Dallas residents blamed "crackpots" who were attracted to Texas in search of a freewheeling, Wild West frontier. One man captured the vexing nature of Dallas when he said, "Dallas cannot be explained in a few words. It is a lot of things."

I spent two weeks in Dallas, or "Big D" as the residents dubbed it, still lugging around the suitcase of dirty clothes I had brought with me from Mississippi. I wrote about two burials—one honoring a police officer who was killed while trying to arrest Oswald, and the second for Oswald, who was buried near his birthplace of Fort Worth, where law enforcement officials had difficulty protecting his grave from desecration.

I wrote about a city on edge as it tried to calm its nerves, find its future, and join a nation in mourning. I quoted a local paper that stated, "Dallas is a city undergoing a dark night of the soul. We are a city trying to find ourselves." And I wrote, "A number of citizens have said publicly that the forces of hate have been allowed to fester in Dallas. Others have insisted that the city is no different from any other and that no soul-searching is needed."

I also quoted another minister, this time a Methodist, who said, "At a nice, respectable dinner party only two nights before the President's visit to our city, a bright young couple with a fine education, with a promising professional future, said to their friends that they hated the President of the United States—and that they would not care one bit if somebody did take a potshot at him."

In the end, defining Dallas was as daunting as the city's own efforts to accept the inscrutable tragedy.

CHAPTER 16

End of a Long Year

BETTY WAS SO GRATEFUL TO SEE ME WHEN I FINALLY RETURNED HOME from Dallas that she didn't mind that I looked like a tattered alley cat dragging in dirty laundry. My daughters circled my legs with hugs. There was a turkey roasting in the oven for a delayed Thanksgiving celebration. "Doesn't everyone celebrate Thanksgiving in December?" Betty joked. It was good to be home.

But the respite didn't last long. Within days I left for Americus, Georgia, one hundred miles south of Atlanta, for the court appearance of Ralph Allen, a twenty-two-year-old white Massachusetts student who had been swept up in a street riot while registering blacks to vote. Two hundred and fifty people were arrested, and thirty-five people were injured, including a police officer hit in the head with a brick. Allen and three other students were held for three months without bond under an antiquated state treason law that called for the death penalty. The charges were eventually dropped, and Allen successfully appealed a conviction on lesser charges.

When I returned to Atlanta a few days later, there was more breaking news to cover. Thousands of black demonstrators assembled in subfreezing temperatures at a small park in front of the downtown Atlanta municipal building to protest the city's segregated schools, hospitals, and hotels. Martin Luther King Jr. had deliberately waited a few weeks since President Kennedy's death to stage this major civil rights rally.

The rally, called Pilgrimage for Democracy, was orchestrated by black leaders discontent with the slow progress of negotiations with white leaders. The organizers, however, were divided in their approach. The older ones wanted a slow route and credited the Board of Aldermen for adopting a resolution urging voluntary desegregation. The younger ones wanted more than resolutions and voluntary action and called for pickets, boycotts, and sit-ins. The elders, at least temporarily, convinced the younger leaders to settle for a rally.

King played a key role in mending the rift. His prominence as a national leader was growing as quickly as his need to control a volatile campaign that showed signs of splintering. He knew his greatest strength came through nonviolent unrest, and he still had his eyes on a national civil rights bill that had not passed before President Kennedy's untimely death. But he walked a fragile line between meeting the pent-up demands of his followers and pushing too aggressively such that the crusade might self-destruct. His responsibility, which he seized with deliberate conviction, was to control the velocity of the movement while also acting quickly when national sentiments were in his favor.

He knew that a nation mourning the death of a president would not tolerate the raw and inflamed violence seen in Selma or Birmingham. For now, King chose to stay away from such unsettled places. Instead, he chose Atlanta for the rally because the city didn't overreact to demonstrations and was better able to host a large, peaceful assembly. It was the first gathering in his hometown in three years.

Atlanta was an educated and professional city whose population was largely civil toward blacks. King himself experienced a bit of an integrated lifestyle there. His children, and the children of Ralph Abernathy, an SCLC leader and King's best friend, attended Spring Street Elementary School with my children. It was the first elementary school in Atlanta to be integrated. Every morning, Coretta Scott King and Juanita Abernathy took turns car pooling their children in a station wagon, while the white children, including my own, took the school bus or walked.

Although Atlanta was far more progressive than some southern cities, it had a long way to go to achieve racial equality. Efforts to integrate its schools after the *Brown v. Board of Education* decision had met legal resistance, and the school board was lethargic about taking action. In 1961, nine black students integrated four white high schools, but after that, efforts to further integrate Atlanta schools lagged.

King appeared unconcerned about his own safety at the rally. In fact, King's view of his own mortality defied rational thinking. The day after President Kennedy was shot, he was asked in a television interview about threats to his life. His answer reflected his acceptance of the inevitable danger of his chosen role. He said that although it was difficult to live with constant threats, "you almost become immune to being afraid." He said that redemption was a product of suffering, and America would be redeemed through its collective pain. He believed that his death, and the deaths of others, were the price to "free the soul of our nation and free our children from permanent spiritual death." He believed that someone must have the courage and fortitude to stand up to racism, even if it resulted in the ultimate sacrifice.

The police protection at the rally was massive. KKK leaders and members of an anti-integration organization attended the event. Acting on police advice, King did not appear at the rally until the end of the two-hour program, when it was time for him to speak. He was ringed by law enforcement, including some black officers, as he entered the park and approached the podium. Below him was a drained fountain that normally flowed in the summertime. It was the first time I'd heard him speak since the funerals in Birmingham. He said:

So, we are assembled here on this cold December Sunday not to embarrass our city or to engage in a negative exposé, but to call Atlanta back to something noble and plead with her to rise from dark yesterdays of racial injustice to bright tomorrows of justice for all. We also assemble here because we are tired. We are tired of being trampled over by the iron feet of oppression. We are tired of being the last hired and the first fired. We are tired of spending our dollars in businesses that will not respect our persons. We are tired of living in the dungeons of poverty, ignorance, and want. We are tired of being harried by day and haunted by night by the humiliating system of segregation.

King was a master at changing his tenor at just the right moment, and a new urgency rose in his voice: "In the absence of legal, political, economic, and moral pressure, not even a city as enlightened as Atlanta is likely to grant the Negro his constitutional rights," he told the crowd in a forceful tone. "Never forget that we have not made a single gain in Atlanta or any other city without some type of creative pressure. History is the long and tragic story of the fact that privileged groups seldom give up their privileges voluntarily. Freedom is never voluntarily given by the oppressor; it must be demanded by the oppressed." The crowd of 2,500 people cheered.

His voice rose to a crescendo as he warned city leaders of their pending choice. "There will be neither peace nor tranquility" until discrimination is eliminated, he said. Then he delivered the sound bite that all the attending news organizations reported verbatim. "The cancer of segregation cannot be cured by the Vaseline of gradualism or the sedative of tokenism."

He mentioned President Kennedy's death in oblique reference to his own people's struggle. "Our determination is not a brag, it is not a boast, it is not a thing we whistle up on the dark hours of the night when we know not from which direction a blow may fall, or an assassin's bullet may speed."

King raised the tempo in calibrated levels that drew the crowd into a feverish pitch. "So, let us rise up and boldly make our determination clear. We must no longer submit to unjust practices. We must revolt peacefully, openly, and cheerfully because our aim is to persuade. We must adopt the means of nonviolence because our end is a community at peace with itself."

Once he had stirred the crowd, he ended abruptly on a final note. "Walk together children, don't you get weary. There's a great camp meeting in the promised land." Then he quickly turned, ringed by a police escort, and left the demonstrators inspired to carry the message with them.

I quickly filed a story about the rally and looked forward to some time off. My first four months at the *Times* had been hectic, and I planned to go with Betty and my daughters to Memphis for Christmas and spend two weeks at her parents' house, where there would be no talk of politics or civil rights. Betty's family, like mine, was not sympathetic to the current racial events. Betty's father, a prominent businessman in Memphis whom everyone called Big Jim, was not an ardent segregationist or a racist, but he disapproved of the disorderly protests. He adhered to societal norms and did not believe in upsetting the economic status quo that was working perfectly well for him and the other well-to-do citizens of Memphis.

Big Jim had a houseful of black servants whom he paid relatively well and cared for under an archaic employment arrangement called "noblesse oblige," an obligation of care that a number of wealthy, decorous ladies and gentlemen extended to their household staffs and families. Based on biblical tenets, an employer assumed a responsibility to act nobly and generously toward his less fortunate workers. Betty's parents, who both grew up in the North, were decent to their help and cared for them during illness, provided them with transportation, assisted them during emergencies, and sometimes paid their doctors' bills. In some ways, the help was part of the family except separated by clearly defined lines, like in the aristocratic English manor homes with "upstairs" and "downstairs" distinctions. But the white authority retained an oligarchic control that didn't provide much advancement for blacks.

My reporting on the civil rights movement remained an unspoken topic each time we visited. We all knew not to tread into territory where none of us would change the mind of the other and strain an otherwise congenial and hospitable household. Betty's parents always accepted us with warm and open arms. It was also a topic that the staff rarely spoke about to the family, even though one time the cook unearthed a pair of my worn shoes from the trash bin and took them home with her. She told me privately that they were a valuable token because I had worn them while walking alongside King.

A few days before Christmas, we packed the car with a trunkful of gifts and left Atlanta for the eight-hour hour drive west through Alabama and Mississippi to Memphis. We were just east of Birmingham when one of the girls needed to visit the restroom. With four children, it was quite a feat to make it far without numerous stops. As I called the *Times* to check in one more time before my vacation, I realized that I should have let a sleeping dog lie. My editor said the Tuscaloosa, Alabama, police chief had announced that five Alabama national guardsmen who were responsible for protecting Vivian Malone and James Hood at the University of Alabama had been the ones who had detonated the bombs near Malone's dormitory.

"Can you get to Tuscaloosa and file a story?" my editor asked.

I was only an hour from Tuscaloosa, and as much as I was looking forward to time with my family, I knew that reporting this story was more important than my vacation. On the way to Tuscaloosa, I stopped at the Birmingham airport and put Betty and the girls on a plane to Memphis. Betty possessed an amazing stamina when reacting to these spontaneous demands on my time. She was my steadfast partner, and she spent long, lonely months caring for our daughters while I was away from home. She hardly ever complained. She understood the significance and relevance of the events, and she rarely put her own needs ahead of those of a nation amid strife. As I kissed the family goodbye, I promised I would be in Memphis by Christmas Day with the trunkload of gifts.

When I arrived in Tuscaloosa, the police chief presented statements and physical evidence that the guardsmen had set off the explosions. The National Guard expressed surprise, but a Guard superior said his men may have been creating a reason to remain on the easy assignment of protecting the school's two new black students rather than be reassigned to dangerous racial skirmishes in other Alabama cities. One of the investigating officers, however, expressed doubt about this theory and said the guardsmen acted in defiance of federal authority, because they resented being federalized to work against George Wallace, whom they honored and trusted. "I've never talked to a single guardsman who didn't like Wallace's stand at the university," a noncommissioned officer in the Guard told me. "We would have gone through fire for him."

I had my own theory that the guardsmen, like some local law enforcement, were not much different from reactionary segregationists. Many years later, I told Paul Hendrickson, a dedicated civil rights researcher and author of a book about the character of white oppressors, that I believed some officers possessed both a self-hate and an outer-directed hate and were prey to the same impulses and secret desires of criminals. The difference was that their behavior was sanctioned by law, the power of authority, and society's desire to maintain order. The Tuscaloosa guardsmen were charged with willfully setting off explosives but not charged with capital offenses because there were no injuries. Two of the five later pleaded guilty and were sentenced to two years in prison.

While I was at the university, I dropped in to visit Vivian Malone. She was friendly, warm, and gracious. Her hair was coifed in a bouffant bob, and she wore a nicely pressed waist-belted shirtdress and a cardigan sweater. She was thin and statuesque, and she displayed a fearless and unflappable conviction. She had been born the fourth of eight children to a couple in Mobile who stridently supported the civil rights campaign. Both parents worked at Brookley Air Force Base, where her father was a maintenance worker and her mother was a cleaner.

In a calm, quiet voice, Malone described how federal agents escorted her and Hood to classes; the university even provided her with a driver. (She later married the driver.) A few students tried to make her feel welcome by escorting her to the dining room. But other students were not so kind. They packed up their books, rose from their desks, and left the classroom when she entered. She was determined to ignore them. She was studious and remained focused on her accounting classes to earn a business management degree. But she described a lonely existence and was saddened that her first day on campus was negative even as President Kennedy used the occasion to introduce his civil rights bill. No matter how much the press, protesters, and provocateurs swirled around her that first day, she responded with a slight and courteous smile.

She said her resolve to remain at the university was strengthened by Medgar Evers, who was murdered the day after she enrolled; his death gave her courage to attend her first classes. She said things had settled down a bit since then, but it was still a constant struggle. I left marveling at how a person so young could display such an abundance of wisdom and fortitude.

Years later on an airplane bound for Washington, I saw Malone for the first time since our meeting in Tuscaloosa, and we agreed to meet for lunch. She was working for the Civil Rights Division of the US Justice Department and earning a master's degree at George Washington University. During lunch, we discussed her job and her move to Washington. She said that her time at the University of Alabama had been impressionable, but that it seemed a long time ago. She still exhibited the calm repose of a gentle and forgiving woman.

After filing my story about the guardsmen to the *Times*, I headed to Memphis to deliver the children's gifts by Christmas morning. What I didn't anticipate was a rare and sudden snowstorm raging across the Delta. By the time I reached Tupelo, Mississippi, the roads were packed with snow and ice, and I pulled over and lashed snow chains to the tires. The snow quickly accumulated, and a drive that normally took four hours turned to eight hours. I wanted to stop and help the stranded drivers along the side of the road, but there were so many that I knew I couldn't assist them all. I was also fearful that if I stopped, I would also become mired in the banks of snow. Finally, just before midnight on Christmas Eve, I arrived at Big Jim's house with the trunkful of toys, feeling a bit like Santa himself.

My vacation ended almost as soon as it began. Two days after New Year's Eve, I was in back in Alabama, where Harold Alonzo Franklin was enrolling as Auburn University's first black student. Wallace, remembering the futility of his actions in Tuscaloosa and the negative national press, decided to avoid another confrontation by promising federal authorities that Alabama state troopers would not prevent Franklin from enrolling. The message to his constituents, however, was the exact opposite. "The forcing of this Negro student into Auburn is a violation of every credited rule I've heard of," Wallace declared with his defiant and inflammatory rhetoric. "He is not a qualified student. The case is under federal appeal, and we plan to resist this in every way."

A light rain was falling when Franklin, a thirty-one-year-old insurance salesman and graduate of a black state university, arrived at the Auburn University library to register for a master's degree program, after a federal judge, whom Wallace called a "judicial tyrant," overruled the university's rejection of Franklin's application for admission. Franklin said later that he didn't really want to attend Auburn because it was considered a "cow college," but he wanted to follow in the steps of Meredith, Malone, and Hood.

Franklin was met by a gaggle of reporters, photographers, and two hundred angry students. We were uncertain about ensuing violence and girded ourselves for sudden outbursts from the protesting students. Wallace assigned Colonel Albert Lingo—the state patrol commander who had reacted violently to the Birmingham protests—to escort Franklin into the university, and Lingo forbade federal officials from accompanying Franklin.

When Franklin arrived, Lingo's men asked him for his student identification, something he didn't own because he was not yet enrolled. Franklin, wearing a charcoal gray suit, blue tie, dark gray raincoat, and no hat, displayed a driver's license and then climbed the library steps through a gauntlet of jeering and laughing students. "I bet the nigger won't have to stand in line to register like we do," a student taunted. University officials met Franklin at the library door and escorted him inside. We reporters and photographers were allowed to follow him and watch as he registered. He appeared nervous but enrolled without incident. Franklin then walked to his dormitory as Lingo drove his car alongside him. The university had vacated an entire four-story dormitory so that Franklin had the sixty-room building to himself. Two white students met him at his room, shook his hand, and said, "We are glad to have you here." Several students helped him carry his belongings to his room. Two white ministers offered to accompany him on the campus during his initial days, but Lingo refused.

The university was integrated without disturbance, and Franklin joked later that he felt safe because the students seemed more likely to fight among themselves than with him. It was the twelfth public institution in Alabama to be integrated during Wallace's first year in office. A month after Franklin's enrollment, a biracial committee in Montgomery integrated and reopened a public park after being closed for five years, and the city hired its first black police officers.

These gains had not been won easily. During the last five months of 1963, 1,800 civil rights demonstrations took place in America, mostly in the South, and about one hundred thousand persons were arrested. One of the favorite forms of demonstration was economic boycotts, and the timing was prime. The early 1960s were boom years for the nation's economy, and some pockets of the Southeast enjoyed business and manufacturing expansion. Business-people and economists were confident that the region would be viable if racial strife did not interfere with economic growth.

City leaders across the South were acutely aware of how televised race riots could hurt their economy. Downtown department store sales dropped off after the Birmingham riots because consumers flocked to the suburbs, and with its steel industry in decline, Birmingham knew it needed to improve its image to attract new business growth. No new companies were interested in moving to Little Rock, Arkansas, after the 1957 civil unrest to integrate Central High School, but by the early 1960s three large industries had moved there after the city undertook a long public relations campaign to repair its image.

Not surprisingly, Mississippi seemed more oblivious to the economic benefits of racial harmony. The poorest state in the nation made only small gains in business growth, and whites were constantly scared that blacks would take their jobs. The less there was to share, the more the establishment clung to their limited resources. While some businesses were worried about bad publicity, most people in Mississippi were too shortsighted to understand the consequences. This was vividly apparent in late January 1964, when I returned to Mississippi to cover the murder trial of Medgar Evers's accused assassin.

CHAPTER 17

Justice Delayed

The First Beckwith Trial

BYRON DE LA BECKWITH JR. WAS A FORTY-THREE-YEAR-OLD FERTILIZER salesman from an old Greenwood, Mississippi, family who had served as a marine in World War II and was a member in good standing of the town's respected organizations—the Masons, the Shriners, the White Citizens' Council, and the Protestant Episcopal Church. Beckwith was also a member of the KKK and a fanatic who believed that neither the KKK nor the White Citizens' Council had gone far enough to oppose evil threats to white society. Medgar Evers was one of the most influential civil rights leaders in the state, and Beckwith wanted to be a martyr for the cause of segregation.

On a warm June night in 1963, Beckwith, hiding in a clump of sweet gum trees and tangled honeysuckle vine, waited for Medgar Evers to arrive home from a civil rights rally. As Evers stepped from his car, Beckwith shot him in the back with a bolt action high-powered rifle. A gun bearing Beckwith's fingerprints was recovered nearby.

Beckwith, who denied his involvement in the killing, was arrested and charged with the murder. The trial, held at the Hinds County courtroom in Jackson, attracted small crowds, mostly black, and uniformed officers stood guard at the doors taking the names and addresses of the spectators. As I entered the courtroom, my memory flashed back to the Till trial and the idiosyncratic workings of the Mississippi justice system.

It was immediately obvious that selecting an impartial jury would be impossible. As with the Till trial, potential jurors were randomly selected from a list of registered voters composed largely of white men. The Southern Regional Council had made strides to register blacks in the South—about

265,000 blacks in eleven states had registered since 1962—but Mississippi still lagged far behind. Of the two hundred potential jurors summoned for the case, just six were black. The district attorney repeatedly asked potential jurors the same questions: Might race impact your verdict? Could you convict a white man for killing a black man who led racial integration efforts in the state? Do you understand that you could be ostracized in your community for reaching a guilty verdict?

The district attorney asked one prospective white juror if he thought it would be a crime for a white man to kill a black man in Mississippi. There was a long pause.

"What was his answer?" the judge asked impatiently as he sat between the Mississippi and American flags, habitually twisting his wedding ring.

"He's thinking it over," the district attorney replied.

Finally, the prospective juror answered yes, it was a crime, but he promised to put the race issue out of his mind for the present time.

"Not for the present time," the judge barked. "It's for all time."

The district attorney dismissed the potential juror.

Three blacks were also dismissed because one had an employment conflict, another had suffered a murder in the family, and the third knew Evers personally. The three remaining black men were skipped over and sent home. Many of the rejected white jurors conceded that their verdict might be affected by the race issue. After three and a half days, the final jury consisted of twelve white men who said they could vote for the death penalty if the state proved the defendant guilty.

Once the trial began, I was reminded how trivial and lackluster the judicial process was in these types of cases. It was bad enough when it happened in the backwater courtrooms of rural Mississippi, but I was expecting a bit more sophistication and balance in Jackson.

Beckwith, wearing a dark blue suit, red tie, and red socks, looked perfectly at ease as he sat at the defense table with his hands folded and his feet propped up in an empty chair. With his dark hair slicked back, he stared placidly from behind his horn-rimmed glasses and occasionally smiled at us in the press gallery.

During the recess, he joked with policemen, smoked a cigar, smiled, and talked with the jury until a bailiff pulled him back. Beckwith seemed surprised when his wife entered the courtroom wearing a brown fur coat and red dress. At the time of the slaying, the couple was separated, and he was

John's grandfather, John Alexander Herbers, born in 1851, owned a liquor store in downtown Memphis.

John's grandmother, Anna Harper Herbers Eder, was slain by a scorned lover in 1909 after she divorced John Alexander Herbers and married Charles Eder.

John's father, John Norton Herbers (Pop), was the only child of John Alexander Herbers and Anna Harper Herbers. He was twelve years old when his parents divorced and left in the care of his father and Catholic boarding schools.

John's mother, Mabell Clare Foster Herbers, was the oldest of seven children of a prominent family in Memphis. Her grandfather was a Confederate captain in the Civil War who served under General Nathan Bedford Forrest.

John as a young boy in Tennessee.

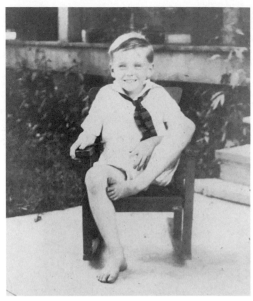

John's father opened and closed a series of variety stores in Tennessee and Mississippi, and moved the family from one small town to another.

John, whom his family called Norton, in a school photograph.

John's mother, Mabell Clare, possessed all the social graces to endear herself with the town's ruling matriarchs even though the family was not wealthy. John poses with his mother and Emily (right) and Sarah (center, holding dolls), two of his three sisters.

John's portrait upon graduation from Brownsville High School in 1942 in Brownsville, Tennessee.

As a teen, John was exceedingly shy with little social life beyond Sunday school. When he asked a girl to the high school dance, she flatly rejected him with no reason.

John and his father in Crystal Springs, Mississippi. As a boy, John worked with his father in the family variety stores.

Upon graduating from high school, John enlisted in the army as a private in World War II.

John served in New Guinea and the Philippines. He was also stationed on Morotai Island, where his company, under the leadership of General Douglas MacArthur, secured air bases seized from the Japanese.

In 1952, John married
Betty Wood in Memphis.
They had met in high
school at a church retreat
and reunited after the war.

John began working at United Press news service in Jackson, Mississippi, in 1952 after stints at the *Morning Star* in Greenwood, Mississippi, and the *Jackson Daily News*. One assignment included covering the 1955 Emmett Till murder trial.

John and Betty in
Jackson, Mississippi.

In 1958, United Press became United Press
International, and John, as Jackson bureau
chief, pursued coverage of racial stories
in Mississippi despite objections from
local newspaper publishers and television
broadcasters who relied on UPI reporting.

John and Betty had four daughters, the last born in 1960.

John was a member of the Class of 1961 Nieman Foundation Fellowship at Harvard University, which provides journalists with one year of independent study. Other fellows included (first row, left to right) Aubrey Sussens, Robert Toth, Peter Goldman, Chanchal Sarkar, Thomas Joyce, Robert Clark, J. Thomas Pugh, Louis Lyons (curator), Joseph Loftus, Lowell Brandle, and Donald Brazier; and (second row) John Pomfret, Andrew Secrest, John Herbers, and Robert Smith.

John Herbers, 1961, at typewriter, in UPI Jackson, MS office.

John returned from Harvard to UPI in Jackson for one year before transferring to Washington, DC, to cover Congress, the White House, and the Labor and Justice Departments. He is pictured here in the UPI Jackson office.

One of John's first assignments for the *New York Times* was in 1963 when four girls died in a church bombing in Birmingham, Alabama. The police used attack dogs and fire hoses on peaceful demonstrators. ©Bruce Davidson/Magnum Photos.

Ross Barnett, the segregationist governor of Mississippi from 1960 to 1964, gave rousing speeches at the Neshoba County Fair. John spent many hours with Barnett, including when Barnett would call him at home and rant about press coverage of civil rights. Eyd Kazery, *Ross Barnett: 1982 Neshoba County Fair*, printed 1998, gelatin silver print, Collection of the Mississippi Museum of Art, Jackson, Gift of Christopher Haddad, 1999.017.

In the summer of 1964, John spent weeks in St. Augustine, Florida, writing about protests at whites-only establishments. An integrated "swim-in" at a whites-only motel pool prompted a sheriff's deputy to jump in fully clothed to make arrests. Originally appeared in the *New York Times* and reprinted by permission.

On July 2, 1964, President Johnson signed the Civil Rights Act into law, outlawing discrimination in the United States based on race, color, religion, gender, or national origin. Johnson spoke on national television surrounded by Attorney General Robert F. Kennedy, First Lady "Lady Bird" Johnson, Senator Hubert Humphrey, Martin Luther King Jr., FBI director J. Edgar Hoover, and House Speaker John McCormack. LBJ Library photo by O. J. Rapp.

John traveled extensively with Martin Luther King Jr. and had a one-on-one interview with him the day before King joined President Lyndon Johnson for the signing of the landmark Civil Rights Act of 1964. John's article appeared three days later in the *New York Times Magazine*.

John worked to meet a deadline for a *New York Times* article about an unusual show of partisanship at the National Governors' Association meeting in 1985. Courtesy David R. Frazier.

John was presented with the 2000 John Chancellor Award for Excellence in Journalism in New York City. Pictured (left to right, back row) are Sander Vanocur, David Halberstam, Jack Nelson, John Herbers, and Bill Minor; and (front row) Ira Lipman and Howell Raines.

John and US Congressman John Lewis reunited in Washington in 2014, almost fifty years after the protests in Selma, Alabama.

John and Betty in 1999.

John admiring the beauty of the Potomac River in Washington in 2012.

living alone in Greenwood. But she arrived at court to support him. He went to the railing to kiss her, and she sat beside him.

Beckwith also had a powerful block of supporters join him at the trial. An army major general stopped by on his way to meet friends at the White Citizens' Council headquarters to shake hands with Beckwith in the courtroom. Former governor Ross Barnett and a Hinds County judge also arrived and chatted with Beckwith.

One of the first witnesses was Evers's widow. Composed and attractive in a royal blue dress and black gloves, Myrlie Evers recounted how she was home with her two children watching President Kennedy's civil rights speech in response to Malone's and Hood's university admissions while waiting for Evers to return from the rally.

The Everses, always anticipating danger, had months before developed an emergency protection plan in which they sent their children to the bathtub for shelter if the family was attacked by gunshots or bombs. "There was this loud blast," Myrlie Evers testified about the night of her husband's death. "Then there was silence. When we got to the door, I saw my husband lying face down and a trail of blood behind him. He had keys in his hand. That is what I found." She said she sent the children running to the bathtub.

Beckwith listened without changing his expression. It was one of his more subdued moments. Most other times he was an active defendant, following his attorneys around the courtroom to inspect photographs and the rifle. When Beckwith met with his attorneys in an anteroom, the door cracked open briefly and we could see Beckwith practice-aiming with the rifle. In the courtroom, he took copious notes in a loose-leaf notebook and seemed particularly interested when an NAACP regional secretary described how she saw him at a rally led by Evers.

Another witness, a Jackson detective, described how "a .30-caliber bullet, fired from a high-powered rifle, entered Mr. Evers's back, emerged from his chest, pierced a window of the home, went through a four-inch wall into the kitchen, struck the refrigerator a glancing blow, broke a glass coffee pot, and then came to rest on a counter." Other witnesses saw Beckwith's car parked near Evers's house about forty-five minutes before the shooting, but the defense contended there was no way to prove Beckwith was the triggerman. Three people testified that they saw Beckwith in Greenwood, ninety-five miles away, within an hour of the shooting. Beckwith denied being in Jackson on the night of the shooting, but he didn't explain his whereabouts. He said a rifle like the one entered as evidence was stolen from his bathroom closet two days before the shooting.

After eleven hours of deliberation, the jury was unable to reach a verdict—voting 7 to 5 for acquittal—and the judge declared a mistrial. Beckwith avoided a conviction that would have brought life imprisonment or death in the gas chamber. Beckwith went back to jail, and the judge set a new trial. The verdict came as a surprise because many in Mississippi, both blacks and whites, expected an instant and unanimous acquittal. The outcome showed that at least five jurors either were unconvinced by the defense's argument or were fair-minded enough to realize the trial was not conducted with utmost justice. Myrlie Evers had prepared a statement for an acquittal, not expecting a hung jury. "The fact that they could not agree signals something," she said after the verdict.

The votes for conviction were partly the result of vigorous prosecution by William L. Waller, a thirty-seven-year-old district attorney and seventh-generation Mississippian with grand political ambitions. He was prescient enough to foresee the potential political windfall of the civil rights movement. Although some believed that Waller was ruining his political career by prosecuting Beckwith, he was eventually elected governor in 1971 by appealing to a coalition of newly enfranchised blacks and poor whites. He was opposed in that election by Charles Evers, who ran as an independent.

Perhaps the mistrial was a result of the widespread national attention surrounding Evers's death. Jackson native and nationally recognized writer Eudora Welty had provided the most cogent and penetrating explanation of Beckwith's motive by explaining how poor, ill-educated whites in Mississippi were threatened by the slightest gains by blacks. In "Where Is the Voice Coming From?," a haunting short story published on July 6, 1963, in the New Yorker, Welty described the stirrings in Beckwith's mind as he plotted and carried out the murder. Narrated in the vernacular of an illiterate man, the story read, "There was one way left, for me to be ahead of you and stay ahead of you, by Dad, and I just taken it. Now I'm alive and you ain't. We ain't never now, never going to be equals and you know why? One of us is dead."

Welty had a unique perspective as a white southerner, but other national artists also described the perverse and paranoid environment of whites' fear of losing ground. Twenty-two-year-old Bob Dylan recorded "Only a Pawn in Their Game," suggesting that Beckwith was not the sole perpetrator but instead a proxy of a pervasive racist mind-set. Dylan first performed the song at a voter registration drive in Greenwood, Mississippi, on July 2, 1963.

Beckwith's jocular smile was gone when his second trial opened two months later in April 1964 in the same courtroom with the same judge, the same attorneys, and the same evidence. Missing were Beckwith's brilliant red tie and matching socks, replaced by more somber navy blue socks, a tie, and a suit. He appeared glum and a little bored by the tedious job of selecting a jury. The final jury included all white males, seven of whom were college graduates and two of whom had migrated from northern states.

But by the second day, Beckwith's spirits were rallied by the support of seventy-five tough-looking Klansmen who sat in the front rows of the court-room and stared stone faced at the witnesses as they testified. I was surprised the Klansmen could stay awake during the trial because the night before they had burned ten crosses in Jackson neighborhoods. The Klan showed up in response to a call for a vigorous prosecution from a few civic and business leaders who were worried about the impact of negative publicity. While white officials were a long way from rejecting the goals of the civil rights movement, they did condemn the killing.

Much of the testimony and evidence was identical to that presented at the first trial, but this time the prosecutor kept Beckwith on the stand for three hours, badgering him to explain his whereabouts at the time of the shooting. Beckwith stuck to his same story as in the first trial. After two weeks, the proceedings ended in another mistrial. A hung jury voted 8 to 4 for conviction, and Charles Evers said the fact that most jurors had voted for conviction was encouraging and "shows progress toward the goal of justice in Mississippi."

Upon hearing the verdict, Beckwith was subdued and showed no emotion. It had been ten months since his arrest, and he was released on a $10,000 bond paid by his friends in Greenwood. The police escorted him home to greeting admirers to wait until the district attorney decided the next step. Beckwith returned to his job as a fertilizer salesman, continuing to collect guns and participate in anti-integration activities. He joined a crowd of whites protesting a movie theater that admitted blacks, and he wrote and distributed racist literature. Mississippi law placed no limits on the number of times an unresolved case could be tried. Yet six months after Beckwith's release, Waller announced he would not seek a third trial unless there was new evidence in the case.

Beckwith remained free for thirty years until Jerry Mitchell, an enter-prising reporter at the Jackson *Clarion-Ledger*, discovered that the state-sanctioned Sovereignty Commission had secretly used taxpayer money to help Beckwith's attorneys investigate members of the jury pool. With this revelation, court officials also found new evidence that Beckwith had bragged about getting away with the murder. Because Beckwith was never acquitted, the state reopened the case, and its long-tortured past, and Beckwith was found guilty for the murder in 1994. He died in 2001 while serving a life sentence in a Mississippi prison. He was eighty years old.

CHAPTER 18

A Long, Hot Summer of Discontent

SUMMER HEAT ARRIVED AROUND MAY IN THE SOUTH AND DIDN'T DIS-
sipate until well into September. With most buildings having no air conditioning, the heat was relentless and unavoidable. It burned people's brains,
seeped into their skin, and produced prickly reactions to the smallest provo
cations. Night brought no relief. Darkness captured the listless air, holding it
tight until a new blazing sun delivered more elevated temperatures. I think
the heat, as likely as anything else, explained the stale and lethargic thinking
and behavior of southerners.

Sultry waves fanned above fallow fields as I drove across Mississippi in
June 1964. Hundreds of college students were arriving for Freedom Summer,
sometimes called the Mississippi Summer Project, to mobilize blacks to vote.
The effort had been spearheaded in McComb in 1961 by activist Bob Moses,
but now the students had a new urgency to their mission.

Lyndon B. Johnson, who had succeeded President Kennedy, introduced
a new Civil Rights Act that was making its way through Congress. Activists
wanted President Johnson, who was running for reelection in November, to
pressure Congress to pass the bill. The Summer Project also came at a significant moment for the civil rights drive. Momentum was lagging as activists
lapsed into a mood of despair over the slow progress of change, and there was
uncertainty about the direction of the movement. Civil rights leaders found
it difficult to focus on both the nuts-and-bolts work of eliminating Jim Crow
laws and sustaining a national public relations campaign. Demonstrations,
boycotts, and direct-action campaigns had some local impact on the laws,
but they had not eliminated large-scale racial barriers, especially in smaller
cities and towns. In addition, the costs of fines, bail, and legal representation

were mounting. Protesters arrested in Birmingham found themselves in court battles a year later, and the number of protesters willing to obligingly accept arrests, beatings, and jail time was declining. The number of deaths was also increasing.

This frustration was fueled by national politics. George Wallace was running for president, and his strong showing in the Wisconsin primary heightened fears among southern blacks that support from the North for the movement was waning. Everyone was weighing the political ramifications of America's race relations. President Johnson feared that increased black power might destroy his white base in the South unless enough blacks voted to turn the tide in his favor. Blacks and liberal whites in Mississippi were forming a Mississippi Freedom Democratic Party as a direct challenge to the exclusively white national Democratic Party. A split in Democratic Party loyalties could hurt Johnson's chances of winning the nomination.

During this period of uncertainty, one thing was clear—the Magnolia State, seemingly impregnable to the winds of social change, would be the focus of what national and local civil rights organizations were calling the "long hot summer of discontent." The Council of Federated Organizations (COFO)—a collaboration of civil rights organizations that included SNCC, the NAACP, CORE, and the SCLC—viewed Mississippi as the epicenter of economic, racial, and societal struggles.

Their goals were twofold: register blacks to vote and educate blacks so they could pass the state's reading and writing registration tests. COFO member organizations recruited eight hundred students, teachers, ministers, and lawyers, who arrived in Mississippi by the busload to work on the Summer Project. They were met mostly with hostility and suspicion, and I wrote an article with the headline, "In the South: Battle Lines Are Drawn for Summer Offensive." I described how the Mississippi legislature passed new laws to prohibit picketing and leafleting, and nearly doubled the number of state police. Local jurisdictions also expanded their police forces and bought more guns. The state published a digest outlining new laws that empowered law enforcement.

With only a single generation separating them from World War II, many whites in Mississippi conflated their fear of invasion by northerners and the federal government with an even larger threat—the influence of communism. Some people were so paranoid that they believed that adding fluoride to the public water supply to prevent cavities was a communist plot. In one speech, King debunked the connection. "I'm sick and tired of people saying this movement has been infiltrated by communists," he said. "There are as many communists in this freedom movement as there are Eskimos in Florida."

Most white racists suspected everyone except their own. Luckily, I could pass as one of them. I understood their language, their gestures, and their habits. Like many southerners of Scotch-Irish or northern European ancestry, I had blue eyes and fair skin. My inexpensive short-sleeved cotton shirts and khaki pants blended in with the local dress. My southern accent grew thicker when I swapped stories with the locals, and I put them so at ease that sometimes they felt comfortable enough to make racist remarks even when they knew I would quote them in a paper for "the Yankees" to read.

One Sunday afternoon, as the two thousand residents of Ruleville, Mississippi, napped after church and a heavy midday lunch, a Greyhound bus pulled into town carrying twenty students, both black and white, 110 pieces of luggage, twenty bedrolls, and one baseball bat. The bus had traveled overnight from Oxford, Ohio. I watched students step down from the bus, shielding their eyes from the blazing white sun. In the distant blue haze, cotton flourished in the rich black soil.

Suddenly, I saw faces emerge in the doors and windows of homes near the bus stop. Seven tough-looking men walked over from a gas station, beer cans in their hands, their mouths agape. The sheriff arrived in his truck with a police dog in the flatbed. The mayor, a stout man in a straw hat, arrived by car and stationed himself on a nearby corner. These were not members of a welcoming committee.

Ten of the students were wide-eyed white girls from the West and Midwest. One of them, Katherine Logan, a brunette in a blue dress, told me, "I really didn't know what to expect. We've been on the bus for twenty-four hours." She seemed surprised by what she saw next.

Striding across the street to meet the students was a large black woman in a pink dress and sandals named Fannie Lou Hamer, a local civil rights leader who had helped organize the Summer Project. Two years earlier, she had been fired after working eighteen years as a sharecropper on a nearby plantation because she had attempted to register to vote. Hamer had picked cotton since she was six years old and left school at age thirteen to help support her family. She had a broad face and a no-nonsense personality. Her involvement with the civil rights campaign had resulted in arrests and beatings by police, but she said she didn't know the point in being scared because she had known brutality all her life.

She led the twenty students on a dirt road to her home, a rundown brick bungalow with torn screens and a front porch of weathered planks that sloped at a precarious angle to the dirt yard. A healthy crop of butter beans and okra lined the side yard. The house was shaded by an enormous pecan tree, where the students were greeted by ten white students who had arrived the week before. One of those students was Len Edwards, a twenty-three-year-old University of Chicago law student and the son of US representative Don Edwards, a California Democrat.

The new students piled their portable typewriters, luggage, and bulletin boards on Hamer's sloping front porch for an introductory meeting. They were handed the names of their black host families and given ominous updates from the previous week: thrown bottles had shattered the windows of black homes, carloads of whites had chased civil rights workers through the streets, and white thugs had thrown a Molotov cocktail into a civil rights meeting at a chapel.

There was no mention of the most dire news that three civil rights workers—two white students from New York and a black man from Mississippi—had gone missing 150 miles away in Philadelphia, Mississippi. Everyone knew from news reports that a hunt for the workers was underway after their burned station wagon had been found in a swamp, but prospects about their present whereabouts were too grim to talk about.

I sat on Hamer's porch, watching the enthusiasm and gumption not only of Hamer, who sat listening in her rocking chair, but also of the students who had ventured here in the face of bodily harm or possible death. They could have easily avoided this assignment. They didn't even know Hamer or her people. They could return to colleges and cities where no one was trying to kill them. Instead, they possessed deep convictions that they could right the wrongs. It was idealistic and naïve but so genuine that you couldn't help think that they might succeed.

I pulled out my portable typewriter, propped it on the roof of my rented car in the shade of Hamer's pecan tree, and typed a story to send to my editors in New York. But to complete the story, I needed to speak with one more person.

After a quick eight-mile drive, I arrived at the air-conditioned plantation home of Senator James Eastland as he prepared to depart for Washington. He farmed several thousand acres of land in the middle of Sunflower County, which was 67 percent black. Few blacks here voted, and probably none would vote for him if given the chance. An unyielding segregationist, Eastland had for years called for state-organized defiance of federal efforts to integrate Mississippi. "I assert that the Negro race is an inferior race," he said on the floor of the US Senate. "The doctrine of white supremacy is one which, if adhered to, will save America."

As I walked up to Eastland's spacious home, I remembered when Betty and I had heard him give a speech in which he proclaimed there were two heavens—one for blacks and another for whites. We were aghast by his comment, but also surprised that he even thought blacks had the chance to go to heaven. That was generous for Eastland.

"I don't think there is any problem here," he told me during our interview, and he seemed unfazed by the arrival of the organizers to his county. Whites were ignoring them, and blacks resented them, he said. I added Eastland's comments and rushed back to my motel room to call in my story to New York. In those days, we dictated our dispatches by phone to a receptionist, and recited punctuation or spelling exactly as we wanted the story to appear in print.

"Dateline Ruleville. Capital R, u-l-e-v-i-l-l-e, Comma, Capital M, i-s-s, Period, Comma, June two-eight, Dash," I spoke into the phone in rapid succession. "In the Mississippi Delta, capital D, comma, the land is black and flat as far as you can see. Period. In late June, comma, the cotton is a foot high and the landscape simmers under a blue haze. Period. Paragraph."

I ended the story with a mention that Ruleville had hired two extra policemen, one black, to maintain order. In the last paragraph, I said that a white Stanford University chaplain with the National Council of Churches was turned away at the local white Methodist church. "You are here as part of the Negro community and should attend the Negro church," Ruleville's mayor, an officer of the church, told the chaplain. "This is no time to antagonize people."

The next day I drove to Hartman Turnbow's house one mile north of Mileston, Mississippi, which consisted of a cotton gin, a general store, and a dozen houses. Holmes County, where Mileston is located, had about nineteen thousand blacks and seven thousand whites. Ordinarily it would be difficult to recognize the remote place, but on this day college students overran the small white house. Turnbow was a short, fifty-nine-year-old man wearing a denim shirt over his expansive belly and a faded white baseball cap. He didn't seem to mind that his farm was being used as an assembly point for thirty students for the Summer Project.

He showed me with some pride four large bullet holes that had been shot in the side of his house a month earlier when he and fourteen other blacks went to the county courthouse to register to vote. Turnbow described his futile attempt: "Sheriff [Andrew P.] Smith met us at the courthouse door. He put one hand on his blackjack and the other on his pistol and said, 'We ain't goin' to have any of that forward stuff here.'"

"Then I told him, 'Mr. Smith, we only want to register,'" Turnbow recounted. "He put one hand back on his blackjack and the other on his pistol and lined us up at the door."

The sheriff allowed Turnbow and the others to fill out voter registration forms but then administered a rigorous reading and comprehension test. Turnbow's formal education was limited to a few sessions of school between cotton picking and chopping time. Turnbow and the others failed the test and went home. Later that night, a gang of whites visited the Turnbow house, shooting guns and throwing Molotov cocktails through the windows. One caught fire inside the house, but Turnbow and his wife extinguished it. Turnbow grabbed his .22 Remington shotgun and fired back. The white gang fled and no one was injured. Turnbow was later found guilty of arson by the local justice of the peace. The case eventually went before a federal judge, who threw out the conviction because he found it implausible that Turnbow would set fire to his own house.

Students also stayed at the farm of David Howard, who had a large house, two tractors, a telephone, and nine children. He and his wife, a substantial woman with bright gold teeth, appeared happy to put aside their chores to host the students. When I visited the Howards' farm, I met one student playing basketball with the Howard boys behind the chicken coop. Another student lay on the living room couch reading James W. Silver's newly published book, *Mississippi: The Closed Society*. Silver, a history professor at the University of Mississippi who had witnessed the riots when James Meredith was admitted, described how the Mississippi orthodoxy of white supremacy was reinforced by laws and official authorities of the state.

The student reading Silver's book was Jerry Parker, a cum laude graduate of Oberlin College who was twenty-one years old but looked no older than seventeen. "Like everyone else, I've had some fears about coming here," Parker told me. "But I believe something needs to be done about what Dr. Silver calls the closed society." I walked to an adjacent bedroom, where four female students rested on a bed—two were black; two were white. One of the white students complained to me that the media had failed to capture the harmonious spirit of the Summer Project, portraying it instead as a source of trouble. "How could anyone want to destroy this?" she said, gesturing to the comfortable rapport between her and the other students.

I left thinking about the students' commitment and about Silver, who was a southerner like me trying to make sense of antiquated and bigoted mores. Silver was not objecting to a minority of misguided folks. He was rejecting a standard of behavior condoned by popular opinion. I related to Silver's dilemma, but my job was to remain objective and report the facts. To do otherwise would compromise my credibility and the exacting standards of a newspaper that prided itself on factual reporting so that readers could reach their own conclusions.

People asked me how I could watch the atrocities during the civil rights movement without taking a more vocal position. I believe that a good reporter is an observer who stands in the corner absorbing as much as can be heard or seen but never becoming partisan. All reporters must leave the corner to search for the truth, but once it is found, offload the material to editorial writers and other sectors of society to reckon with. The search for truth requires an objective seeker, especially when that search goes against public opinion. A dedicated reporter can spend a lifetime finding the truth without becoming an advocate in the public arena.

CHAPTER 19

Bloodshed at the Beach

WHILE MISSISSIPPI WAS NOTORIOUS FOR ITS JIM CROW LAWS, THERE WAS another, lesser-known bastion of intolerance where civil rights leaders focused their efforts in the summer of 1964. St. Augustine, Florida, the nation's oldest city, was a stronghold for far-right conservatism steeped in an obsession about white genealogical origins. A beach community of fifteen thousand people located thirty-five miles south of Jacksonville, St. Augustine was a seemingly inappropriate locale for launching the campaign's summer efforts. Although the town was a popular visitor destination, with 80 percent of its economy reliant on tourism, it was, politically and socially, a backwater town that rejected its Latin American history, black heritage, and any larger national identity. While St. Augustine was not one of the most segregated cities in the South—it had nominal school integration and a few black police officers—the city was, at the same time, vehemently opposed to any further racial progress. One journalist described it as "schizophrenia by the sea." Despite its quaint streets, historic buildings, and fine old families, the city displayed the vilest kind of racism. It was a stronghold of the crazed right, which preached shrilly that the civil rights movement was analogous to communism. King called it "the most lawless city" in the nation. The sheriff's office was an arm of the KKK, and a story floated around town that a black maid found matching his-and-her KKK robes in her employers' closet.

It was the perfect staging ground for a critical test of not only King's ability to hold the imagination and allegiance of millions of blacks but also to reinforce loyalty to nonviolence. With white backlash reaching a peak, a new militancy by both blacks and segregationists was on the rise, and even whites sympathetic to the cause of racial justice were beginning to fear that black demands for "Freedom now! Freedom now!" were about to pull the pillars of society crashing down.

A new black dentist in town, Dr. Robert B. Hayling, who was a member of the local branch of the NAACP, seized upon the idea that St. Augustine's upcoming four-hundred-year anniversary would also be a perfect time to bring national attention to the city's discriminatory practices. Hayling and other black leaders considered their demands to be quite modest: desegregating public facilities including separate black and white beaches, hiring more black police officers and firefighters, and establishing a biracial commission to devise a plan for further desegregation. Because the city was concerned about its image as a tourist destination, King surmised that demonstrations at whites-only lunch counters, motels, and restaurants would impact the local economy and perhaps force white business owners to consider changes. These economic boycotts, considered more strident than mere street marches, could also fortify King's strategy of nonviolent disobedience, which was being questioned even among some journalists who believed that a more militant approach was needed.

As he set up his headquarters in St. Augustine, King told reporters he was steadfast in his nonviolent approach, which was bolstered by the arrival of out-of-town white ministers and rabbis sympathetic to the cause. He aptly quoted Saint Augustine of Hippo, the Latin philosopher and theologian who advanced the concept of a just cause for war because an "unjust law is no law at all" and, therefore, "morally null and void." King's strongest weapon was the ethos of passive resistance in which protesters would "pose themselves for martyrdom and force the oppressor to commit his brutality openly, with the rest of the world looking on." King said he would plague the community "lovingly" until discrimination ended. This was done by filling up the jails, putting a burden on law enforcement and the courts, and appealing to the nation's conscience through the media by showing thousands of peaceful people subjected to unprovoked beatings and arrests. Rather than instinctively fighting back, demonstrators were trained to curl up into balls to protect themselves during clubbing. Rather than lash out, they prayed for their oppressors while they withstood beatings. By doing this, the nation saw them as the long-suffering victims of white oppression rather than violators of the laws.

Sometimes the practice even suppressed violence. Once, I saw white segregationists kick and club crowds of praying demonstrators. When there was no return of blows, the attackers would suddenly walk away. King believed if blacks freely submitted themselves to violence, the oppressor would realize his injustice, cease his behavior, and eventually redeem himself and society. Blacks said the strategy shifted the violence they had known for years from the jail cells and dark alleys into open view. If the nation witnessed the violence, then someone—the government, the church, the white moderate—might be stirred to consciousness.

"Civilization and violence are antithetical concepts," King said. "[N]onviolence is not a sterile passivity, but a powerful moral force which makes for social transformation." Under his approach, demonstrators would reject revenge, aggression, and retaliation and harbor no hatred for whites. "Hate is too great a burden to bear," he said.

Yet theory and practice are not always aligned, and nonviolence had its limitations. As an increasing number of protesters were sacrificed for the cause, some leaders splintered from the main organizations and called for meeting violence with violence. In Monroe, North Carolina, Robert Williams, a former NAACP leader, urged blacks to arm themselves, and militant leaders from other cities joined the Monroe movement. After a riot in the Monroe town square, blacks kidnapped a white couple and held them hostage for several hours. Williams fled to Cuba, where he found asylum, but he left behind a town torn by bitterness and misunderstanding.

During one Nashville sit-in, a group of black high school students and militant whites fought the police. Nonviolent leaders saw this as detrimental to the racial progress already achieved in Nashville, which proudly called itself "the answer to the South." Five of the forty city council members were black, and the city was slowly integrating lunch counters, schools, restaurants, hotels, hospitals, parks, and playgrounds. Now the city was caught by surprise when black youths suddenly flooded the streets in a wildcat demonstration. A local newspaper editorial described the demonstrators as "untrained, misdirected, without sensitive leadership."

Fueling the sentiment for black retaliation was Malcolm X, a charismatic Muslim leader who preached a message of black pride and black power. In persuasive and passionate speeches, he enjoined blacks to fight racism "by any means necessary" including violence. "You don't have a peaceful revolution," he said. "You don't have a turn-the-cheek revolution. There's no such thing as a nonviolent revolution." Malcolm X was the antithesis of King's nonviolent movement, and his message was attractive to many who wanted quicker changes. He approved of many of King's goals, but not his methods. The two men had only one face-to-face meeting, and it appeared to be by chance in Washington in the spring of 1964 when King attended the Senate debates over the Civil Rights Act. As King left a news conference, Malcolm X, tall and lanky, emerged from the crowd to shake his hand, and King greeted him. Malcolm X stood a head taller, and the two men smiled and posed for the cameras. The meeting lasted less than a minute.

Although King advocated nonviolence, he was not passive. He invited confrontation. Protest leaders would deliberately plant demonstrators in crowds to taunt and tease police officers or segregationists with the hope they would lash out. King was constantly trying to find the right combination of militancy and moderation. At one Frankfort, Kentucky, rally, King told a crowd of ten thousand people that blacks must continue to press for equal rights at the risk of being called immoderate. "If moderation means slowing up in our fight," he said, "then moderation is a tragic vice which members of our race must condemn. The time is now to make real the promises of democracy."

When King opened a field office in St. Augustine in June 1964, he knew that the locals would serve up just the kind of terror and oppression needed to advance the movement's public relations campaign. I arrived in St. Augustine in June as King and the SCLC arranged for hundreds of black and white protesters from around the nation to descend on the town and stage sit-ins at white restaurants, wade-ins at white beaches and swimming pools, and marches around the town square and former slave market. Movement leaders understood the growing impact of television and wanted images of peaceful blacks being brutally beaten to reach America's living rooms.

The plan worked. Tough white gangs from the swamps and byways of nearby St. Johns County roamed the city attacking peaceful demonstrators, white sympathizers, and even white businessmen who tried to voluntarily desegregate stores and restaurants. The gangs patrolled the streets in cars carrying guns, two-way radios, and whiplash antennas. Townspeople called them Manucy's Raiders because their leader was Holsted Richard "Hoss" Manucy, an illiterate forty-five-year-old pig farmer and former bootlegger who had been laid off from his job and convicted for beating a black man. Manucy's men were said to hunt alligators in the swamps by day and beat up blacks by night.

Manucy was 220 pounds of brawn and belly. He wore a T-shirt, jeans, and a battered black cowboy hat that hid a shiny bald spot. Small tufts of black hair curled around his ears, and he was usually in need of a shave. Manucy lived at the end of a road five miles from town with his fourteen children and a yard littered with dogs, automobile parts, empty bottles, and broken toys. Pigs rooted for acorns under a tree in the yard.

Manucy's Raiders were also known as the Ancient City Hunting Club, a white supremacy organization with about 1,500 followers. Manucy founded the club in 1961 because he was a Catholic, like most of the county's residents, and was therefore banned from becoming a member of the Protestant-only KKK. Despite being ostracized by the Klan, he praised the organization and was responsible for bringing a Klan leader from Atlanta to march through black neighborhoods in St. Augustine.

Most whites in St. Augustine had simply tolerated Manucy's Raiders; they never considered the Raiders much to worry about because they thought that Manucy exaggerated the number of men under his command. But he gained influence when the local sheriff made Manucy and some of his men special deputies to help contain the demonstrations. When black protesters were arrested, the man who opened the jailhouse door for them was Manucy himself, grinning from ear to ear. Manucy bragged to me that his men were better organized than the protesters. "That's the only way we can win. We've got a better communications system among ourselves and the police, I guess," he said. "We don't carry no guns ourselves. Out on the street, I mean. Sure, we have them in our cars. I think every white citizen has got a gun in his car."

Both the demonstrations and the violence escalated in a short period of time. A beach cottage where King was staying was firebombed twice, and the jails were brimming with hundreds of arrested protesters, including the mother of Massachusetts governor Endicott Peabody. A white restaurateur who served four blacks during a sit-in found the windows at his home, car, and restaurant broken the next day, and he discontinued serving blacks. Gunshots were fired through Hayling's home, killing the family dog, who had been standing behind the front door, and Hayling and three other blacks were beaten at a Klan rally outside town. A black student attending adult education courses in a predominantly white school was beaten on his way to class. A white shrimp fisherman was shot and killed when he drove through a black neighborhood.

By day, downtown St. Augustine was a picture of tranquility, with elderly white men playing checkers in the former slave market and tourists visiting Spanish buildings in horse-drawn surreys. But at night, demonstrators filed out of churches and marched to the town square. Almost every evening, Manucy's Raiders would pull some of them aside and beat them. Police used tear gas to break up crowds, including those that threw rocks at the demonstrators. Andrew Young, one of King's right-hand men who was bludgeoned during protests in St. Augustine, recounted years later, "We were living in the presence of death all the time."

Law enforcement authorities tried to reduce the violence. One night, white men and youths lurking in the shadows hurled bricks at police who were guarding civil rights demonstrators from a cursing mob. The mob broke through the police line, slugged and kicked several demonstrators, and burned marchers with acid. The city removed the bricks that bordered flower beds in the palm-tree-lined park adjoining the former slave market and installed seven mercury vapor lights to illuminate dark corners of the square. Governor C. Farris Bryant sent in state troopers with tear gas to break up and arrest the white mobs. Four white St. Augustine teens were charged with disorderly conduct, and a fifth was charged with carrying a large chain.

King asked federal authorities for extra protection, but Bryant assured the White House that he could maintain order without federal troops. What King didn't realize at the time was that he was probably better off without them. FBI director J. Edgar Hoover despised King, and FBI agents sometimes sided with local authorities. When Hoover called King the "most notorious liar in the country," King replied that Hoover must be "under extreme pressure" to make such a statement. It is now known that the FBI considered King a national security threat and wiretapped and bugged his office, home, and motel rooms.

After reporting from St. Augustine for six weeks with no time off, I went home to Atlanta for the weekend to see my family. When I arrived, Betty and my four daughters were standing in the driveway dressed in bathing suits, flip-flops, and floaties ready for a beach trip to Panama City, Florida. As I was packing the car, my editors called and said to get back to St. Augustine because more protesters had arrived and the violence had worsened. Betty and I traditionally built a wall to separate our positive home life from the atrocities I saw daily. But I had been away from my family for so long and could not bear to leave them again, so we made an exception. I looked at my family and said, "Riots or no riots, we're headed to the beach."

At 5:00 a.m. the next morning, our family drove to St. Augustine instead of Panama City. I checked the family into a Howard Johnson's motel on the beach outside of town, and the girls swam in the motel pool. That night, I went to a church eight blocks from the town square where four hundred black and white protesters had assembled. King, in his booming, resonant voice, urged them to "march tonight like you never marched before." They left the church carrying signs mounted on poster boards declaring, "I Am an American Also," "My Father Died Defending This County Too," and "Segrega-tion Must Go." As they walked toward the square they softly sang, "We Love Everybody in Our Hearts." I remember how calm and seemingly unafraid they were. The weather was hot and humid, yet the marchers wore no shorts or untidy shirts. All the men wore long pants and starched white button-down dress shirts, while the women wore skirts and dresses.

When they arrived at the square, they were met by a crowd of about sixty white people carrying signs, one that proclaimed, "Martin Luther Coon / And All His Little Coons / Are Going Down." Suddenly, a screaming white mob began hurling bricks and broke through a line of state troopers the governor had dispatched a few hours earlier. Several large white men with buzz cuts exited a drugstore and rushed at a few of the demonstrators, using the sticks from their placards to beat them on the head and shoulders. The protesters never resisted but curled into fetal positions as blood splattered onto their clean white shirts.

A local police officer standing outside the drugstore never moved, instead planting his feet hip-width and crossing his arms over his broad belly as he watched the melee. It was during these times that I had difficulty being a mere observer. My instinct was to rush into action to protect the abused and to punish the bully. But I held back, knowing my job was to report the scene back to the nation.

The troopers mistook one of the white marchers for a member of the mob and shoved him into the all-white crowd. The mob pushed him out to the street and beat and kicked him. At this point, a state trooper with a dog ordered the white mob to disperse, and when they refused he threw a tear gas bomb into their midst. This halted them for only a moment, and the mob hurled bricks at the police. It took more tear gas and threats to break them up. "Niggers have more freedom than we do," the whites shouted.

One person beaten in the clash was Reverend William England, a white chaplain from Boston University who had arrived in St. Augustine the night before. "They [the mob] grabbed me and tried to pull me into the bushes," he told me afterward, "but I fell down and they stood and kicked me for a while." The police did not intervene. A slender teenage black boy threw his body over England, and the assailants slowly walked away. Gradually, the white mob faded into the night and the marchers returned to their church. Six people were injured, and the police arrested some members of the mob for disorderly conduct and carrying concealed weapons.

The next day, King and seventeen companions, including England, arrived at one of St. Augustine's finer whites-only restaurants at Monson Motor Lodge overlooking Matanzas Bay. Like many demonstrations, this one was staged to gain optimal news coverage, and we in the press were notified beforehand. As King and his aide Ralph Abernathy tried to enter the restaurant at noon, they were confronted by its owner, James Brock, president of the Florida Hotel and Motel Association, whom I had seen during the night marches acting as a sheriff's special deputy and carrying a shotgun, billy club, pistol, and flashlight. Brock told King that he and his fellow diners were not welcome at the restaurant, and then the two men entered a calm but intense twenty-minute discussion about the civil rights movement. It was a strange interaction. King tried to rationalize with Brock, asking him if he understood how his people were humiliated by being forced to use separate facilities. Brock replied that he would integrate his establishment only if asked by white citizens or if ordered by the federal courts.

"You realize it would be detrimental to my business to serve you here," Brock said. "I have unfortunately had to arrest eighty-four protesters here since Easter." Then he turned to the reporters, smiled, and used the moment for a promotional plug as he spoke into the television cameras: "I would like to invite my many friends throughout the country to come to Monson's. We expect to remain segregated." Brock had received letters from around the nation praising him. Some people in town said Brock was not a bad guy and was just trying to restore some order to the city.

As King and Brock spoke, a burly white man impatient for his lunch bullied his way through the crowd and shoved King out of the way. The sheriff arrived, arrested King and his companions, and took them to jail for breaking the local segregation laws. They were charged with disturbing the peace, trespassing, and conspiracy. It was King's seventeenth arrest in racial disturbances throughout the South.

Later that evening, as King was transferred to a safer jail in Jacksonville, white segregationists staged a counterdemonstration. Two hundred KKK members, including their lawyer from Atlanta, marched through the dark, narrow streets of a black neighborhood dressed in white robes and waving Confederate flags. The lawyer egged on the crowd, calling King "a long-time associate of communists" supported by a "Jew-stacked communist-loving Supreme Court." Following the KKK marchers were at least one hundred police officers, several police dogs, and about thirty news reporters, photographers, and television cameramen. We were a strange-looking parade.

As we passed Big Daddy's Blue Goose Night Club, a crowd of black men came out and jokingly applauded. "They don't need all those policemen down here," one man from the night club said. "We aren't going to hurt anybody." A group of white youths broke through a line of state troopers and police dogs, but fifty troopers chased them for two blocks to keep them from causing further trouble. Troopers searched the area and found sulfuric acid, chains, and clubs that belonged to the white youths.

The next day, I drove through another black neighborhood to see if demonstrators were planning a protest. A trooper stopped me and asked me nicely to leave, which I did. Shortly after, the police stopped me again and this time took me to the station and fined me fourteen dollars for running through a stop sign. They were not kind, but they let me go. It was a trumped-up charge simply to harass me. I knew perfectly well I had come to a complete stop at the sign because I always took extra precautions to obey the laws, knowing I was being watched. That same day, I saw some KKK members writing down my license-plate number while I was parked near the town square. Some news reporters and cameramen hired bodyguards for protection. I didn't feel it was necessary because even the most violent segregationists understood that attacking the press only brought them unwanted national attention. The streets were dangerous, but because I was in familiar territory, I was less fearful than some of the northern journalists.

However, I grew increasingly uneasy about my family's safety, even though they were staying at a motel away from the rioting. Late one night, Betty and I were startled from our sleep by the sound of roaring cars and pickup trucks. A gang of whites drove in circles around the motel, firing their rifles into the air. The hoodlums were content to keep their distance and were probably only intent on scaring us, which they did. After they drove away, Betty and I hurriedly woke the girls, packed them into the back of our turquoise Ford, and drove out of town. As I looked at the fading lights of St. Augustine in the rear-view mirror, I was relieved to escape harm and return to Atlanta.

CHAPTER 20

Purifying Prelude

WITHIN A FEW DAYS, I WAS BACK IN ST. AUGUSTINE—WITHOUT MY FAMILY—
where King was upping the ante. When a county grand jury proposed a thirty-
day ceasefire so a biracial committee could be created to negotiate a truce,
King immediately rejected the idea and said demonstrations would continue.

A week after King's arrest at Monson's, seventy protesters, including sixteen
rabbis from northern cities, reappeared at Brock's motel. Brock once again
ordered them to leave. When they refused, he began assaulting the group's
leaders. As one rabbi was pushed aside, another would come forward to stand
his ground. A crowd of white businessmen and townspeople stood by and
shouted. While everyone watched the shoving, a small group of black men
and women in swimsuits jumped out of an automobile and dove into the
motel swimming pool. They were joined by two white men who were civil
rights workers staying at the motel.

I watched as Brock quickly fetched two containers of muriatic acid, a
cleaning agent, and poured it into the pool. A fully dressed white policeman
dove into the pool to arrest the swimmers while other officers clubbed them.
I walked across the street where King, who was out of jail on a $900 bond,
watched the dive-in. "It was raw police brutality," he told me. "Cattle prods
were used on our demonstrators and people were actually beaten." He was
right, but the local laws were not on his side—they still forbade integrated
swimming.

Forty-one people, including all the rabbis, were arrested, but no one was
seriously injured. The next day, my article appeared on the front page of
the *Times* with an Associated Press photograph of a full-clothed policeman
suspended in midair above the demonstrators as he jumped into the pool to

drag them out. The photograph was printed in papers around the world and proved an embarrassment to the United States and St. Augustine, which was beginning to seriously worry about its marred reputation.

Although every day was consumed by writing about yet another outbreak, I felt the story in St. Augustine needed to be told with a deeper explanation about how King's campaign was critical to moving the Civil Rights Act toward passage. The *New York Times Magazine*, which dedicated thousands of words to a few topics each Sunday, was the perfect forum to capture the impact and future of the movement.

King agreed to meet me for an interview on a steamy Wednesday afternoon at one of the safe houses where he stayed with host families. It was the only time I saw him without a battery of aides, an audience, or other journalists in the room. Despite the intense pressure of the campaign, he appeared calm and measured as we sat on a screened porch sipping iced tea and orange juice to talk about his goals for the summer. He was short and beefy and dressed immaculately in a snow-white shirt. His appearance had changed little since I first met him. He was a little heavier, but there was no flabbiness to him. His broad, sloping face and thick neck gave him a sense of power, yet that was the only hint of the extraordinary life he led.

It was hard to believe he was only thirty-five years old, not because of his appearance but because of the veneration in which he was held by all who were willing to sacrifice their lives for him and the cause. As a black leader, he was unique. The movement's power was fueled by his personality and his ability to arouse an audience that wanted to see, hear, and touch him. His assistants introduced him to crowds as "the Moses of our time" and "the spiritual leader of the world." Both his followers and his detractors referred to him as "the Lawd."

He had barely graduated from Boston University with a doctorate in systematic theology when he rose to national prominence by leading the 1956 Montgomery bus boycott, an assignment he accepted with some reluctance because he was only twenty-seven years old, recently married, and the new pastor of a church in Montgomery. He moved to Atlanta a year after the bus boycott to copastor the Ebenezer Baptist Church with his father and establish the SCLC. By 1964, the SCLC had grown to more than sixty full-time workers at more than one hundred chapters across the nation.

Neither the SCLC nor King had claims on administrative efficiency. But King's sheer brilliance, charisma, and oratory skills made him the most prominent and recognized American black leader since Booker T. Washington or Frederick Douglass. Although his life was repeatedly threatened, he moved around St. Augustine that summer with no visible protection. He said he needed to be among the people for the campaign to succeed. He was optimistic about St. Augustine and the nation because he was leaving the next day to join President Johnson in Washington as he signed the Civil Rights Act into law; Congress had passed the legislation on July 2, 1964. King was a realist and knew that the South's acceptance and application of the law would take time, but its passage was a major step in starting to change hearts and minds. And it boosted morale for the campaign.

"Even if we do not get all we should, movements such as this tend more and more to give a Negro the sense of self-respect that he needs," King told me during the interview. "It tends to generate courage in Negroes outside the movement. It brings intangible results outside the community where it is carried out. There is a hardening of attitudes in situations like this. But other cities see and say, 'We don't want to be another Albany [Georgia] or Birmingham,' and they make changes. Some communities, like this one, had to bear the cross."

I asked him if he remained committed to nonviolence even though hundreds of his followers were being beaten and arrested. In gentle yet forceful terms, he articulated his conviction that repudiating violence was the most effective means of achieving change. If classical nonviolence did not work in its purest sense—that being reconciliation and equal dignity of the races—then blacks must accept, at least for the time, a lesser victory: a white man's acceptance of blacks for his own self-interest.

I pressed on, and he was not uncomfortable or offended by my line of questioning—he had grown accustomed to scrutiny of his tactics. But what about nonviolence in the future? Are blacks soon to abandon it, as some predicted?

"I still feel that Negroes by and large in the United States are willing to follow tactical nonviolence," he explained. "By that, I mean they believe in it in a pragmatic sense, not as a way of life as I do. I think the Negro will continue to accept nonviolence if it can bring about concrete victories. I think this will be the test of the summer, so to speak." He wanted St. Augustine to be a "purifying prelude" to a future of continued nonviolence as he carried the campaign to other cities.

With humility and eloquence, he described the longings of his people. "We will make progress if we freely admit that we have no magic; if we accept the fact that four hundred years of sinning cannot be canceled out in four minutes of atonement," he said, evoking religious themes from the core of his belief. "Neither can we allow the guilty to tailor their atonement in such a manner as to visit another four seconds of deliberate hurt upon the victim."

I left feeling I had been schooled at the feet of the philosophers, historians, and theologians I had encountered during my Nieman year at Harvard. I rushed back to my motel to compose an article that captured both the details and expansive ideas of a historic moment. Because the *New York Times Magazine* did not have a daily deadline, the editors were notorious for massaging our words for weeks before publication. I sent the article to the magazine editors on Thursday, and to my surprise they rushed the story into print on Sunday without any changes.

After King left St. Augustine, the protests reached a feverish pitch, and for the first time my southern accent did not allow me to blend in with the white crowds. Some suspected me to be an outsider with northern connections. One evening, a dozen of Manucy's men mistook me for an FBI agent and began harassing me. (Manucy's men did not always pick up on everything around them and didn't realize that some FBI agents were more likely to be their friends.) I was standing in a crowd of about five hundred whites in the former slave market when one of these men pointed me out and yelled, "That's one there." I sidled over to some state patrolmen sitting in their parked car, hoping that Manucy's mob might be deterred and leave me alone.

Two women approached me, both carrying Confederate flags and one wearing a low-cut blouse and shorts stretched like a drum over her ample midsection. I recognized them as part of the female cheering section for white gangs who beat demonstrators.

"Would you hold our flags while we get a Coca-Cola?" the one wearing shorts asked sweetly as she pushed her flag toward me. I tried to ignore her, but she persisted. Finally, in a momentary loss of discretion, I mumbled something about preferring the American flag. That set off a signal for some of her boyfriends to take over.

"What are you messin' with our women for?" one of them said. I inched closer to the state troopers as more gang members congregated and angrily accused me of offending southern womanhood. The troopers finally chased them off, but when I crossed the street, a mob of thirty or forty men followed me. Foolishly, I thought the troopers would again disperse the crowd. Instead, they put me in a patrol car and escorted me to the city limits. "Get out of town until they cool off," they ordered.

I walked back to get my car and hurriedly drove to a pay phone to call my editors in New York. "I'm in danger here," I told them. "The police told me to leave town. They won't protect me or let me stay any longer." My editors advised me to return to my office in Atlanta. They reminded me there were plenty of other protests throughout the South to cover. When I got back in the car, I heard the local radio announcer brag that the white crowds had succeeded in running off another "Yankee agitator" of the northern press. It was the only time I was forced to leave an assignment, and I was humiliated. The one salve to my injured pride was that the *Times* replaced me with Homer Bigart, a two-time Pulitzer Prize–winning war reporter who was one of the greatest journalists of the twentieth century.

As I drove from town, the last thing I saw under the dense vegetation of the park were the silhouettes of hundreds of black people headed to a beating by those who proclaimed to be the true stewards of the American revolution. That scene from the car window reminded me of when I was a small child watching rough-hewn black farmhands gather on the town square in front of my father's store to share stories. On this night more than a generation later, however, blacks were headed to the town square to try to claim their rights. I shuddered to think of their destiny. After that night, whenever whites— including my own extended family—spoke harshly about blacks, I recalled those people in St. Augustine marching into certain violence, determined to bring about the most far-reaching social change of the American twentieth century.

CHAPTER 21

A Hooded Society of Bigots

AS THE SCRATCHY LAST REFRAIN OF "THE OLD RUGGED CROSS" FADED out on a portable record player and a twenty-five-foot cross burned bright against a dark sky, a chubby man in a gray suit and bow tie stepped to the speaker's stand.

"People in other parts of the country like to think of niggers as human beings because they have hands and feet," the man said. "So do apes and gorillas have hands and feet. If a nigger has a soul I never read about it in the Bible. The only good nigger is a dead nigger."

He raised his arms, and about three hundred men and women—most of them garbed in white cotton robes, hoods, and masks—cheered in unison. Some in the audience murmured similar sentiments: "The nigger is a willing tool of the communist Jews and is being used to destroy America. They want to pump the blood of Africa into our white veins." The faces in the audience were hard and humorless, baked and lined by rough lives and too much exposure to the glaring sun. Children, some wearing hoods and sheets tailored to their diminutive sizes, played chase and brushed against their parents' robes, unaware of what was being said.

It was a typical Saturday night meeting of a fringe group of the KKK. The speaker was J. B. Stoner, an Atlanta attorney, and the gathering was held in a plowed field just north of the Jacksonville, Florida, municipal airport. Earlier in the day, the group had paraded through downtown Jacksonville to protest the Civil Rights Act. It was one of many Klan gatherings held from the North Carolina coastal plain to the pine barrens of Louisiana that I attended as a reporter in the 1960s.

The Klan was at that time more active, and possibly stronger in both numbers and influence, than at any time since its heyday in the 1920s. A resurgence began in the mid-1950s in reaction to school desegregation, reaching a new peak in the mid-1960s in response to growing black activism and the advancement of the Civil Rights Act. Of sixteen widely publicized racial murders in the South from September 1963 to April 1965, Klan members were implicated in eleven of them. None of those eleven cases, however, brought a felony conviction against a Klan member.

In the mid-1960s, the Anti-Defamation League estimated that since 1959, at least forty-three people involved with the civil rights movement in the South had been killed because of their activities; since 1955, about one thousand instances of racial violence, reprisals, and intimidation had been recorded; and since 1954, 227 bombings had been reported. If the Klan was not directly responsible for this proliferation in violence, it at least created a climate of hate in which others felt free to act.

Federal law enforcement officials said the Klan was a fragmented, poorly disciplined collection of angry human beings. Yet the Klan had become such a disruptive force on the national scene that President Johnson called for a congressional investigation and legislation to control Klan activity.

"My father fought them many long years ago in Texas, and I have fought them all my life because I believe them to threaten the peace of every community where they exist," President Johnson said in a nationally televised speech. "I shall continue to fight them because I know their loyalty is not to the United States of America but instead to a hooded society of bigots."

This strongly worded declaration came from a son of the Deep South who understood racism like President Kennedy never could. President Johnson also understood the complexities behind the Klan's evolution since its early inception as a purely social organization. Its genesis dated to just after the Civil War, when soldiers returning to Pulaski, Tennessee, found their town exceedingly dull. On Christmas Eve, 1865, six young Confederate veterans— including one coincidentally named John Kennedy—met in a law office and created a secret club purely for social diversion. Because secrecy requires disguise, the founders created a fictitious name based on their studies of the Greek language. The word *kuklos* means "circle" or "band," and because all the founders were of Scottish descent, they added the word "clan." For consistency and euphony, they settled on the name Ku Klux Klan.

To heighten the society's entertainment and mystery, they made disguises from the most readily available materials: sheets and pillowcases. Soon, the young Klansmen were riding through town in their bedsheet costumes. Superstitious blacks mistook the pranksters to be ghosts of the Confederate dead. Others joined the group, and it became sport to rouse a black person at night, demand a drink of water, and then appear to drink it without pausing (the water was funneled into a pouch hidden under the robe). "That's the first drink I've had since I was killed at Shiloh," the prankster would say.

Some figured out quickly that the disguise could intimidate freed blacks and carpetbaggers, and the Klan morphed into a vigilante group intent on opposing congressional Republicans who supported postwar Reconstruction. When simple intimidation failed, rougher members of the Klan resorted to violence. They invaded homes or entire towns and flogged, mutilated, and murdered blacks and carpetbaggers. When Klan leaders could no longer control the local klaverns, or chapters, the imperial wizard, Nathan Bedford Forrest, the former Confederate general, disbanded the KKK in the early 1870s.

Once the Klan was disbanded, white southerners remembered it not as a terrorist group but as a legitimate instrument of law and order to restore power to white Democrats. They considered the Klan to be knights of courage, righteousness, and chivalry. Surprisingly, the rest of the country came to accept this myth, and the Klan was twice revived—once in the 1920s and again after World War II.

In the 1920s, the Klan was glorified in D. W. Griffith's epic film *The Birth of a Nation*, which millions of people watched and President Woodrow Wilson showed at the White House. The movie and its popularity helped a backwater Protestant preacher named William J. Simmons organize a new KKK as the protector of traditional American values in a nation shaken by World War I and the influx of new Jewish and Catholic immigrants.

Millions of mostly Anglo-Saxon, Protestant Americans from Maine to California joined the hooded order. The Klan played a significant role at the 1924 Democratic National Convention when it opposed New York governor Al Smith because he was Catholic. The next year, an estimated forty thousand Klansmen dressed in sheets and caps paraded down Pennsylvania Avenue in Washington in a show of strength. By 1926, however, the Klan had fallen into rapid decline after newspapers across the country exposed its corrupt and exploitative leadership and its violence toward minorities. Membership dwindled to a few thousand, and by the start of the Depression in 1929, it was reduced to an ineffectual organization limited to the South.

The second resurgence occurred in response to the 1954 *Brown v. Board of Education* decision and subsequent efforts by the federal government to secure full rights and privileges for black citizens. The Klan view of the world was shaped by fundamentalist religion, a host of myths that blacks were innately inferior to whites, and a belief that "real Americans"—Protestants of British descent who came to North America by divine will—risked losing their superior position.

The Klan in the 1950s was a fringe element of society that most whites in the South disparaged because of its extremism. In fact, many southerners never took the Klan seriously because most members were from the lower rungs of society with no economic or social standing. The Klan members I saw at rallies were portraits of despair. Even some blacks laughed at their sheets and robes.

Despite its reputation, by the 1960s the Klan showed signs of new strength from Virginia to Texas. In 1964, federal and state authorities estimated there were about ten thousand Klan members, and the first public Klan wedding since 1926 was held at night in a cow pasture near Farmville, North Carolina, as five thousand people watched. The bride wore a lace gown; the groom wore a white satin robe and peaked hood.

There were four main Klan organizations and a scattering of smaller ones, including one klavern with a single member in Gulfport, Mississippi. But the number of members was not as significant as their influence of intimidation. "I can take five men in a city of twenty-five thousand and that is like having an army of men. That five can almost control the political atmosphere of that city," Calvin F. Craig, the Georgia grand dragon of the United Klans of America, told me.

When a handful of residents in Bogalusa, Louisiana, invited former US representative Brooks Hays of Arkansas, who had served as a mediator during the integration of Little Rock Central High School, to give a speech on racial peace, the KKK threatened to bomb the church where Hays was to speak, and his appearance was cancelled. The Klan also sent leaflets to homes near the church warning that Klan members were part of every business in town and would retaliate. "Those who do attend this meeting will be tagged as integrationists and dealt with accordingly by the Knights of the Ku Klux

Klan," the leaflet stated. Klan activity in Bogalusa dated to the Reconstruction era. In the 1960s, the Klan burned scores of crosses in Bogalusa, including three crosses on the front lawn of a young local newspaper publisher
who opposed them. The operator of the local radio station who supported
Hays's appearance told me that he had temporarily moved his wife and
child out of town because of Klan threats.

The Klan wielded even greater control when its members were law
enforcement officials or were friendly with city leaders. Sheriffs often did
nothing when black churches were burned by the Klan. The FBI estimated
that at least thirty sheriffs, policemen, and state highway patrolmen belonged to the White Knights of the KKK of Mississippi until some elected
officials fired them. Klansmen driving through some towns gave a Klan
salute to the sheriff. If the salute was reciprocated, the Klansman knew it
was friendly territory. The Bogalusa city council obtained a special ruling
from the state attorney general that a meeting of three hundred masked
Klansmen did not violate a state law prohibiting the wearing of masks in
public except for special occasions like Mardi Gras or religious celebrations.
When one Bogalusa citizen learned that a cross would be burned in front
of his house at a certain time, he called the city police to alert them. When
the time came, the cross was burned but the police were nowhere to be
seen.

I found the Klan leaders to be humorless young men in their thirties and
forties who extended their vitriol beyond hatred of Jews, Roman Catholics,
and blacks. Some worked closely with the John Birch Society with the
greater mission of fighting subversion by communists or the federal government. Acting as if the Civil War had ended just yesterday, these Klansmen
believed that a surrender to federal authority was a sign of weakness and
a ceding of their heritage. They maintained that because the Klan had
restored white rule after Reconstruction, why couldn't it do so now?

Mississippi was the home of the most violent, most secretive, and new-
est Klan organization in the nation: the White Knights. With two thousand members, it was the second-largest Klan organization in the country.
Meetings were guarded with secrecy and security; during one rally, two
Klan surveillance planes circled overhead and kept radio contact with their
guards on the ground. The only public information about the organization
came from informers who infiltrated its ranks or from the group's own
literature, which it distributed from airplanes and cars.

The White Knights' imperial wizard was a thirty-nine-year-old bachelor who operated a small business in Laurel, Mississippi, and publicly disclaimed any connection with the organization. The grand dragon, the number two man, was a former sheriff who lived near Crystal Springs, Mississippi, where my mother resided. During one of my visits to Crystal Springs, I took my daughters for a walk around town. When we passed the cotton mill and sheet factory, I jokingly told them we should pass quietly because that was where the KKK made their hooded uniforms. They clung to my legs as we slipped quietly by. I laughed to ease their fears—and my own—because my tall tale was likely true.

The Mississippi White Knights had been part of the Louisiana-based Original Knights of the KKK until February 1964, when civil rights workers arrived in Mississippi and the White Knights split off to form their own group. They expanded rapidly, charging a ten-dollar initiation fee called a "klectoken" and another ten dollars for a robe and hood. About sixty chapters of the White Knights were established. White Knights leaders formed a Klan Bureau of Investigation (KBI) and issued a list of punishments for violating Klan purposes: (1) a warning visit to the defector's home or workplace; (2) a burning cross; (3) bombing, burning, beating, or a volley of shots fired at night into a dwelling; and (4) extermination.

According to federal officials, the White Knights were responsible for at least five murders as well as scores of bombings, church burnings, and beatings. When federal officials put pressure on the organization, three hundred Klan leaders held a statewide "klonvocation" to invoke a ninety-day moratorium on violence. But that didn't stop the Klan from delivering its message. One edition of the *Klan Ledger*, a mimeographed newsletter distributed in several areas of Mississippi, printed an open letter to President Johnson. "The White Knights of the Ku Klux Klan is sovereign to Mississippi as regard to work and administration of the invisible empire," the paper said. It continued:

> We are spiritually connected with our Klan brethren in our sister state of Alabama through Christ, Our Lord and Savior. Possibly some of our brother Klansmen are impetuous and short-tempered. Some of them may occasionally engage in rash actions as a consequence of their being goaded by Communists who are protected by your unlawful decrees, but in spite of their shortcomings, we will still choose to stand by our Christian American patriots of the Klan—sinners

though they may be—rather than to leave them and join your secret society of sex perverts and atheistic murderers.

The largest and most geographically expansive Klan organization, with five thousand members, was the Tuscaloosa-based United Klans of America, Incorporated. Four of its members were responsible for the Birmingham church bombing. Unlike the White Knights, the United Klans were public relations minded. They posed for hours for photographers and allowed reporters to interview them, saying, "We're above board. We've got nothing to hide." They had elaborate plans to build private settlements with schools, churches, and stores where Klansmen and their families could live undisturbed by state or federal authorities.

The United Klans' imperial wizard was Robert M. Shelton Jr., a third-generation Klansman. He was a small, lean man with sunken cheeks and sagging eyebrows. His square jawbones flanked a deep chin cleft. He wore a shiny purple satin robe over his business suit and a matching open hood exposing his full face. Shelton was a high school–educated businessman who sold tires to Alabama state agencies, but he described his occupation as "Ku Kluxing." His professional approach gave the Klan some middle-class respectability. When hosting regional Klan meetings, he rented the ballroom of the upscale Dinkler-Tutwiler Hotel in Birmingham. The highest-ranking officers—"dragons," "cyclopes," "titans," "kligrapps," "klokards," and "kludds"—were accompanied to the ballroom by their wives, who wore evening gowns. The ladies had auxiliary klaverns, and children at the rallies wore multicolored silk robes and peaked caps.

Shelton agreed to meet me in Atlanta for an interview before he left for weekend rallies in the Carolinas. Because he was running behind schedule, one of his associates, Calvin Craig, invited me to tag along to a board meeting, where I could meet Shelton. Craig was a thirty-six-year-old crane operator and a Georgia grand dragon who had run as a Democrat for the state senate. He lost by only six hundred votes.

It was after midnight when I arrived at Craig's small home in an old section of Atlanta. It was the only house on the block with the lights on, and several cars with shortwave radio antennas, including Shelton's Cadillac, were parked in front. The modest living room was filled with stacks of Klan propaganda—copies of the *Fiery Cross*, the organization's newspaper, which claimed 250,000 readers, and leaflets that accused civil rights leaders and public officials of being communists. Shelton, dressed in a well-tailored dark suit, was seated on a sofa drinking coffee and eating cookies. He eased back into the cushions and talked at length about the democratic structure of the Klan, his plans to establish Klan insurance businesses, and the effectiveness of his KBI.

I was relieved when I finally left in the wee hours of the morning. The next night, I followed Craig and Shelton to a Hemingway, South Carolina, rally in a cornfield, where the mood was vastly less civil. I was met by a "security guard" resembling a paratrooper in a dark gray uniform who was glad to hear I was from Mississippi. He told me he admired the Klan leadership in Mississippi because they had a "coon license that lets you hunt coons year-round." Klan members exchanged introductory greetings. "Ayak," said one, meaning "Are you a Klansman?" Another answered, "Akia," meaning "I am." (My *Times* article describing the rally included a glossary sidebar with Klan terminology.) I met the United Klans' grand dragon, a thirty-six-year-old former sailor, bricklayer, and lightning rod salesman who had traveled from Salisbury, North Carolina. A thirty-foot, burlap-wrapped cross, soaked in fifteen gallons of kerosene and 120 pounds of motor oil, burned in the background. Shelton stood before the crowd and stirred them with warnings about the "beatniks, sex perverts, tennis-shoe-wearing white trash" invading the South.

I left the rally early and headed to Birmingham because I had an interview with Matt Murphy, the United Klans' imperial counsel. He was a tall, heavyset, rumpled man with gray hair and deep lines in his face. His moods alternated between amiable and brooding. Murphy was one of the few attorneys in the South who bragged about being a Klansman; he was the black sheep of an aristocratic southern family. His cousin, a banker in Greenville, Mississippi, was a voice of moderation on racial issues, and Murphy showed me a letter from another cousin pleading with him to abandon the Klan. But he did not heed his family's advice.

Whenever a Klansman got into trouble while on Klan business—which was happening with increasing frequency—Murphy showed up with the bail money and represented him in court. He was also one of the Klan's best publicists. "Doctors, lawyers, people of means—everybody is flocking to the Klan," he told me. Murphy said he believed the root of the country's problems was the Federal Reserve Act passed during President Woodrow Wilson's administration because it gave monetary control to a group of "international

Jew Zionists" who had financed the Russian Revolution and advanced communism in America. He handed me a worn book with a red cover entitled *The Negro a Beast*. Murphy explained that the book's message was that "the Bible and divine revelation, as well as reason, all teach that the Negro is not human." I flipped open the book to an illustration of a white woman being ravished by a black man.

"This is the only copy in existence," Murphy said, without explaining where he had obtained it. "It was written during the Reconstruction when it wasn't safe for the author to be known. I'm thinking of having it reprinted for distribution." I didn't know what to say so I just listened. I discovered later that the book had been written by Charles Carroll and published in 1900 by the American Book and Bible House in St. Louis.

Murphy said the Klan was even attracting upper-class followers and cited J. Emmett Thornhill, a self-made millionaire oil man who was a Klan leader in McComb, Mississippi. Thornhill lived in a $125,000 house, raised black angus cattle, and maintained a stable of Cadillacs. Although he had only a third-grade education, Thornhill was good with numbers and real estate purchases. He bought and leased scrub land in southeast Mississippi and developed holdings for forty oil wells.

When there was civil unrest in McComb, which was often, Thornhill was seen often on the town's streets alongside police. He recruited Klan members, hosted Shelton at his home during Klan rallies, and donated a K-9 dog to the McComb police force when civil rights activists arrived in town. Thornhill claimed that he was harassed by FBI agents, who hid in bushes on his farm and frightened his cattle. Murphy said Thornhill, who was born poor, was not going to have his comfortable life threatened by a change in the social order. Not since the Civil War had so many men like Thornhill fought so hard in a state as poor as Mississippi.

Another poor state—Louisiana—was home to the thousand-member Original Knights of the KKK, which recruited Roman Catholics to expand its membership. Its imperial wizard was Houston P. Morris, a thirty-year-old former mill superintendent who devoted all his time to the Klan. I met him at a Klan rally in Hamburg, Arkansas, just over the Louisiana line. "Our purpose is to preserve Christianity and keep the communists from taking over," he said.

The fourth major Klan organization in the South thrived in Jacksonville and St. Augustine, Florida. The Knights of the KKK of the North Florida Klan had about a thousand members and was one of the most militant groups in the country. At one rally in Jacksonville, I watched as Klansmen erected two wooden crosses with crude dummies. One was labeled LBJ for President Johnson, the other MLK for King. The crosses were set afire, and as the flames consumed them, a leader took out a pistol and fired bullets through the effigies.

The North Florida Klan's chief leader was Don Cothern, a tall, moustached automobile mechanic from Jacksonville. He and other Klansmen were in St. Augustine in the summer of 1964 during the civil rights demonstrations. Cothern's organization worked mostly under the command of "Hoss" Manucy, who denied being a Klan member. "Whoever heard of a Catholic in the Klan?" Manucy said. But a federal judge deemed that Manucy's gun club was a KKK front. The Florida state attorney told me he had escaped an attack by the North Florida Klan in St. Augustine. "I was amazed and astounded at the intensity of the feeling on the part of the segregationists," he said. "It overwhelmed anything I had ever encountered before, and it reminded me of movies I have seen from the 1930s when Hitler was rising to power."

CHAPTER 22

Paradox in the South

THE NONVIOLENT STRUGGLE HAD PRODUCED RETRIBUTION BUT ALSO rewards. The Civil Rights Act outlawed segregation and discrimination in America based on race, color, religion, gender, or national origin. Not since President Lincoln signed the Emancipation Proclamation had blacks been offered such hope. To gain its passage, however, Congress watered down a section that addressed voting biases, and President Johnson promised King that he would introduce a separate voting rights bill the next year to address the problems.

I was surprised to see how quickly some major southern cities complied with the Civil Rights Act even when met with pronounced resistance elsewhere in the region. I tried to explain the idiosyncratic and multifaceted reaction to the new law in an article beginning, "Many Southerners do not know quite how to feel about the South these days. It has long been a land of paradox and contradiction—a mosaic of many shades and differences. But the contrasts that have emerged this summer have been more pronounced than usual."

I explained how something historic was happening: many southern communities were taking great strides to settle their race problems, knowing they would eventually face federal mandates if they did otherwise. The act required that racial discrimination be eliminated in public schools and gave the US attorney general authority to file lawsuits to enforce that provision. The Southern Education Reporting Service found that even though most southern school districts were still segregated in 1964, as much progress to integrate was made in that year alone as in all the previous nine years combined since *Brown v. Board of Education.* Unexpected advances in school integration occurred in Louisiana, Tennessee, and Virginia.

All southern states—even Mississippi—had some form of school integration, and some citizens realized that it was not as terrifying as they had anticipated. Three public school districts in Mississippi were desegregated without incident, and two more black students enrolled at the University of Mississippi without federal intervention. Although it took a federal court order to desegregate Alabama schools, those in the cities of Montgomery and Gadsden were integrated peacefully. The Gadsden school superintendent told me, "People are taking it soberly; they want to abide by the law." Three black students were enrolled at Bullock County High School in the small town of Union Springs, Alabama, without any significant loss of white student enrollment. All told, twenty-four formerly all-white elementary and secondary public schools in Alabama accepted black students. The University of Alabama and Auburn University had several black students. This was a significant step compared to the year before, when Governor Wallace had used state troopers to prevent integration in schools in Alabama.

With exceptions, compliance with the accommodations section of the act was more far reaching than some black leaders had anticipated. In St. Augustine, the owner of Monson's Motor Lodge followed the law and served blacks patrons even as he was ridiculed by white segregationists. St. Augustine city officials and demonstrators called a truce, the Florida governor appointed a biracial committee, and businesses announced they would comply with the new law even in the midst of continued KKK opposition. "Whether or not we agree with the civil rights bill or not, and I do not, it is time to draw back from this problem and take a look down the long road at the end of which somehow we must find harmony," the governor declared. "Upon one thing we can all agree, we cannot solve this problem through violence. Violence is anarchy and anarchy is the enemy of freedom." That is not to say that the changes were always decisive or lasting. The biracial committee never met because too few whites agreed to serve, communication between white and black leaders failed, dentist and activist Robert Hayling was eventually forced to leave town, and the city did not integrate its schools until they were ordered by the federal courts in 1970.

Yet, even in Mississippi, private businesses were complying with the new law in small ways. Two days after the law was enacted, a dozen blacks including a Los Angeles banker and a Boston engineer checked in for the first time

PARADOX IN THE SOUTH

at three whites-only hotels in Jackson, where, in an about face, the mayor (who had called the law "repugnant") and Chamber of Commerce urged compliance with the act. The hoteliers said they would abide by the law and instructed the white bellhops to carry the black guests' luggage to their rooms. Some newspapers that circulated in Mississippi urged compliance as well. The New Orleans *Times-Picayune*, which had previously opposed the act, and the *Memphis Commercial Appeal* now acknowledged it was the "law of the land." The Jackson papers made no comment, although they didn't condemn the law either. Jackson's decision not to test the law in the courts, contrary to the governor's wishes, was such a dramatic turn that my article about it landed on the front page of the *New York Times*. The softening of resistance in Jackson came as business leaders worried about attracting industry and tourism, because national attention was focused on the Summer Project and the three missing workers.

King acknowledged to me that some formerly segregated places were now "almost open cities." When coastal communities suffered cutbacks in the tourist trade, their leaders finally pressured legislatures to ignore the orthodoxy of segregationists. The influence of the White Citizens' Council was waning. Even in cities like Montgomery and Birmingham, white businesses were finally making changes. Because of this, King planned to shift the focus of his campaign to the smaller, recalcitrant communities like Selma and Tuscaloosa. King predicted that the testing period of the new law would last five years. Over a longer period, he envisioned a national revolution in the structural institutions of education, government, finance, and politics.

While the new law spawned advances, it also unleashed a backlash. The body counts and incidences of terror were staggering. This was particularly true in Mississippi. In the two months after the act's passage, ten black churches in the state were burned, and the KKK attempted to set fire to the home of a black contractor in Natchez. Fifty miles from there, several white men were arrested for bombing black homes, and the authorities confiscated four high-powered rifles, several carbines and pistols, fifteen dynamite bombs, a five-gallon can of explosive powder, several thousand rounds of ammunition, and a stock of hand grenades, clubs, and blackjacks. In Moss Point, Mississippi, a nineteen-year-old black woman standing at a voter registration site was wounded by gunfire from a passing car.

The bodies of a black sawmill worker and a black college student who had participated in campus demonstrations were discovered in the Mississippi

River. Both bodies were bound in rope and wire, and one was decapitated. I interviewed the mother of the college student as she sat on the unpainted porch of her house on a sixty-acre farm near Meadville, Mississippi, where she had lived all her life. She was soft spoken and said she did not understand why anyone would kill her quiet, well-behaved son. "He didn't have any kind of enemy, white or colored," she said. The crime went unsolved until 2007, when the FBI learned that several Klansmen had picked up the sawmill worker and student hitchhiking and beat them with bean poles. One Klansman stuffed them in his trunk, drove to Louisiana, chained them to an engine block and train rails, and threw them alive into the river. A Klansman and a former police officer were arrested and convicted for the murders.

Violent reactions to the new law were so prevalent that I could barely keep up reporting about them. One night I attended a civil rights rally near Indianola, Mississippi, where 250 blacks gathered in a concrete block building. Suddenly we heard a low-flying airplane overhead. "It must be the KAF [Klan Air Force]," said one man, who ran outside. The plane dropped a flare and released a small explosive, which went off near the building without doing damage. Then the plane roared off into the darkness, leaving the meeting participants in a state of fear and confusion.

The backlash forced some blacks to retaliate. Gangs of black youths roamed the streets of Memphis, damaging property and hurling bricks and bottles at police cars. Some younger civil rights leaders were advocating for a more militant approach, and we all watched and waited to see what would happen next.

King arrived in Mississippi in late July 1964 with a set of far-reaching goals. He sought money and support for the newly formed Mississippi Freedom Democratic Party. King planned to attend the Democratic National Convention in Atlantic City, New Jersey, later that summer to ask national leaders to recognize the Mississippi Freedom Democratic Party in exchange for its pledge to endorse President Johnson's programs. Their support was important to the national party, which recognized the future potential value of black voters at a time when conservative southern Democrats were shifting loyalties to the Republican presidential candidate, Barry Goldwater, a US senator from Arizona who had defeated George Wallace in the primary election. Goldwater opposed the Civil Rights Act and wanted state control over segregation.

King knew that gaining legitimacy for the Mississippi Freedom Democratic Party would pressure President Johnson to fulfill his pledge to introduce a voting rights law. "The regular Democratic Party of Mississippi does not represent the people, particularly the Negro people," King told reporters in a press conference. "The church burnings, harassment, and murders in this state are a direct result of the fact that Negro citizens cannot vote and participate in electing responsible public officials who will protect the rights of all the people." King knew that the next phase of the movement was to harness the power of politics by enfranchising blacks. "In 1963, only 1,636 Negro persons were registered in the entire state," he said. "Some method must be devised to enable the 400,000 unregistered Negroes to vote." He asked President Johnson to appoint "voting rights marshals" to accompany blacks when registering, and he wanted federal election monitoring included in the national party's civil rights platform.

I traveled with King to Greenwood, Mississippi, where he poked his head into the Red Rooster night spot and beckoned the patrons to follow him outside. He invited others from shanties along the street, and then he climbed onto a crude wooden bench in front of the Savoy Café to speak. "You must not allow anybody to make you feel you are not significant," he declared from his makeshift podium. "Every Negro has worth and dignity. Mississippi has treated the Negro as if he is a thing instead of a person. Above all things, they have denied us the right to vote. We have got to show the world we are determined to be free." Although the small crowd was excited to see him, they were quiet and fearful. Some in the audience told me they never expected to hear talk like this in Greenwood. Most were astonished that King so blatantly and publicly stood up to the white establishment.

Later that night, as King spoke at a rally of one thousand people at the Elks Lodge, a small airplane without lights flew overhead and dropped leaflets signed by the White Knights of Mississippi. One man in the audience ran outside to retrieve one of the leaflets and read it to the audience. The leaflets called King "the Right Rev. Riot Inciter" and stated, "If the agitators should overrun the law, and a violent disorder erupts, it will then be the right, the duty, and the moral obligation of the white man in Leflore County to restore law and order and replace it into the hands of the duly elected and appointed officials."

This whipped up the audience into chanting "Freedom, Freedom." King seized the moment to stress a broader theme. He drew a thunderous ovation when he attacked Goldwater, who, King said, "articulates a philosophy that gives aid and comfort to the segregationists." Other speakers urged the crowd to support President Johnson in the fall election, and the crowd broke into a swelled rendition of "We Shall Overcome." The speeches resonated more deeply than King and other leaders had anticipated. The audience spilled into the street and began marching furiously toward the downtown. They advanced several blocks before the rally leaders persuaded them to disperse. It was one of many times I saw King and other leaders struggle to reach a delicate balance of inciting action without violence.

King stayed in Mississippi for five days to boost morale, visiting a different town each day, including Philadelphia, where the three civil rights workers had gone missing one month earlier. He went to the town's black community center, which sat atop a red gravel hill across the street from a hotel owned by Charles Evers. A gaggle of boys scrambled to the center's front door and stared in amazement when King arrived in his black Oldsmobile followed by fourteen cars carrying his entourage, which included SNCC leader John Lewis, FBI agents, and news reporters. We stirred up a cloud of orange dust upon our arrival.

Dark clouds loomed overhead as King emerged from his car, bounded up the stairs, and challenged a teenager to a game of pool while his staff rounded up an audience. After losing a game of eight ball, he climbed atop a bench and told sixty curious listeners that he was there in the interest of the three missing civil rights workers. "Three young men came here to help set you free," King said. "They probably lost their lives. I know what you have suffered in this state, the lynchings and the murders." One old woman approached him as if he were the Messiah and said, "I just want to touch you."

As we left the community center, there was a clap of thunder, the skies opened, and fat drops of rain splattered on the crusty gravel road. Little boys in ragged clothes watched in astonishment and confusion as we all piled into the caravan of cars and rolled away. From the car window, I saw groups of whites and Choctaw Native Americans standing on the sidewalks, staring and pointing at us. They looked very much like the people I knew from the small towns where I'd lived as a boy, watching the world change before their eyes.

CHAPTER 23

"I've Got Bitterness in My Heart"

DAVID NEVIN, A REPORTER FOR *LIFE* MAGAZINE, DESCRIBED PHILADELPHIA as a "strange, tight little town" where fears of outside influences were "nearly pathological." Most of the 5,600 residents had never seen so many outsiders converge on their town and believed that civil rights workers, black leaders, federal agents, and reporters would take over their lives. Some cars bore bumper stickers pronouncing, "You Are in Occupied Mississippi—Proceed with Caution." Their fear, which overshadowed reason, was fed by the Klan and the overt brutality of the Neshoba County sheriff, Lawrence Rainey.

Rainey, a large man with a balding head and an eighth-grade education, had avoided prosecution for fatally shooting a black motorist and beating black suspects in his custody. Rainey's deputy, Cecil Price, a hefty man with a penchant for brandishing his guns, was the last person known to have seen the three Congress of Racial Equality workers who were stationed in Mississippi that summer with the Summer Project and who had gone missing. Price had arrested and jailed Michael Schwerner, twenty-four, of Brooklyn; James E. Chaney, twenty-one, of Meridian, Mississippi; and Andrew Goodman, twenty-one, of New York City for speeding in their blue Ford station wagon. Most white people in the county said that word of their disappearance was a prank or that they had fled to Cuba. One rumor was that they were in Chicago, laughing it up and drinking beer in a bar.

While King was in Philadelphia, he and his entourage drove twelve miles east to the charred remains of Mount Zion Methodist Church, which was destroyed by arson after Schwerner and Chaney had made speeches there urging blacks to register. The Summer Project planned to use the church sanctuary as a school to help blacks pass the registration tests. The church had seen trouble before when several elders had been beaten and left injured on a roadside by a gang of twenty-five whites, some wearing law enforcement uniforms.

When we arrived at the church, King emerged from his big black car, stepped through the ruins, and climbed onto a blackened brick foundation, which he used as a metaphor for his belief that good rises from the ashes of destruction. "As I stand here on the site of this church, I have mixed emotions," he said. "I feel sorry for those who were hurt by this. On the other hand, I rejoice that there are churches relevant enough that people of ill-will will be willing to burn them. I think this church was burned because it took a stand."

The black congregants, Goodman, Schwerner, and Chaney were an unlikely mix working toward the same goal. Schwerner, known as "Mickey," was Jewish and dark haired and sported a beard. He and his wife had moved to Mississippi and opened a community center for blacks, and he was hated by the Klan, who vowed to "exterminate" him. Goodman, also Jewish, was a white college student from an intellectual and socially progressive family in Manhattan who had arrived to work with Schwerner less than twenty-four hours before he went missing. Chaney was a local black man from Meridian who had become interested in civil rights and the NAACP when he was fifteen years old. He had participated in two Freedom Rides in Tennessee and Mississippi to integrate interstate buses and was an emissary between Summer Project workers and church leaders.

The disappearance of the three men attracted an unusually large amount of attention. Some observers said this was because two of the victims were white. That was partly true, but other reasons were that the nation's eyes were now focused on the South's civil rights abuses and that the local authorities were so lax in their efforts to find the men. The FBI, at the bequest of President Johnson and the Justice Department, stepped in to investigate, and J. Edgar Hoover himself visited the state to announce the opening of a Mississippi FBI bureau in Jackson with 150 new agents.

Even after the FBI arrived, the investigation was painstakingly slow because many residents were intimidated and tight lipped. Weeks of searching turned up nothing. Crystal Springs was one hundred miles from Philadelphia, and I traveled there on a hot dusty August afternoon to meet Betty, who was visiting my mother with our four daughters. As soon as Betty and I sat down to lunch in a local diner, a young boy ran in from the street and cried, "They found them. They found the three people in Philadelphia." They had been missing for forty-four days.

I grabbed Betty, kissed her, and left my half-eaten BLT and vanilla milk-shake at the lunchroom counter. I bolted to Philadelphia, trying hard not to speed because getting pulled over by a Mississippi cop who didn't like reporters could delay me by hours.

The FBI broke the case by paying $30,000 to an unnamed informant. I followed the FBI agents as they drove to Old Jolly Farm, a 250-acre hard-scrabble corn and cattle farm in the red-clay hills five miles southwest of Philadelphia. The farm was owned by Olen Burrage, a KKK member who also owned a prosperous trucking company that hauled timber and corn. The FBI presented Burrage with a search warrant to dig up a dam that he had recently built to form a pond for watering livestock and fishing. The agents told Burrage they would pay him for any damage to the dam, and he complied with the warrant.

Cars packed with perspiring FBI agents, wearing open-necked shirts, bumped down the gravel road toward the pond, passing the home of a care-taker, his wife, and their seven children. The scrub pines and bitter weed wilted in the hundred-degree heat. Once we arrived, the agents walked di-rectly to the barren dam, which was 250 feet long and 25 feet high. With a dragline, they dug down 20 feet in one spot and immediately found three mangled bodies, draped over each other in a heap. It was a grisly scene that I regretted witnessing. One body had outstretched arms reaching over his head; another wore white socks and loafers. All had been shot, and Chaney had been severely beaten.

Accompanying the agents was Deputy Price, whom FBI agents asked to help remove the bodies. The chief FBI investigator was interested in seeing Price's reaction to the discovery, because Price was a suspect in the murders. The agents wrote in their reports that "Price picked up a shovel and dug right in, and gave no indication whatsoever that any of it bothered him." Price also helped the FBI agents unload the bodies from the back of their station wagon for an autopsy in Jackson.

The next day, I drove behind two carloads of men returning to the dam. They were six members of a coroner's jury that included Rainey, Price, and the coroner, Fulton Jackson, a stringy-looking funeral home employee with sad, bloodshot eyes. Their mission was to survey the scene and conclude the cause of death. It was downright bizarre to watch Price and Rainey—who were believed to have some role in this heinous crime—participate in the inquest. At the other end of the farm, Burrage was busy answering questions from reporters and friends who had gathered at his home. "I told them [the FBI] to look all they wanted," said Burrage, a brawny forty-two-year-old man with a straw cap pushed back from his black hair. He had a friendly and helpful approach. "I went down there late yesterday to check on my cows, and all I could see was a swarm of people and a dragline on top of the dam. I tell you, I don't know anybody that would kill them and put them on my property. All night I wracked my brain trying to think of something that would help in the investigation."

I also interviewed the farm's caretaker, who told me that he had seen nothing unusual at the dam before the FBI arrived. "There's very little traffic on that road," he said. "I don't believe anybody could come up, particularly a stranger, if I didn't know about it." I found the contractor who had been hired to build the dam. "I don't know anything about it," he said, and returned to his work building another dam nearby.

Everyone in Philadelphia was in a mood of fearful expectation, trying to avoid any association with the crime. Small groups of men stood around the town square and in the courthouse talking about what was likely to happen next. They speculated about the identity of the informer and criticized the FBI. "I think most people here were shocked that the FBI would pay informants large sums of money," a businessman told me. "I, for one, did not know the FBI operated that way." A man who was rumored to be the informant, and who supposedly witnessed the burials, lived three miles from the dam, so I traveled to his small house but found no one there. A neighbor would only tell me that he was in Jackson.

The mayor said that some people praised the FBI's work and welcomed its massive investigation. But most townspeople were in denial, he said. "Maybe it was wishful thinking, but most people here believed that it was a hoax," the mayor told me. "Most people were shocked to find that it did happen." It was just like Mississippi to be fighting to the bitter end. White folks in Philadelphia went about their business as usual, but there were rumors that at least six townspeople would soon be arrested, some of them prominent members of the community and even law enforcement officials.

The discovery of the bodies, however, did not interfere with the opening of the annual week-long Neshoba County Fair, started in 1898 and held just three miles south of Burrage's farm. Nestled in a grove of ancient oaks, the fair was originally conceived as an annual picnic for Confederate Civil War veterans. When the fair expanded to include the civilian community, cars and truckloads of children, relatives, and servants arrived to set up residence in more than two hundred unpainted shacks and narrow, two-story cabins built around the speaker's square. The upper stories slept up to fifteen people, and the first floors were for cooking and eating. The front porches, decked with rocking chairs, were reserved for storytelling and listening to gospel music.

A visitor, if of the right color and demeanor, could walk into any shack at high noon and be offered a plate of fried chicken, cornbread, and vegetables from gardens back home. After lunch, crowds gathered for speeches, harness races, livestock shows, and music. Although Neshoba County banned alcohol, 115-proof moonshine liquor was consumed in copious quantities. The fair had all the flare of the wild frontier. "Our biggest problem here is keeping it sloppy and old," Willard Hays, the fair secretary, told me when I visited. "We have to fight hard to keep the people from streamlining it. Children roam at will and nobody worries about them. We hire guards to see that nothing happens to them. If one gets too close to the rides, one of the carnies catches him by the diapers and pulls him back."

J. B. Hillman, the eighty-six-year-old fair chairman and a retired lawyer who was as much an institution as the fair itself, told me that people were determined not to let the murders dampen the festivities. "We were all surprised when the bodies were found out by the fairgrounds," Hillman said. "But we are not going to let it interfere with the fair." What Hillman didn't acknowledge was that racial discord was always present because politicians could be born or broken over the issue. One who succeeded was James K. Vardaman, who had stormed the fair pavilion at the turn of the twentieth century with racist rhetoric, comparing blacks to "hogs," saying that lynchings were necessary to retain white supremacy, and calling for a complete ban on black suffrage. His followers were called "rednecks" because they sported red kerchiefs at political rallies. Vardaman served as both state governor and US senator.

When I attended the fair, the speakers included Republican candidates who just a decade earlier would not have been welcomed in a solidly

Democratic and populist state. But President Johnson's advocacy of civil rights had positioned Goldwater as the new favorite candidate at the fair. This was the first time since the Civil War that Democrats in Mississippi and the South were defecting from their party and embracing a Republican candidate. I wrote an article with the headline, "Mississippi Fair Likes Goldwater—Pennants Indicate Ardor of Whites for Arizonian," and I described how automobiles, trucks, and cabins at the event were emblazoned with Goldwater bumper stickers and banners. "You can tell just from talking to people here that Goldwater will take at least 60 percent of the vote in Mississippi," one businessman told me. "Our only problem is whether to support him on a Republican or a Democratic ticket."

About six hundred fair attendees, including farmers in denim overalls and FBI agents in button-down suits, gathered to hear political speeches. A Jackson physician and Goldwater supporter summarized to me his list of expectations: He wanted communists ejected from government, the impeachment of US Supreme Court Chief Justice Earl Warren, the elimination of foreign aid, the removal of the United States from the United Nations, and an FBI hunt for communists rather than civil rights violators. "The close personal friends of President Johnson must be smoked out," he said. "They can show us their true mettle by being for Goldwater in the next election."

I left the county fair to attend Chaney's funeral and burial on a sandy hill three miles south of his Meridian home. The contrast to the fair was striking. Five hundred people, mostly black, filled every pew in the stifling, hot church and crowded into doorways to see the memorial service. They poured out their bitterness through songs and tears, and pointed fingers of blame. "I believe the people in Washington and Jackson are just as much to blame for this death as the people who pulled the trigger," David Dennis, an assistant program director for the Mississippi Summer Project, said in his eulogy. "I've got bitterness in my heart, and I'm not going to ask you not to be bitter either tonight." Shaking the pulpit in anger, Dennis continued, "I know what is going to happen when they find those men. A jury will come in and say, 'not guilty.'"

Another speaker, a chaplain at Tougaloo College in Jackson and a leader in the Summer Project, said, "I'm glad Dennis got angry tonight." But then he tempered his message and warned: "Our hatred should be aimed at destroying the system, not the individuals." It was a heart-wrenching scene, especially compared to the frivolities of the county fair. Chaney's mother and other relatives, sitting in the front pew, sobbed and moaned as Chaney's twelve-year-old brother cried out: "I want my brother! I want my brother!"

The landscape of my childhood was a bloody battlefield, and in my mind, Mississippi was the meanest, most backward place in the nation. The region I called home was a national symbol of intolerance and irrational hate, and I found it difficult to believe that anyone with a clear conscience would not be changed by what the nation was witnessing.

CHAPTER 24

"I'm Innocent"

TWO MONTHS AFTER THE PHILADELPHIA MURDERS, NO ARRESTS HAD been made. Instead, mass confusion and duplicative efforts roiled federal and local officials as they waged a turf war over legal jurisdictions. Outdated Mississippi laws governing prosecutorial rights and grand jury proceedings kept federal officials in limbo. This put President Johnson in an awkward position, because four days after the bodies were found he had stated that the nation could expect "substantive results" from a federal investigation in a "very short time."

In addition, layers of mismanagement and obstruction caused more delays. Mississippi officials held autopsy reports in secret and gave no explanation why to the news media or federal authorities. Three juries convened—coroner, county, and federal—each working in apparent isolation. Except for Price, who witnessed the exhumation, other members of the coroner's jury never saw the dead bodies and claimed it could not reach a cause of death without the autopsies.

The county grand jury, consisting of eighteen white men, investigated the abduction and murders. But its proceedings were secret and would not be made public for six months. This grand jury also had not seen the autopsy report. Circuit Judge O. H. Barnett, an outspoken segregationist and first cousin of former governor Ross Barnett, ordered the county grand jury to investigate the murders because Neshoba County had been "indicted and tried before the whole world" by "socialistic-minded liberals." He assured jurors they would be fully supported by the "most courageous sheriff in all America: Lawrence Rainey." The jury subpoenaed thirty witnesses, including federal agents, who refused to appear.

Meanwhile, a twenty-three-member federal grand jury was impaneled in Biloxi. The jurors were all white men except for two women, one who was white and the other a black cook in a restaurant. The federal grand jury had limited power because Mississippi law allowed only the county grand jury to return indictments for murder or kidnapping. Therefore, it was obvious the federal grand jury would issue no murder indictments even though the FBI said it had enough evidence. US attorneys were working to turn up new leads that might force the state courts to consider murder charges, but they were proceeding with care to build an airtight case knowing the state's dismal history in getting convictions in these types of cases.

In the meantime, the federal grand jury was considering the possibility of issuing indictments on the lesser charge that the victims' civil rights had been violated. Federal authorities also reasoned that if they could not seek murder indictments, then perhaps they could bring charges against perpetrators for other crimes that intimidated blacks in Philadelphia. In one instance, whites clubbed a young black man after the murders of the three workers. Another instance involved Wilbur Jones, a young black member of the armed forces visiting his mother, who was abducted by police because they said his goatee made him look suspicious. The police turned him over to a gang of whites, who threatened him and ran him out of town. Jones testified before the federal grand jury; the FBI concealed his identity with a cardboard box over his head, with slits cut for peepholes, and drove him around town hoping he could identify the perpetrators.

In September, Price was subpoenaed to appear before the federal grand jury. I watched the pudgy, dark-haired, twenty-six-year-old deputy arrive at the Federal Building wearing a gray business suit with a silk handkerchief in his pocket. This getup was accessorized with a felt fedora with a crisply shaped gutter dent and a front brim snapped down above his large, thick-framed sunglasses. He clenched a cigar in his teeth. As he approached our gaggle of reporters, he smiled broadly and handed us a printed card that read, "Regardless of what you have heard or seen about me, I'm innocent." With nothing further to say, he then placed the card so it could be read from his breast coat pocket. The grand jury also subpoenaed a missionary Baptist minister, a bootlegger, a barber, a county jailer, a policeman, a used car dealer, and an electronic equipment dealer (the latter two who served on the governor's staff). All of them were suspects in either the murders or other racial violence.

During the county grand jury proceedings, I noticed a handbill posted on the courthouse bulletin board next to official notices of public business. The handbill was published by the National States' Rights Party and stated, "Jew-Communists Behind Race Mixing." Below the words were pictures of Karl Marx and Nicholas Katzenbach, the US deputy attorney general responsible for escorting black students at the Universities of Alabama and Mississippi. This propaganda was given official sanction on a government bulletin board where jury members saw it each day as they filed into the courtroom. This not-so-subtle form of intimidation epitomized how local authorities and the legal establishment condoned and perpetuated racism. It also underscored the obstacles federal officials faced in bringing justice. In the eyes of most white residents in Philadelphia, the true crime was not that three young men had been murdered or that local law enforcement officers were in league with a lynch mob, but that there had been "federal encroachment" into local affairs with the intent to reelect President Johnson.

The county and federal grand juries met simultaneously but worked at cross-purposes. Neither side trusted the other. The Justice Department ordered federal agents to ignore subpoenas from the county grand jury and to pass on findings only to the federal grand jury. Judge Barnett warned federal officials that it was time to "put up or shut up" and cooperate with the county grand jury, but they ignored his warning. By late September, the county grand jury adjourned without issuing murder indictments for the triple slaying because it said federal officials refused to cooperate with their investigation. Upon adjourning, the county grand jury concluded that local law enforcement had done a respectable job maintaining order "in the face of drastic provocations by outside agitators."

Finally, in October there was some slight movement. The federal grand jury arrested five Neshoba County law enforcement officers, including Price and Rainey, for an incident that had occurred two years before the arrival of Schwerner, Chaney, and Goodman. According to the indictments, Rainey arrested five black men for stealing cows and, with the four other defendants, stripped the men to their waists and beat them with leather straps. The officers were charged under an 1870 statute that made it a federal crime for law enforcement to deny a person's rights under the Constitution. These arrests were far short of the murder charges US attorneys wanted, but they felt it might eventually open the way for future indictments.

The immediate reaction from the local residents was outrage. I watched as FBI agents arrived at the Federal Building in downtown Meridian, forty miles from Philadelphia, with Rainey and Price in custody. A rowdy crowd of two hundred white people cheered for the defendants as they emerged from two FBI cars. The crowd jeered at us and shoved the photographers as a giant Confederate flag waved above our heads. Rainey and Price, both wearing police uniforms but without their guns, smiled broadly as they walked into the building. Rainey had his omnipresent Red Man chewing tobacco pouch bulging from his front breast pocket. A delegation of about forty whites accompanied the other defendants in separate cars. Rainey and Price laughed and talked in the building corridors while waiting for their bonds. Both men appeared invincible. They had seen this routine played out before with no consequences, and they appeared unfazed by the presence of federal authorities. All the defendants were released after posting bonds—$2,000 each for Price and Rainey, and $1,000 each for the others.

In late November, the FBI finally announced that it knew who murdered the three civil rights workers, but, without an autopsy, it lacked the evidence needed to obtain a conviction or to publicly name the men. Rainey mocked the agency, crowing that if the FBI knew the murderers' identities, why didn't it do something? The FBI had tried unsuccessfully to convince the Mississippi governor and attorney general to indict the men for murder, but they both wanted the FBI to act first. It was early December, more than five months after the murders, when the FBI finally decided not to wait any longer for murder indictments. They arrested Rainey, Price, and nineteen other men on conspiracy charges in connection with a KKK plot to murder Schwerner, Chaney, and Goodman.

During the early morning hours, four FBI agents wearing trench coats apprehended Rainey and Price at the Neshoba County courthouse as the two men returned from a "whiskey raid" on moonshine stills. When they told Rainey he was under arrest, he removed his badge and revolver and handed his office keys to his secretary. As he walked out the front door, a group of white men cursed at the FBI agents. The crowd chased away a CBS cameraman and threatened an Associated Press cameraman with a knife. Price, still wearing his badge, was escorted out a side door of the courthouse. By this time, some townspeople who were tired of the case and its toll on the community, including moderate leaders and members of the clergy, said they were relieved to see justice prevail to end "this damaging and deteriorating experience of the past five months."

The FBI said Rainey conspired to murder the civil rights workers but had not participated in the actual slaying. Price, however, was more directly involved. The FBI said he unlawfully arrested the victims and then turned them over to a lynch mob that he himself joined; ten other defendants took part in the murders. Some of the accused, including a Baptist fundamentalist minister named Edgar Ray Killen, were free on bail after having been charged two months earlier for beating blacks in a separate incident. Others arrested included a tavern bouncer, a Philadelphia policeman, and several leaders of the KKK White Knights including the grand cyclops of a chapter in Meridian. Most of the twenty-one men arrested were KKK members.

I attended the men's arraignment hearing at the Federal Building in Meridian. They stood silently before US commissioner Esther Carter, an administrative figurehead appointed by a federal judge from southern Mississippi. US commissioners, first empowered by Congress in 1793 when there was a shortage of lawyers in the American frontier, were still used in rural areas of the South to accept bail and inform defendants of their legal rights. Carter, a county deputy court clerk, was called to serve as commissioner in this case. A Mississippi native, she was a delicate, middle-aged woman with gray curls who appeared in court wearing a beige dress, four strings of pearls, and bright earrings. Some defendants bowed their heads as if contrite; others stared defiantly at Carter across a long wooden table. Rainey, leaning back in an armchair, kicked one leg over his knee and stuffed chewing tobacco in his right jowl.

For the first time, the FBI publicly described in lurid detail how the three young men met their deaths on a dirt road a few miles outside Philadelphia. After Price arrested Schwerner, Chaney, and Goodman for speeding, he called Killen and told him he was holding them at the jail. Killen organized a group of Klansmen at a Meridian drive-in to plan what they called a "butt ripping." Five hours later, Price released the three workers from jail and coordinated with Killen to ambush them. As the young men drove away from Philadelphia on a deserted highway, Price and ten other armed men followed and pulled them over. They forced the civil rights workers into their cars and drove on a dirt road to join other Klansmen. There they shot Schwerner, then Goodman, and beat and shot Chaney. Rainey was visiting his wife in the hospital at the time, so he was charged with conspiring to cover up the murders. Burrage had agreed to let the Klansmen bury the bodies at his farm. Burrage was among those charged with conspiracy. Price was not there when the bodies were dumped, but shortly after midnight, he and Rainey met for an update.

All the men were released when they posted bonds totaling more than $100,000, and Rainey and Price returned the same day to their law enforcement jobs. They were greeted at their courthouse office by supporters with smiles and handshakes. A defense attorney told me that a fund, like the one for Byron De La Beckwith's defense, was being formed to help pay the men's legal costs.

I described the disparate reactions of the townspeople. One white minister who had moved to Philadelphia just a year before the murders occurred preached about the community's debt to justice. "I am quite sure than some of you would prefer it if I didn't make reference to past events of our community," he said from the pulpit. "However, I feel I would be derelict in my calling as a minister of the Gospel if I did not lift up our responsibility. We must at all costs hold high the ideals of truth and love and justice, giving them our highest allegiance and deepest loyalty."

That same minister challenged town leaders at the weekly Rotary Club luncheon. After scarfing down ham and potato salad, he rose from the table and told his audience that they faced a biblical dilemma like that of Sodom, where the Lord sought ten good men to forestall the city's destruction. "It has been the method and purpose of God to sustain his people when he found just ten good men," the pastor said. "It is up to you to see how many good men he finds here." He received a polite response at the end of his speech, and some in the audience told me that the federal government was the primary target of the town's anger.

I drove across the railroad tracks to the other side of town, where the pavement ended at the black neighborhoods with small homes perched atop orange clay hills. I spoke to one woman, a divorced mother of six children, whose only income was fifty dollars a week in public welfare that she begrudgingly accepted because, after joining the freedom movement, she could no longer get a job.

"If they don't get a conviction, I don't think it will be a place where people can live. They can't help but be afraid." She paused and grimaced, showing three gold teeth. "They are wondering what will happen if they let the sheriff off. They are afraid."

I visited another community ten miles east of Philadelphia where a black farmer, who had attended the burned Mount Zion Methodist Church, expressed a similar opinion. He had just returned from hunting and leaned against his shotgun. "If they do get a conviction, it will be the first time," he said. "If they get away with it, I don't know." He did not work in the civil rights movement, and because he was the owner of a three-hundred-acre farm, he said he could speak more freely than most blacks, who were poor. He said Rainey and Price had visited his community in early June asking blacks about civil rights activities, but had not returned since.

Some blacks said they suspected that the money raised to pay the defendants' lawyers would surpass the $20,000 needed to rebuild the Mount Zion church, which was not insured. A trustee of the church told me the congregation had received $5,000 in restoration pledges, most from outside the South.

On the day of the preliminary hearings, rain clouds hung over the Meridian courthouse as crowds hurried to get one of the two hundred seats in the second-floor courtroom. The marshals allowed no one to stand. The audience was a mixture of black and white civil rights workers and the wives and relatives of the defendants. Also in the audience were members of the Mississippi Sheriff's Association, who were urged by its president to show support for Rainey.

Fannie Lee Chaney, the mother of James Chaney, sat behind a row of white women and stared over the railing at Rainey and the other defendants, who sat in the jury box. Most of the defendants appeared uncomfortable in their Sunday suits. Price wore a blue suit with a red tie and pocket handkerchief. Commissioner Esther Carter arrived five minutes late and took a seat directly in front of fourteen lawyers seated at the defense table. She appeared a bit nervous and spoke so softly that those in the back of the courtroom had difficulty hearing her. Because Carter was not a lawyer, Judge Sidney Mize appointed a law clerk to whisper advice in her ear throughout the hearing.

The Justice Department's young lawyer, Robert Owen, announced to Carter that the department had obtained a signed confession from one of the accused men. The defense attorneys, who came from Philadelphia and Meridian, immediately challenged Owen. "We don't believe you have any proof," one of them railed. This brought snickers from the defendants, who had looked rather glum to that point. Carter fluttered her eyelashes and called for order. An FBI agent testified that one defendant, Horace Doyle Barnette, a twenty-five-year-old meat salesman who had moved to Louisiana, signed a confession to the murders "after a bout with his conscience." The defendants looked disheartened, and the defense attorneys jumped to their feet again. "We object to that. This is hearsay," one defense attorney said. "This is a confession by an individual in a foreign state to Mississippi. He is not even here. These people's rights are in jeopardy."

Carter sustained the objection. Owen paced the courtroom and quoted case law that hearsay evidence was permissible to show probable cause. Carter refused to reverse her ruling. "I sustain the objection," she repeated, looking sternly at Owen. One by one, the defense attorneys demanded that they see a copy of the confession, but Carter refused. She repeated that the FBI agent's testimony of a signed confession would not be admitted as evidence. With that, she dismissed all the charges.

"Agent testimony is used in every district in the country," Owen responded in a state of disbelief. He said Carter's action was without precedent. But the Justice Department opted to let the defendants go free rather than reveal the evidence for its case. Its strategy was to wait for the federal grand jury to see the confession. After the hearing, a group of blacks protested briefly in the corridor until marshals quickly hurried them down the stairs.

The defendants, smiling and congratulating one another on their first-round victory, departed the courthouse as free men. Their attorneys quickly released a written statement saying the defendants and Mississippi had been treated unjustly because King had pressured the president and the Justice Department to indict them. "We think they are playing politics with the lives of these people," the statement read. "It is most unfair to this section of the country and to these defendants and their families." King responded from Norway, where he was accepting the Nobel Peace Prize, by calling for a national economic boycott of Mississippi products.

Two months later, a federal grand jury in Jackson handed down new conspiracy indictments, but Judge William Harold Cox, a die-hard segregationist, threw out the charges, saying the crime was subject to state, not federal, laws. The Justice Department appealed, and the US Supreme Court eventually overruled Cox. A trial was finally held in 1967 with an all-white jury and Cox as the presiding judge. Price and six others were found guilty of conspiracy; Rainey, Burrage, and six others were acquitted. The jury was unable to reach a verdict in the case of Killen. Cox sentenced the guilty men to three to ten years in prison. Price served four years, returned to Philadelphia, and died in 2001. Rainey finished his term as sheriff in 1968 and died of cancer in 2002. Decades after the murders, the informant was identified as a highway patrolman who had acted as an intermediary to disperse the reward to those providing information he took back to the FBI.

No one was found guilty of murder. Then, in 1998, Jerry Mitchell, the same journalist who had unearthed additional information about Byron De La Beckwith, launched a series of investigative pieces in the Jackson *Clarion-Ledger* about civil rights cases that had died out long ago. He interviewed one of the former defendants, an imperial KKK wizard, who admitted that he had escaped justice in the Philadelphia murders. The victims' families called for a reopening of the case, and in 2005, a county grand jury delivered the first murder indictment. It was against Killen, who, at age eighty, was found guilty of manslaughter and sentenced to sixty years in prison. The conviction came on the same day as the forty-first anniversary of the crime. In 2013, the US Supreme Court rejected an appeal from Killen, and he died in the Mississippi State Penitentiary in Parchman on January 11, 2018. In 2016, the Mississippi attorney general said finding additional evidence for convictions after fifty-two years was unlikely because many witnesses were dead or had refused to cooperate, and the case was closed for good.

CHAPTER 25

The War in Men's Souls

THE SUMMER OF 1964 HAD BEEN AN OUTRIGHT WAR. CONFLICTS REACHED a new peak when hundreds of civil rights workers from all over the nation poured into the South to aid black activists. Their presence triggered a visceral reaction, and the costs of the war—both in personal casualties and property damage throughout the South—were high. A four-month tally by the Council of Federated Organizations revealed that in addition to the murders of Schwerner, Goodman, and Chaney, eighty individuals were beaten, more than one thousand people were arrested, and thirty-five incidents of gunfire had resulted in the wounding of three blacks in the South. In addition, thirty-five black churches were burned and thirty homes and other buildings bombed. Blacks appealed to President Johnson for protection. Almost every day, a person was beaten by a self-appointed guardian of racial orthodoxy and few arrests were made. Blacks accepted the violence directed toward them as the price of freedom, but they also showed considerable impatience with the federal government for not bringing more pressure on the perpetrators of violence. Lawlessness was on the rise, and violence seemed to have lost its shock value. When three men beat a young black civil rights worker with a wooden board and a pipe at the Leflore Theater in Greenwood, the FBI quickly made arrests under provisions of the Civil Rights Act. The theater was owned by a national chain and was one of several theaters in Mississippi complying with the new law by admitting blacks. But the arrests prompted hooded men to break into a local television station and beat the announcer as he read news about the arrests. Gunshots were then fired into the home of the victim of the movie theater attack.

Nowhere was the setting as complex and mystifying as in Mississippi. On the surface was apparent serenity among pastoral rural scenes, especially in the autumn, when the sky was a deep blue and the green land had not yet been touched by frost. The brain-dulling heat and haze of summer was lifted and the fields and forests were visible for miles. The Gulf Coast had white sandy beaches, shrimp boats, and thriving industries. Jackson had clean new buildings and virtually no slums. Greenville had more sophisticated, well-heeled, and well-traveled residents than most northern cities its size. People were, at first glimpse, friendly and open.

But not all was as it seemed to be. As in most wars, virtually every man, woman, and child—black and white—was emotionally involved. Change wreaked havoc on the time-honored, whites-only world. Many southerners watched from the sidelines as small bands of white men, called nightriders, terrorized demonstrators in the streets and citizens in their homes. Most nightriders were in their twenties and thirties and were employed in labor or service jobs, although some were former army demolition experts or the sons of wealthy oilmen. Some had little education, but others had a certain amount of drive and intelligence. Paul Hendrickson's illuminating book *Sons of Mississippi: A Story of Race and Its Legacy* describes the dichotomy of their personalities in a chapter appropriately entitled "Sometimes Trashy, Sometimes Luminous."

Whatever their backgrounds, the nightriders viewed themselves as the last line of southern defense, and most did little to conceal their activities or identity. They stood in bunches on street corners as blacks lined up to register to vote or eat in all-white restaurants. Suddenly, one of these steely-eyed men would step out from his gang and brutally slug a peaceful protester.

Their violence was directed at three categories of people: blacks and whites engaged in or sympathetic to the civil rights movement, blacks not engaged in civil rights work but who just happened to get swept up into a demonstration, and whites who defended a segregated system but condemned the use of violence against demonstrators. The first two groups had been regular targets of violence for some time. But it was another matter altogether for the third group, which included white public officials, to become prey.

Judge W. H. Watkins, a segregationist who opposed the Civil Rights Act and presided over several circuit courts in southwestern Mississippi, seemed a likely ally to the nightriders. In 1964, he freed nine white men convicted of bombing the homes of three black families in McComb because he said the defendants were from good families and deserved a second chance. During the sentencing, Watkins lectured the defendants for thirty minutes, saying, "What you have done has been, to some extent at least, provoked by outside influences. Their [civil rights workers'] presence here was unnerving and unwanted, and some of them are people of low morality and unhygienic." But he wanted order in McComb and added, "Being provoked is no excuse for a crime such as bombing or attempted burning of a home." He granted their clemency with the condition of no more violence. Locals viewed his order and his lecture as a probation on the entire town, and the nightriders burned a cross in his front yard a few weeks later.

Natchez mayor John Nosser also felt the nightriders' wrath. Nosser was a segregationist, but he also believed in abiding by the law even when he disagreed with it. He surprised many people in Natchez by promising black citizens equal protection and the right to vote if they qualified. He also hired blacks in his grocery store. One evening, a blast of dynamite tore out a wall of his two-story, white-columned house while he was in the living room with his family. The damage was extensive, but no one was injured. It was the third explosion in eleven days to property he owned. Nosser thought whites probably bombed his property, but said either blacks or whites could be responsible because he had stepped on the toes of both.

There was no middle ground. Eric Johnston, the director of the State Sovereignty Commission and the publisher of a weekly newspaper, was a segregationist who rejected the label "moderate" because that implied a compromised belief he did not support. But because he condoned nonviolence and promoted ethical approaches toward resolution, he was rebuked by extremists. "The Ku Klux Klan, the Americans for the Preservation of the White Race, the Citizens' Council, the John Birch Society—they're all against me," Johnston told me. "Nobody is for me."

Charles Dorrough, mayor of Ruleville, Mississippi, where the Summer Project students gathered, clearly identified with and represented his conservative white constituents. But he was also president of the Mississippi Municipal Association and felt a responsibility to uphold the law. Following passage of the Civil Rights Act, he set up a program to train blacks to work in Ruleville industries that had previously hired only whites. The town also hired a black policeman, not to advance integration but to ease racial tensions and abide by the new federal law. Nevertheless, a cross was burned on Dorrough's front lawn, and literature attacking him and the aldermen as traitors was distributed in the white community. Local business leaders came to Dorrough's defense and posted a $500 reward for information leading to the arrest of those who had burned the cross and defamed him.

Edgar Thatcher Walt, a thirty-five-year-old Greenwood native and editor of the *Greenwood Commonwealth*, was a conservative who endorsed maintaining the white status quo. But when the KKK became active near his town, he wrote a mild editorial criticizing cross burning and other illegal activities. He and his family were immediately threatened and harassed, and Walt found it necessary to sit up one night with a shotgun resting in his lap to protect them. He went to the town leaders and asked them to publicly denounce the terrorism, but he received little support.

"I decided then I did not want to raise my children in this town," Walt told me. He found another newspaper job in Mississippi and gave his two-week notice. Before he moved, however, he and his wife took their two children and a neighbor's child to see a movie at the Leflore Theater, where a gang of whites congregated nightly warning theatergoers to stay away.

Walt entered the theater anyway and told the gang he would notify the authorities if there was trouble. After the movie, Walt and his family had barely gotten home when telephone threats began. Then there was an explosion on his front lawn, and although Walt called the police for help, none came. He spent another long, sleepless night on guard with his shotgun.

The next day, a friend told Walt he had overheard a conversation at a gas station about a plot to kill him. Walt packed up his family and left town immediately. He also called the publisher at his new job to say he would not be reporting to work as planned. "I felt like it wouldn't be safe for me anywhere in the state," he explained to me, and so he found a job several hundred miles away. A few days later, another reporter told me he'd asked a Greenwood policeman about Walt. "He left town before we could get him," the officer replied.

Desperately trying to maintain a system of black suppression, white segregationists created a world rife with rumor, fabrication, and paranoia. They were convinced that black men were determined to rape white women and that black restaurant workers contaminated their food. They believed rumors that the NAACP instructed maids to harass employers by hiding valuable items so they appeared to be stolen, giving the lady of the house a moment of heightened concern and fear.

For some, the real war in Mississippi raged in their white souls. Even moderate whites struggled with their consciences. In some white families, one or two members had thought their way out of the Mississippi orthodoxy. Most times, these family members remained silent despite their urge to offer an opposing view. "I just don't talk about it anymore when I go home," a young man in Jackson told me. "But I find it hard not to when the subject is always under discussion."

I felt the same frustration with my extended family, who did not understand why I was writing about civil rights for a northern newspaper. They were not overt racists or mean-spirited haters of black people, but they certainly did not support troublemakers who upset the traditional southern lifestyle. My family believed in abiding by the established rules of society. Like most people, they didn't question whether something was right or wrong or should be changed. To question would have exposed themselves to the withering scrutiny of small-town doctrine.

Betty and I coexisted with our extended families by not talking about race. But once we left their homes, we taught our daughters differently. One Sunday after leaving my parents' home, I stopped the car at the curb a few blocks away, turned to my four daughters in the back seat, and instructed them to never to use the words my mother had just used to describe blacks. Those words so offended me and evoked images of the nightriders and people screaming at blacks sitting at whites-only lunch counters. One daughter challenged my instructions. "Why didn't you tell Grandmother not to use those words?" she asked. My answer was as simple as I could explain, even to myself: "She's my mother. You always respect your mother. And some people's minds can never be changed, no matter how many times you try. But you, you are never to use those words."

Perhaps it was southern politeness or fear of scorn that rendered some whites silent even when they sympathized with the plight of blacks. Sometimes when a white person questioned the system, others were relieved to find they were not alone. One young office worker told me she had summoned the courage to tell a coworker that she disagreed with segregation. "You do?" the coworker responded in surprise. "Why, I do, too." They kept a quiet, mutual pact.

Because of such secrecy, the number of people harboring these beliefs was probably greater than I knew. They formed little cells to talk among themselves but never took an active role in the movement. They felt they didn't fit anywhere. They had nothing in common with the unkempt, revolutionary civil rights workers coming to Mississippi nor would go so far as to support interracial relationships. But they sensed something was terribly wrong in Mississippi without knowing how to change it. Did their silence make them complicit? Were they innocent compared to the segregationists or the nightriders? Or was their silence merely a lesser evil?

King worried that white moderates were more pernicious than the KKK or the White Citizens' Council. He wrote from his jail cell that such people were "more devoted to 'order' than justice," preferring "a negative peace, which is the absence of tension, to a positive peace, which is the presence of justice." He said the "shallow understanding from people of good will is more frustrating than absolute misunderstanding from people of ill will."

Some blacks constituted another silent contingent. They accepted their lot and thought the movement was futile. They wondered why other blacks would subject themselves to a cause that could never reverse the history, politics, and sociology of discrimination that gripped the region. I directed that question to organizer Andrew Young. He told me that blacks subjected themselves to violent assaults during the protests because there could be "no resurrection without a crucifixion." Some of my colleagues thought his comment was cavalier and indifferent. But I understood. He believed that from sacrifice rose salvation.

Sacrifice produced gains, which were spotty and ambiguous but seemed substantial in a system of intractable prejudice. Although the Summer Project registered only a fraction of the eligible black voters in Mississippi, it created forty-seven Freedom Schools and tutored 2,500 black students. Another civil rights organization established thirty community-based projects with 250 workers and encouraged blacks to serve on local agricultural committees to administer federal crop programs. Thanks to pressure from the FBI, Mississippi removed KKK members from the highway patrol, and some local police forces fought back bands of terrorists who burned and bombed black homes and churches.

A greater systemic shift occurred in national politics. From 1962 to 1964, the number of blacks registered to vote in eleven southern states rose from 1.4 million to 2.2 million. Mississippi and Alabama, where blacks still had the greatest difficulty registering, lagged with fewer than 25 percent of eligible blacks registered. Blacks in the South voted in unprecedented fashion in

1964 and helped reelect President Johnson, who carried six southern states, including four that otherwise would have voted Republican. A *New York Times* banner headline pronouncing "Johnson Swamps Goldwater" was accompanied by my front-page article with a lead declaring: "President Johnson carried a majority of Southern states tonight by turning the normal voting pattern inside out." President Johnson won in large part because of the black vote, a phenomenon never before seen in a presidential election.

The southern sweep, however, did not include the most racist states of Mississippi, Louisiana, Alabama, Georgia, and South Carolina, where the lowest percentage of black voters in the South were concentrated. Those states rejected their long-held Democratic loyalties and voted solidly for Goldwater. It was the first time since Reconstruction that South Carolina and Mississippi voted for a Republican president. In Alabama, President Johnson's name was not even on the ballot. Seven Republican congressional candidates in districts that had been held by Democrats since Reconstruction rode to victory on Goldwater's coattails. President Johnson's earlier prediction that passage of the Civil Rights Act would cost Democrats in the Deep South proved to be true, a shift that would have profound political implications for decades to come.

Goldwater's defeat left many southern whites shocked and confused. They had believed that national support for segregation had momentum and that the Civil Rights Act would be repealed in a matter of time. They channeled Goldwater's defeat into a new determination to fight back at the same time that civil rights leaders were demanding that President Johnson deliver on his promise of a Voting Rights Act. Both segregationists and integrationists were poised for the next battle.

CHAPTER 26

Hope in Selma

IT WAS A COLD, BLUE DAY ON JANUARY 2, 1965, WHEN MARTIN LUTHER King Jr., now recognized on a worldwide stage, headed to Selma emboldened for a new and rejuvenated "march on the ballot boxes." He vowed to continue his commitment to nonviolent resistance, and it seemed to be holding up among the growing number of supporters who were joining the movement. Whether or not my *New York Times Magazine* article had any impact, there was, after passage of the Civil Rights Act, a drift among organizers back to preserving a strategy of nonviolence.

Children gathered under a chinaberry tree in front of Brown Chapel Methodist Episcopal Church in downtown Selma to prepare for King's arrival. They practiced their anthem with raised voices of "A-a-men, A-a-men," clapping their hands on the upbeat. The Romanesque Revival–style chapel was an imposing red-brick structure with twin towers built in 1908 by a black mason. Across the street, a deputy sheriff with a stare as steely as his revolver kept an eye on the youth.

Selma had been relatively calm since the 1963 protests. But civil rights activists were returning to the city as its next staging ground. "We're going to turn Selma upside down and inside out in order to make it right-side up," King told his supporters.

Alabama still had poll taxes that mainly affected black voters, and the Alabama Supreme Court, in response to the Civil Rights Act, also instituted a more difficult literacy test. Blacks who arrived to register at the Dallas County courthouse were greeted with a sixty-eight-question list about government minutia and the US Constitution. Each applicant was asked eight questions from the list and given a dictation test to determine his or her ability to write. Sample questions included: "If no national candidate for vice president receives a majority of the electoral vote, how is a vice president chosen? In such cases, how many votes must a person receive to become vice president?" (Answers: the Senate, and fifty-one votes.) The test was rarely given to whites, especially wealthier white men, who never took it. One federal official candidly remarked that if all Alabamans on the voter rolls had taken and passed the test, the state would have the most intelligent electorate in the nation.

Unofficial barriers, yet equally powerful, also prevented blacks from obtaining the right to vote. I interviewed Lonzy West, a forty-year-old house painter with an eighth-grade education and eleven children, who first tried to register in 1963 in Dallas County. "I was standing in the registration line," West recalled, "when this white man I had contracted some work with came up to me and said, 'Lonzy, what are you doing here?' I said, 'I'm trying to register to vote,' and he said, 'Well, we'll see about that.' After that my work fell off, and there was only one white lady who would hire me."

Like St. Augustine, Selma had all the ingredients King and his lieutenants needed to stir a pot of angry backlash and catch the nation's attention: a 50 percent black population, widespread racism, antiquated discriminatory laws, and Sheriff James Clark, who still ruled the county with a chokehold. Black boys played a game called "Jim Clark and the Negro" in which they taunted each other saying, "I'll be Jim Clark, you be the Negro. I'll hit you on the head, you fall down."

Upon his return to Selma, King found that some things had changed since 1963. The SCLC and other organizing groups had developed durable bases in the city, and white leaders better understood King's tactics of inciting trouble. The monolithic city government had been replaced with new leaders who wanted to avoid their city becoming like Birmingham. Despite the county's egregious registration laws, city leaders reluctantly complied with some parts of the Civil Rights Act to preserve the peace and reputation of the community. Although Clark was still in charge of voter registration, many influential white citizens were urging the city to avoid arresting protesters in hopes that they would become discouraged by the lack of attention and go away. "We are hoping," one white resident told me, "that Dr. King will leave town and let us deal with the problem in our own way." Even the fashionable country club set turned against Clark, and city leaders put pressure on him to exercise restraint.

But King, the SCLC, and SNCC believed that Clark and George Wallace would not respond calmly to their demands. In the 1964 general election, 111,000 blacks in Alabama were registered, a dramatic increase from 6,000 in 1947. But their numbers still paled in comparison to the 946,000 white voters in 1964. The plan was to register 370,000 black voters in Alabama, which was 80 percent of the eligible black vote in the state.

Another difference in Selma since 1963 that benefited organizers was increased federal support. A few days before King's arrival, the Justice Department filed suit in the US district court charging that Alabama's voter registration requirements targeted blacks and violated the Civil Rights Act. But the Civil Rights Act did not have enough teeth to eradicate the disenfranchisement in states like Alabama, and King and other organizers were now pushing for a Voting Rights Act that would outlaw poll taxes and literacy tests.

When King arrived at Brown Chapel on that cold January day, seven hundred people had joined the children to hear his words. "If they refuse to register us, we will appeal to Governor Wallace," he told the crowd. "If he doesn't listen, we will appeal to the legislature. If the legislature doesn't listen, we will seek to arouse the federal government by marching by the thousands at the places of registration. We are not asking, we are demanding the ballot." The crowd roared with applause. I stood in the back of the church, knowing that their campaign had reached a pinnacle that the president, Congress, and the nation could not ignore.

"When we get the right to vote," he continued, "we will send to the state house not men who will stand in the doorways of universities to keep Negroes out but men who will uphold the cause of justice, and we will send to Congress men who will sign not a manifesto for segregation but a manifesto for justice."

The crowd roared again. One person who was not at the rally that evening was Sheriff Clark. He was seven hundred miles away in Miami, where the Alabama Crimson Tide football team had lost the night before to the Texas Longhorns in the Orange Bowl. Clark's substitute outside the church during King's speech was Wilson Baker, the city's new police chief, whom Clark had defeated in the county sheriff election a decade earlier. While Clark controlled his deputies and a sanctioned posse, Baker was in charge of the city police and part of the new city administration seeking a more moderate course in race relations. He was a large, genial man originally from North

Carolina who had pledged to keep the peace "someway somehow," and he vowed that whites would not cause trouble for demonstrators. To prove his point, he had recently arrested two white youths who set off a tear gas bomb in a black neighborhood near Brown Chapel.

Within days after his speech, King led hundreds of protesters in sub-freezing temperatures from the church to the courthouse. A small gaggle of reporters, including myself, followed them during the nine-block walk. Under pressure from the city, Clark, who had returned from Miami, met them with a more welcomed response than in the past. He led them to an alley entrance of the three-story stone courthouse and said he would allow fifty people at a time to register. I stood in front of the courthouse near King as he was approached by two white men—James Robinson, a Birmingham member of the National States' Rights Party, and George Lincoln Rockwell, head of the American Nazi Party from Alexandria, Virginia. A group of helmeted police looked on.

The two men questioned King about what he was doing. He explained he was accompanying blacks to register, and he invited both men to speak at his rally that evening. For some reason, his suggestion ignited their fury, and they seized upon each other. Robinson turned on Rockwell and accused him of being a spy for the FBI. "Where are your Nazis, Mr. Ratwell?" Robinson screamed. Then J. B. Stoner, the KKK's attorney from Atlanta, joined the chaos and announced there would be a rally for white segregationists that evening on the outskirts of town.

The confrontation deescalated and the white supremacists left, going their separate ways. King and eleven other black leaders stood in front of the courthouse for a while longer and then headed back to the Albert Hotel, a magnificent four-story Gothic structure built by slaves one hundred years earlier to resemble the Doge's Palace in Venice. The hotel had been used as the Union army's headquarters after Confederate soldiers surrendered in the Battle of Selma in 1865, and it was where other reporters and I stayed overnight.

King approached the front desk to check in as the hotel's first black guest when Robinson suddenly wormed his way through the crowd and approached him. "I want to talk to you," Robinson said. I was standing on the second-floor balcony that ringed the lobby and had a bird's eye view of what happened next. Robinson drew back his arm, swung, and hit King twice on the right temple. King offered no resistance. But SNCC's John Lewis did.

He pinned Robinson's arms to his side. But Robinson kicked King twice, catching him lightly on the inner thigh near his groin. Lewis and Robinson fell across the red carpet in a struggle.

A white woman in tight slacks and a leather jacket stood in a corner shouting to Robinson, "Get him. Get him." Baker, who was standing nearby, collared Robinson and dragged him to a patrol car. The black leaders accompanying King helped him to his feet, and all were given hotel rooms as required by law. I hurriedly ran to a pay phone to call in a news story to the *Times* that King had been assaulted by a white supremacist leader. King later told reporters he suffered nothing more than a headache from the attack. Lewis, committed to the nonviolent movement, said later that this attack tested his limit of reserve. Robinson was charged with assault and disturbing the peace, fined $100, and sentenced to sixty days of hard labor.

In many southern cities like St. Augustine and Philadelphia, reporting the news was fairly straightforward because a handful of black leaders organized the demonstrations and rallied their troops. John Lewis and Andrew Young of the SCLC consistently called me about when and where meetings and marches would take place. I also regularly dropped by leadership headquarters to check in on press conferences and rally announcements. But reporting from Selma was more challenging because the movement there tended to be decentralized and orchestrated at the grassroots. There were more than just a few black leaders, and I had to scramble around town to different makeshift offices to find out where the next set of demonstrations or rallies was planned.

The city's strategy to temper its reaction worked for a while, but Clark was able to restrain himself for only so long. The day after the assault on King, more blacks went to the courthouse, and Clark was in no mood to accommodate them. When the prospective voters refused to line up in the alley outside the courthouse, Clark arrested sixty-two people on charges of unlawful assembly. One of the protesters was Amelia Boynton, an insurance agent and local civil rights leader. When she ignored Clark's orders to leave the sidewalk, he roughly grabbed her by her coat collar and pushed her swiftly for a half block to a waiting patrol car. Boynton, wearing a dress, hose, and black pump heels, stumbled down the street as Clark hustled her along.

King watched the encounter from a parked car across the street. He stepped out of the car, walked to an adjacent federal office building, and asked the Justice Department to file a court injunction against Clark. "It was one of the most brutal and unlawful acts I have seen an officer commit," he told reporters. Although clearly a rough and wrongful arrest, given King's seasoned eyes, these words appeared to be for effect. This was not the first time Clark was the subject of a federal complaint, including a lawsuit that claimed he used his office to avoid compliance with the Civil Rights Act. Clark angrily refused the pleas of city officials and business leaders to control his outbursts, and Baker was left to contend with him. Baker's city police escorted protesters on their third consecutive march to the courthouse, but Clark again sent them to a side entrance. When they refused, John Lewis engaged Clark in a five-minute discussion in which Clark told him, "You are here to cause trouble: that's what you are doing. You are an agitator and that is the lowest form of humanity."

Clark warned Lewis that if the black applicants did not use the side entrance, he would arrest them. Then he counted off sixty seconds and carted many of them off to jail. A second group to arrive was also arrested. When a third wave arrived and stood on the corner, Clark barked, "Captain Baker, they are blocking the sidewalk. Will you clear it?" Baker instructed them to clear the sidewalk by forming a line that extended one and a half blocks. Clark still barred them from entering the courthouse. By this time, the two men's relationship was so strained that they stopped speaking to each other even as they stood only ten feet apart. Two officers ferried messages between them. Finally, Clark shouted to the people waiting to register, "You are under arrest." By day's end, I watched him arrest 150 demonstrators.

Two days later, I followed a hundred black teachers from Brown Chapel to the courthouse. Before now, the teachers' presence in the protests had been rare because they answered to an all-white school board who warned that the teachers' involvement could erode gains already made for black students. Clark and his men met the teachers at the courthouse and repelled them by jabbing them in the ribs with nightsticks and pushing them down the front steps. "You can't make a playhouse out of the corridors of this courthouse," Clark told them. "Some of you think you can make it a Disneyland."

The tense confrontation lasted about thirty minutes as at least three hundred adults and students cheered from across the street. After being pushed back a second time, the teachers returned to Brown Chapel, where they were buoyed by supporters. "This is the first time in the history of the movement that so well organized and dramatic a protest has been made by any professional group in the Negro community," King told a crowd of about eight hundred people that evening. It was the fourth demonstration in one week, and 223 people had been arrested. The NAACP Legal Defense Fund sought an injunction to bar Clark from making more arrests.

It was clear this would be a long and drawn-out campaign. My room at the Albert Hotel became my home away from home for weeks, and Betty sent me homemade cookies and "we miss you" messages from my daughters with colorful drawings of flowers. Every night when I fell to bed exhausted, I wondered, "If I am weary and ready to go home, what must it be like for the demonstrators who were threatened with violence and physical harm?"

The demonstrators' spirit was irrepressible, and their determination was emboldened when the federal government intervened. A federal judge said that one hundred people could wait in line at one time to register and issued an injunction to curtail Clark's behavior. However, neither he nor the demonstrators abided by the judge's orders, and three days later I witnessed one of the most brutal assaults so far of the Selma demonstrations. I was standing with a group of reporters near a two-hundred-person registration queue as King approached reporters to answer questions. Clark grabbed King by the arm and ordered him to return to the line. At that moment, a large fifty-three-year-old black woman named Annie Cooper, who worked as a motel clerk, stepped forward and punched Clark in the face.

Three deputies wrestled Cooper to the ground. As she flailed and kicked in the struggle, she cried, "I wish you would hit me, you scum." Clark was fuming mad and accepted her invitation. He clutched his billy club with two hands and brought it down on Cooper's head, sending a loud whack through the crowd. At King's urging, no one moved. Those present watched in horror as the officers rolled her over, restrained her with two pairs of cuffs, and hauled her away bleeding from a wound over her right eye. King, who was standing a few feet away, called the sheriff's action unnecessary. "We have seen another day of brutality," he told the crowd a few minutes later. "We still have in Dallas County a sheriff who is determined to trample over Negroes with iron feet of brutality and oppression."

In the struggle, Clark lost his green tie, his cap with the emblazoned "scrambled eggs" logo, his badge, and, for a moment, his club. He showed no signs of injury, although he said, "If that eye isn't black, it soon will be. She knocked the hell out of me." One sheriff's deputy caught in the melee lost some skin on the back of his neck and gained a knot on his cheek. Cooper was charged with two counts of assault and battery and held under a $2,000 bond. When I later asked Clark for more information about Cooper, he answered, "She hasn't got a Miss or Mrs. in front of her name. She says she's a secretary at a motel, but I think she's a bouncer." He also noted that Cooper weighed 226½ pounds on the jailhouse scale, 6½ pounds more than he did.

I wrote about the scene in an article on the front page of the *Times*. Yet my words were dwarfed by an accompanying photograph. It showed two deputies holding Cooper to the ground while Clark, raising his billy club in a double-fisted grip, was poised to land a blow to Cooper's head. Only the back of Cooper's head was visible in the photograph, but Clark's face, framed by wisps of hair circling his balding scalp, displayed an evil grimace. The graphic photograph generated national attention and support for the Selma campaign as it entered its fourth week. Hundreds of people, black and white, arrived to join the protests. King emphasized that voting was the key to equality because he said there would be no poverty, no segregation, and no sheriffs like Clark if blacks could elect officials who represented their interests. "This is our intention," he said, "to declare war on the evils of demagoguery."

CHAPTER 27

Pulling at the Fiber

BY EARLY FEBRUARY, MORE THAN SEVEN HUNDRED PROTESTERS, INCLUD-
ing King and five hundred students, had been arrested at the courthouse.
Most were released within hours after arrest, but King, as he had in Birmingham and other cities, refused to post his $200 bail and remained in jail as
a sign of protest. His arrest had come about two weeks later than the campaign's planned timeline, mainly because of Baker's restrained reaction. As
King lay on his cell bunk reading the book of Psalms, demonstrators gathered
for another day of protests at Brown Chapel. Clark, shivering from the cold
in his Eisenhower-style military jacket, arrived at the chapel to arrest John
Love, a SNCC leader from New York who Clark said was contributing to the
delinquency of minors because he encouraged students to join the protest.
I watched as Clark and his men hauled away Love, who wore his trademark
outfit of sneakers, tailored dungarees, a red jacket, and one earring. Later in
the day, Andrew Young called a press conference in a back room of Brown
Chapel to explain the next moves.

Young said if the campaign subsided now, local blacks would be intimidated into submitting to more suppression. Therefore, a new strategy would
be employed to gain more media attention by recruiting students, mainly
from high school, to skip school and join the protests. More importantly,
the campaign would expand to the nearby town of Marion, near Coretta
Scott King's hometown, where sixteen blacks had been recently arrested for
attempting to enter an all-white restaurant.

King spent his third day in jail directing the campaign through detailed
letters to his assistants. On February 3, more than one thousand students
were arrested for truancy when they protested in Selma and Marion. Most

of them had gathered in front of the courthouse in Selma, clapping and singing "Ain't gonna let Jim Clark turn me round" and "I love Jim Clark in my heart." Clark smiled at them, paced the street, and talked to his deputies, his posse, city police officers, and state troopers. I stood next to a mechanic at a Chevrolet garage across the street who told me, "There's going to be some niggers killed here before this is over. They'll be killed like flies."

At first, almost everyone at the protest seemed in good humor except Baker, who was trying to control Clark's behavior. Clark let the students sing for a while, but then he barked orders through a portable loudspeaker: "All of you under-aged are under arrest for truancy and the others for contempt of court. Turn that line around and let's go." The students, still singing, followed three officers through busy streets to an armory, which was the only place large enough to handle the mass incarceration. Their arrests brought the total number of people arrested in one month in Selma and Marion to 2,800. This caught President Johnson's attention, who came forth and publicly denounced the infringement of voting rights in Alabama and pledged vigorous legal action. Six US House Democrats also announced plans to come to Selma to observe the registration process.

The Dallas County Board of Registrars made some small, incremental changes. It hired more clerks to process applications, it opened its office thirteen days a month rather than two, and it processed 113 black applications. A federal judge in Mobile also ordered the board to stop using the state-prescribed literacy test because it was too time consuming for the clerks to grade and process, but he did nothing to curtail Clark's actions.

During his fourth day in jail, King expressed disappointment that the judge's order did not go further. Black leaders also feared that small improvements in the registration process would take steam out of the campaign, and they regrouped to consider their next move. It became complicated when Malcolm X showed up unexpectedly as hundreds of demonstrators gathered at Brown Chapel. Because of his growing popularity, his militant message was one of the greatest threats to the nonviolent movement. Even some of King's lieutenants and many of the SNCC students aligned their thinking with Malcolm X and had encouraged him to visit the South because they were impatient for change and didn't trust the white establishment to redress their grievances. Yet, other leaders felt that Malcolm X struggled to find rapport with those advocating nonviolence who, so far, had been rewarded by passage of the landmark Civil Rights Act. It was understandable that some in Brown Chapel were unsettled by his surprise appearance as King sat in jail and as demonstrators were about to march to the courthouse where Clark and his deputies were waiting with guns, nightsticks, and cattle prods. A succession of speakers had roused the audience to a delicate balance of restrained frenzy when Malcolm X walked through the door. Leaders did not want him pulling at the fragile fiber of their message.

Yet the leaders reluctantly allowed him to speak because they had a policy of open meetings. As he stepped to the altar, I wondered how the crowd would receive him. Would his fiery and militant message tip the balance and send the marchers to an incursion with the sheriff's posse? Perhaps he understood the sensitivity of this moment because, compared to his speeches in Harlem, he was restrained and shifted blame to the federal government for not protecting human rights. He had, in recent months, adopted a more moderate tone and was less confrontational with other civil rights leaders. But in this speech he did not abandon his traditional philosophy of strict black nationalism. He compared himself to the field hands during slavery who, unlike the slaves working inside, were unwilling to protect their masters. His remarks contained strong tones of overt action and predicted that even King would someday abandon his nonviolent technique.

"But before I sit down, I want to thank you for listening to me. I hope I haven't put anybody on the spot," he said. "I'm not intending to try and stir you up and make you do something that you wouldn't have done anyway." This produced a few chuckles from the audience that gave way to laughter and applause. But Malcolm X was not amused, and he remained stern:

> I pray that God will bless you in everything that you do. I pray that you will grow intellectually, so that you can understand the problems of the world and where you fit into, in that world picture. And I pray that all the fear that has ever been in your heart will be taken out, and when you look at that man, if you know he's nothing but a coward, you won't fear him. If he wasn't a coward, he wouldn't gang up on you.

The tension in the sanctuary was palpable as I waited to see the audience's response. There was polite applause, but by the time the march began, it was clear that Malcolm X had not connected with this audience. The pacifist approach, with its ultimate goal of assimilation rather than estrangement, was rooted deeply in this crowd. The marchers left the church and filled the streets in peaceful protest.

After five days of imprisonment, King walked out of jail calling for more demonstrations. He joined about two hundred adults and twice as many children and teenagers carrying leaflets saying "Let our parents vote" to the courthouse steps. Clark, accompanied by Baker, emerged from the courthouse in a short-sleeved shirt and white riot helmet to read a court order banning demonstrations. Protesters responded by slumping to the sidewalk to await their arrests. But Clark and Baker turned and went inside the courthouse. White business and civic leaders had finally gotten through to Clark, mainly because he had gone too far the day before when he forced 165 children and teenagers who were demonstrating at the courthouse to walk two miles into the Dallas County countryside by jabbing them with nightsticks and cattle prods. The *Selma Times-Journal*, consistently critical of the demonstrations, even published a one-page editorial denouncing Clark's actions.

The next morning, Clark was hospitalized with exhaustion and complained of chest pain. About two hundred demonstrators knelt in a chilly rain in front of the courthouse to pray for his recovery, as a handful of deputies looked on with puzzled frowns but made no attempt to make arrests. Except when he had gone to the Orange Bowl, this was the first time the hefty sheriff was not on hand for the demonstrations, and his absence was notable. "It just wasn't the same without Jim Clark fussing and fuming," one demonstrator told me. "We honestly miss him."

Clark's wife told me that her husband was resting, and she expected him to recover in a couple of days. She said she awoke at 3:00 a.m. and found him reading a newspaper, fretting over complaints that some of his officers had mistreated some of the arrested demonstrators and held them in substandard conditions at a makeshift jail outside of town.

As the campaign entered its seventh week, a total of 3,400 people were arrested and more reinforcements arrived to lend support. The sheer number of protesters was overwhelming, even for Clark. On February 15, 2,800 demonstrators marched at courthouses in three counties—Dallas, Perry, and Wilcox. There was no violence and few arrests. The largest demonstration was in Selma, where 1,400 adults stood in a five-block line that stretched into a white residential neighborhood shaded by enormous oak and magnolia trees. Clark, who was out of the hospital, watched from inside the courthouse. White city officials met with black leaders, and the city issued a parade permit for Baker to administer.

King, who had been home in Atlanta with a cold, arrived in time to lead the permitted march. Demonstrators walked two abreast to the courthouse where blacks signed an appearance book that gave them priority on future registration days. King, wearing a black topcoat and hat, complained to me and other journalists that the registration process was still too slow. He shook hands with people standing in line, saying, "I see you people want your freedom. God Bless you."

I had followed King and his aides on many occasions, but on this day, he seemed more emboldened by the number of protesters and their enthusiasm. He went to the First Baptist Church, where he met with students who had skipped school for two weeks to participate in the marches. Many had been arrested at least once during the protests. King applauded them for their dedication but encouraged them to return to school because he said they would be most effective if they studied hard and received an education.

We left the church, and I piled into a car with other journalists to follow King to Wilcox County, where no blacks were on the voter rolls even though there were four black residents for every three whites. When we arrived, about seventy blacks formed a line in front of the old jail across the street from the courthouse. "How's the registration coming?" King asked as he bounded from his car. "You all want to vote, don't you?" Monroe Puttaway, a fifty-year-old farmer, told King, "I filled out the form like I have three times before but I cannot get nobody to vouch for me." Under Alabama law, many counties required prospective voters to have another voter sponsor them, but blacks here found no one willing or able to do that. A member of the board of registrars who overheard the conversation stuck his head out a door and said to King, "That's the state law. But we haven't opposed any of them registering."

King asked to see P. C. "Lummy" Jenkins, the county sheriff for the previous twenty-six years, who was a legend for his unorthodox, iron-fisted authority. When Jenkins sought to arrest a black suspect, he simply sent out word and the accused showed up at Jenkins's office to turn himself in. King found Jenkins on the courthouse lawn and asked if he would vouch for blacks to register. "I'm in politics myself," Jenkins said, "and maybe that wouldn't look right. Maybe some other whites would vouch for them. I'm not against their voting. We just want everything orderly. We love peace and quiet."

Our group then followed King to Marion, in Perry County, where four hundred people waited outside the courthouse while another three hundred were inside registering. They greeted him with a roar of applause, and he urged the people to keep waiting. Then he returned to Selma to prepare for another day of demonstrations with hopes that Clark would act unreasonably. When momentum lagged, black leaders consistently relied on Clark and his militant venom to bring the movement back to life.

The next day, about one hundred people gathered at the Selma courthouse in a chilly rain. Reverend C. T. Vivian, one of King's assistants from Atlanta, led some of the registrants to another entrance to escape the weather. I saw Clark order them to leave and prod them with a nightstick. Vivian accused him of acting "like Hitler" and challenged Clark to hit him. Clark's deputies tried to calm their boss, saying they would handle the demonstrators. But Clark would have none of it. He threw a blow to Vivian's lip with his right fist. Vivian did not fight back. The deputies carried Vivian away, blood running from his mouth, and charged him with criminal provocation and contempt of court.

I followed King as he spent the afternoon trying to find Vivian. He went to a hospital for blacks that was staffed mainly by white Catholic nuns from New York; they were wearing white robes and surrounded King to shake his hand and pose for pictures to send to relatives back home. They brought out a small black baby wrapped in a blue blanket that King spent a few minutes admiring. Then King, six members of his staff, the nuns, and two priests enjoyed coffee and cookies while talking about the racial situation in Selma. The nuns told King that Vivian had been sent to jail, but once King arrived there, the deputies turned him away and told him to see the sheriff, who had left for the day.

That evening, King and a caravan of cars carrying his assistants, FBI agents, and newsmen traveled fifty miles southwest of Selma in a blinding rainstorm to Gee's Bend, a small farming community in Wilcox County. We skidded and slipped over mud roads for more than an hour before arriving at Pleasant Grove Baptist Church, where 250 blacks were waiting patiently. The gospel choir hit a high pitch when we entered the church, amplifying the electric energy that King created wherever he went. "I came to Gee's Bend tonight to tell you we are going to stay with you and work with you until Negroes get the ballot," King told them. "When you get the ballot, things in Gee's Bend are going to change. You won't have to send your children to the terrible school you have here, and they will do something about your roads." The congregation responded with "Amen"s.

Despite his bad cold, King returned to Selma that night with a renewed belief that the campaign needed to embrace more aggressive approaches like night demonstrations and economic boycotts. Night protests were more volatile and uncontrollable than the daytime protests, and New York had banned them the previous summer because some in Harlem had become so violent. King and other black leaders had so far held back on conducting night protests. But now he called for them in Selma and Marion. In his strongest speech since the Selma campaign began, he told an audience of five hundred people at Brown Chapel that the white power structure must take responsibility for Clark and his men and ensure there was not one impediment to blacks registering to vote.

"It is time for us to say to those men, 'If you don't do something about it we will engage in broader forms of civil disobedience,'" King told the crowd. People in the audience voted to institute a boycott against the downtown businesses whose white owners and managers had fired employees who participated in the marches. The boycott would target most aggressively the business owners who were members of Clark's posse. Black leaders decided to hold off on night demonstrations in Selma for three days to give the white community time to meet a list of demands that included faster voter registration, biracial negotiations, and paved streets in black neighborhoods. But that did not mean that night protests could not be staged in Marion.

CHAPTER 28

A Wild and Woolly Night

ON FEBRUARY 18, ABOUT FOUR HUNDRED PEOPLE ASSEMBLED IN MARION, which seemed like a good place to stage the first night protests because it had been calmer there than in Selma. But the night took a wild and woolly turn.

A handful of other reporters and I arrived in Marion as demonstrators gathered at Zion Chapel Methodist Church, which sat across the town square from city hall and the white-columned county courthouse built by slaves in 1856. It was a cool night, and a large orange moon hung heavy in the sky. The red brick church, accentuated by a high-pitched steeple, was packed to the brim. Reverend C. T. Vivian, who was free from jail after his confrontation with Sheriff Clark, gave a rousing speech before ushering everyone outside, where some fifty sheriff's deputies and state troopers clad in helmets and riot gear waited. The protesters walked two abreast past the law enforcement officials and their commander, Colonel Albert Lingo, the same public safety director as in Birmingham and at Auburn University.

The street, deserted except for the marchers and police, was dim because the city had deliberately turned off the streetlights. The marchers walked a mere half block before Marion's police chief blared commands through a loudspeaker: "This is an unlawful assembly. You are hereby ordered to go home or back to the church." The marchers stopped walking but refused to move and remained in a line reaching back into the church. One leader at the head of the line, Reverend James N. Dobynes, knelt and prayed.

I watched from a corral that the police had built in front of city hall to cordon off reporters despite our objections that we should be able move about freely. Suddenly, the troopers without provocation prodded Dobynes and two other leaders with nightsticks, pushing them into the flailing clubs of the county sheriff's deputies. Protesters began screaming and running back into the church, but most remained stranded on the steps, where troopers beat, pushed, and shoved them. About one hundred protesters ran behind the church to a street lined by Mack's Café, a funeral parlor, and a physiotherapy clinic.

The troopers ran after them, beating them with nightsticks, and I could hear screaming and loud whacks ringing through the square. Some blacks retaliated by throwing bricks and bottles. I wanted to break free from our quarantined space, but the police held me back with threats and poised nightsticks. Standing near us was Clark, wearing sports clothes and carrying a nightstick. "Don't you have enough trouble of your own in Selma?" one reporter asked him.

"Things got a little too quiet for me over in Selma tonight and it made me nervous," he replied.

Some of the fleeing protesters took refuge at the commercial establishments, and the troopers followed, clubbing those huddled on the porches. I couldn't see from the corral, but I learned later what happened. Ten troopers, armed with shotguns, followed protesters into Mack's Café and began overturning tables and striking anyone they found, including Viola Jackson. When her twenty-six-year-old son, Jimmie Lee Jackson, lunged at a trooper to protect her, the trooper shot him in the stomach. The bullet entered Jackson's abdomen near his navel and came out the left side.

I saw people frantically running past our pen of reporters and photographers. A television cameraman turned a bright light on the crowd, and a gang of ten white men began harassing us. It was times like this when my southern appearance—sunburned neck, light-colored hair, and southern drawl—probably saved my life. I was standing next to Richard Valeriani, an NBC television reporter, when I noticed a middle-aged white man wearing a hat and tan overcoat behind us swinging a blue-painted wooden ax handle. He paced back and forth in obvious anger. I thought he was preparing to wield his club on the fleeing blacks, but instead the man suddenly delivered a mighty blow to Valeriani's head. Valeriani staggered and fell like a bag of potatoes, blood spewing from his pate. Perhaps the angry assailant recognized Valeriani from his television newscasts, but it was more likely that he focused on Valeriani rather than me because of his black, tightly curled hair, Italian facial features, and northern accent.

Other journalists and I rushed to Valeriani's side and screamed at the police to get him to a hospital. After receiving several stitches, he amazingly was working from his hospital bed with a portable typewriter and back on the beat in two days. It was not until the next day, when NBC executives raised a stink with local officials, that police arrested the perpetrator. Valeriani was not the only media victim of the mob that night. Other white toughs, some carrying guns in their belts, attacked two UPI photographers and destroyed their cameras by stomping on them. At least one trooper and several city police officers stood by and watched the smashing. I stood helplessly in the pen watching with despair.

The protesters who sought refuge in the church remained for another half hour, singing "We Shall Overcome." As they slowly left in small groups to return home, the troopers prodded them along the sidewalk with their clubs. By night's end, at least ten protesters were injured, and a state trooper suffered a head injury from a bottle thrown from the crowd. The police finally allowed us to leave the restricted confines, and I scrambled to find a pay phone to call in my story to New York. But at every turn, police moved me along so that only when I returned safely to Selma could I make my call. I went to bed that night and lay awake wondering how to muster enough resolve to return another day to scenes of brutality.

When daylight came, I reluctantly headed back to Marion. Hundreds of demonstrators were already in formation, facing two platoons of troopers with helmets and guns glittering in the sunlight. "This is an unlawful assembly," the Marion police chief announced. The protesters turned and went back inside the church. "We aren't interested in getting clubbed no more," said one protester, who was a bricklayer and president of a local civil rights organization.

Reactions to the protests were immediate and unapologetic. The Marion mayor explained that the protests the previous night had turned violent because marchers had gotten "outside leadership from Selma and they were determined to take over the town. Of course, we can't have that." Governor George Wallace, who had been unusually quiet about racial issues in recent months, said he regretted the outcome in Marion and ordered an investigation. But he blamed "career agitators" with "pro-communist affiliations" for the violence and banned all-night demonstrations in the state. In Washington, Nicholas Katzenbach, who had been appointed US attorney general only a week earlier, said the Justice Department would conduct a full investigation. King was in bed with a fever at his Atlanta home but said he would return shortly to resume the campaign in Selma and Marion.

The next day I went to Selma's Burwell Infirmary to visit Viola Jackson and Cager Lee Jackson, her eighty-two-year-old father and a retired farmer, whom state troopers had also attacked. Both father and daughter had lacerated scalps and bruises. Jimmie Lee Jackson remained in critical condition at another hospital across town. My lead that day read, "Three generations of one Negro family were in Selma hospitals today because of Thursday night's assault by state troopers on a crowd of demonstrators in the Marion Town Square."

Cager Lee, a small, stooped man, sat in a chair beside his daughter's bed. A bandage covered a knot on the back of his head. He was part of a group of blacks who had run to the churchyard when troopers dispersed the protesters. He described to me what happened. "The man with clubs come. . . . They hauled me off and hit me and knocked me to the street and kicked me. It was hard to take for an old man whose bones are dry like cane," he said. "One of them knew me. He say, 'Why that's Cager. What are you doing here, Cager?' and they let me up." Cager Lee Jackson, born in 1883, understood the significance of protest. He had tried unsuccessfully five times to register to vote. "The last time the voting referee asked questions so fast I couldn't understand them," he said. "I haven't heard from them yet."

Viola Jackson, who had five stitches in her head, said she and her seventeen-year-old daughter were in the café when troopers stormed in. "'If you don't live here, get out,'" she recounted their warning. "Two of them hit me on my head. They knocked me down and started beating me on the floor." Cager Lee then picked up the story of what happened next. He said he saw his grandson run out of the café with the troopers following and hitting him. Jimmie Lee ran past the church to the post office, where they clubbed him. "I walked by where he was lying and I heard him say, 'I've been shot,'" Cager Lee recalled. "I heard them say, 'You threw a bottle' and he said, 'I didn't throw no bottle.'" I left Cager Lee and his daughter sitting in the hospital room, each holding their head in their hands.

I did not learn until I returned to my hotel in Selma that night that Malcolm X, just thirty-nine years old, had been assassinated in Harlem while addressing members of his Organization of Afro-American Unity. The assassins were members of the Nation of Islam, a rival group that had also firebombed his home a week earlier. His wife and children, sitting in the front row of the Harlem gathering, ducked safely for cover, but they witnessed his killing.

The next day, King arrived in Selma and spoke to about seven hundred people crammed into Brown Chapel. His message was clear—the melee in Marion followed by Malcolm X's assassination underscored a greater need for nonviolence. Except for a few incidents of retaliation, the demonstrators' overall restraint had been remarkable. King reminded the audience that the passive approach was imperfect and the tolls were high. But change was coming, he said. The Selma campaign was forcing President Johnson to advance a Voting Rights Act, and Dallas County had processed about two thousand registration applications from black residents. That was not enough, King said, and he announced the next phase of demonstrations—a motorcade from Selma to Montgomery in the coming days to convene at the state capitol. "We will be going there to tell Governor Wallace we aren't going to take it anymore." He was impassioned, but calm and firm, as his audience cheered.

While he spoke, fifty state troopers and members of Clark's posse waited outside the courthouse with guns, nightsticks, and riot gear. And at the same time, former Mississippi governor Ross Barnett was stirring up a crowd with a speech at a White Citizens' Council meeting near Selma, accusing integrationists of trying to "diffuse our blood, confuse our minds, and degrade our character as a people." He railed on, saying, "The complete and happy removal of the Negro from our land would not change our attitude, nor would it change the hatred that these people have for us. We face absolute extinction of all we hold dear unless we are victorious."

Other reporters and I followed King as he and his assistants left Brown Chapel to a waiting car. A plainclothes state investigator approached King and asked why state agents had been run out of the church. "I didn't know they had," King said. "Our meetings are open to everyone." At that point, about twenty state troopers crowded around King's car, and the investigator asked him why he had been critical of state troopers. "That's another matter," King replied. "I intend to be critical of the state troopers and the state law." After a moment, the troopers dispersed and let his car pass.

We accompanied him to Good Samaritan Hospital for a five-minute visit with Jimmie Lee Jackson, who remained in critical condition. "He seems to be in good spirits," King said, emerging from Jackson's room. "I told him we were very concerned about him and he was very much in our prayers. I prayed with him." Jackson required twelve stitches in his head, and he was charged with assault and battery with intent to murder a patrolman. James Bonard Fowler, the trooper who had shot Jackson, was not indicted by a grand jury. Decades later, Fowler told an Alabama journalist that he was not a racist and had acted in self-defense. He was eventually indicted in 2007, pleaded guilty, and was sentenced to six months in jail. He died in 2015.

Tensions in Selma were reaching a boiling point. Some observers said it was a carryover from Marion and the growing number of protesters who fed the fury. Others claimed that Clark and his militant style were gaining support among white extremists. I noticed an increase in the number of hostile-looking white citizens gathering near the courthouse, and King said his life had been threatened. City leaders refused to negotiate with local black leaders unless outsiders left town, which was an unrealistic request because King was calling for bigger demonstrations, including the planned march to Montgomery.

CHAPTER 29

Bloody Sunday

EIGHT DAYS AFTER THE MARION PROTEST, ON FEBRUARY 26, 1965, JIMMIE
Lee Jackson died in Selma's Good Samaritan Hospital. His two funerals were
attended by more than four thousand people. The first was at Brown Chapel,
where Jackson's hollow-cheeked grandfather stood outside in a misting rain
beneath a banner proclaiming, "Racism Killed Our Brother." Inside, mourners
viewing Jackson in an open casket linked arms in a human chain of unity.

The second funeral was at the church in Marion where protesters had
gathered on that fateful night. Jackson—a woodcutter, father, Baptist deacon,
and Vietnam veteran—had joined the protests after several unsuccessful attempts to register to vote. King spoke at Jackson's funeral in Marion, leaving
few absolved of blame. He enumerated those responsible for Jackson's death,
including the federal government, which he said spent millions of dollars
daily on the Vietnam War rather than protect rights at home; politicians who
bred hatred and racism; white ministers who remained silent; officers who
permitted lawlessness; and cowardly blacks who stood on the sideline. As
always, he also offered purgation and inspiration. "We must not be bitter,"
King preached to the crowd. "We must not lose faith in our white brothers."
Then he led a procession of about one thousand people on foot and in cars
through a steady rain to Jackson's burial place on a lonesome hill beneath
long-needled pines.

Many people were beaten and arrested in the Selma-Marion campaign,
but Jackson was the first to die. It emboldened civil rights leaders to plan a
fifty-mile, four-day march to Montgomery on Sunday, March 7, to deliver
a petition to Wallace. The petition called for repeal of the poll tax, longer
periods for voter registration, appointment of blacks to state boards and

agencies, and impartial law enforcement. Black leaders clearly did not expect Wallace to meet all their demands, but the march would dramatize their call for national support.

In the days leading up the march, King traveled to Washington to pressure President Johnson to send the Voting Rights Act to Congress. His departure gave me an opportunity to go home for the weekend to see my family. One daughter was turning nine years old, and I wanted to be there for her birthday party. In two months, I had gone home only a few times because initially I was the only *New York Times* reporter covering Selma. But as the protests grew larger, Claude Sitton hired another young southerner named Roy Reed, who arrived in February to help me. By early March, more *Times* reporters arrived for intermittent stints in Selma and Montgomery, and the *Times* stationed reporters in New York, Washington, and Detroit to write about the national reactions to events in Alabama. I could finally afford to go home while others covered the first day of the march to Montgomery. I would be back in Alabama on Monday for the second day of the march. Like many others, I expected the first day to be not much different from that of scores of other marches. Organizers also believed that the first day was simply a drill in which marchers would face state troopers blocking their path, sustain mass arrests, and return to try another day.

In fact, King himself planned to not be present the first day so that he could preach at his home church in Atlanta. His travels had left his parishioners without their pastor, and he felt obliged to be with them when he could. I also heard rumors later that King had received death threats, and his associates were advising him against returning to Selma for a while. They discussed postponing the march until he could safely be there. But at least six hundred demonstrators, some whom had traveled from distant parts of the country, were prepared to march, and it seemed doubtful that the momentum could be stopped. They decided the march should proceed, but King told black leaders to limit the number of arrests. The goal of this demonstration was to eventually walk to Montgomery, not fill up jail cells.

What King and other the organizers did not know was that Wallace had worked out a plan with law enforcement officials in a meeting at his office to bypass arrests and show aggressive force. They had a three-pronged plan. The first line of defense was Lingo's state troopers, whose numbers had swelled from four hundred to six hundred. Their military gear was emblazoned with Confederate flags, and demonstrators dubbed them, in one of their kinder appellations, as "Wallace's storm troopers." The second group was composed of Clark's deputies and a volunteer posse of hundreds of men. One Selma citizen told me that many of the volunteers had been "looking for an excuse to knock some heads." The troopers wore crisp blue uniforms, while the posse men dressed in more casual khakis or dungarees. The third group was the city police under Wilson Baker's authority. The Selma mayor, a chief supporter of Wallace, instructed Baker to have his men join Clark's forces. But Baker threatened to resign rather than work with Clark, and some city council members intervened on Baker's behalf to reach an agreement that the city police would not assist Lingo or Clark.

I went to church with my family on Sunday morning, enjoyed a full afternoon meal, and took a nap. That evening, ABC news interrupted its regular broadcasting to show disturbing footage from Selma. Demonstrators had assembled in front of Brown Chapel, some wearing clothes from that morning's church service and others carrying bags packed for a long journey to Montgomery. John Lewis of SNCC and Reverend Hosea Williams, one of King's most trusted advisors and an SCLC leader, led the march, which was fitting because neither man was a big national name or celebrity. The Selma campaign had evolved more organically than campaigns in other cities, and these two men represented the grassroots efforts of many organizers. Both wore suits, ties, and canvas overcoats. Lewis, who had a knapsack strapped to his back, looked as if he were carrying the weight of the world on his shoulders. The procession left the church and walked a mile to the Edmund Pettus Bridge, which spanned the Alabama River and carried Highway 80 in the direction of Montgomery. The bridge was named for an Alabama Confederate brigadier general who became a US senator and a grand dragon of the KKK.

I could see on television that the bridge was closed, and the only space remaining for the demonstrators was a narrow sidewalk abutting the bridge railing. Because the bridge rose to a camelback hump, it was impossible to see from one side to the other. Only when the demonstrators reached the crest did they see their destiny: fifty troopers blocking all four lanes of Highway 80 with several dozen posse men, some on horseback, behind them. They were armed with tear gas, nightsticks, cattle prods, shotguns, pistols, carbines, and whips. Along the highway, a crowd of white spectators waved Confederate flags.

Lewis and Williams paused momentarily at the sight of the militia. Then they advanced to within fifty feet of the troopers and stopped again. Major John Cloud, the officer in charge, bellowed instructions through a bullhorn that the demonstrators should turn around. "May I have a word with the major?" Williams asked. The major refused. Williams asked again and received the same answer. "You have two minutes to turn around and go back to your church," the major commanded. There was no space for the demonstrators to turn around, and within seconds the major ordered, "Troops advance."

Williams and Lewis stood their ground, neither moving, while the troopers lowered their gas masks and walked toward them. Without pausing, they rushed upon Lewis and Williams with their nightsticks, and the demonstrators spilled over each other like falling dominoes. A wave of blue uniforms swelled over the marchers, batons whirling and cracking. The posse followed, galloping in on horseback while the white spectators egged them on. Lewis went down with a quick club to his head. He instinctively curled into a fetal position to ward off as much physical damage as possible. A trooper hit him again. Others ran and fell, hitting the pavement wounded and crying. Then, from the blue sea of troopers rose a mist of gray tear gas smoke.

I learned later from news dispatches that the demonstrators frantically ran back to the chapel, but not all of them could fit inside. Posse men and 150 troopers moved in to chase and beat those who remained on the street. "Get out of town," the posse men shouted. Some black men and boys retaliated, throwing bricks and bottles at the troopers. Ambulances, some staffed by medical volunteers from New York, ferried the wounded to the hospital and a small clinic. About ninety people were treated for injuries, including Lewis, who had a fractured skull and a concussion.

Before Lewis went to the hospital, though, he addressed the crowd at Brown Chapel. "I don't know how President Johnson can send troops to Vietnam. I don't see how he can send troops to the Congo. I don't see how he can send troops to Africa, and he can't send troops to Selma, Alabama," he said. "Next time we march, we may have to keep going when we get to Montgomery. We may have to go on to Washington."

Like many Americans, President Johnson watched the carnage on television. The unprovoked assault struck a chord in the nation like none of the previous clashes, perhaps because of the large number of casualties, the unprovoked aggression on subdued demonstrators, the presence of white protesters, or the number of national clergy who were present. The day was tagged "Bloody Sunday." King wrote later that if he had known the outcome of the march, he would have forsaken his church duties to be there. The Justice Department announced it would investigate whether law enforcement used unnecessary force. King called for another march on Tuesday and sought a protective federal court order, which the Justice Department supported.

I rushed to Selma on Monday. King also arrived that day to begin negotiations with local and federal officials before Tuesday's march. A federal district court judge refused to grant the protective order without first holding a hearing scheduled for Thursday morning, and he also issued a temporary injunction banning more marches until after the hearing. President Johnson told King to abide by the ban and refused King's request for federal protection.

King and other black leaders stayed up most of the night agonizing over what to do. "I believe we have a constitutional right to march whenever we get ready, injunction or no injunction," Lewis said. King conferred by phone until 5:00 a.m. with Attorney General Katzenbach and LeRoy Collins, the head of the Federal Community Relations Service, a new office created by the Civil Rights Act to be a peacemaker in racial conflicts. The men told King they had spoken with the federal judge, and he was likely on Thursday to grant them permission for a march, so they urged King to wait. But 1,500 ministers, nuns, and other sympathizers from all over the country were ready to march.

King decided the march would go on as planned. "All morning I had been agonizing. I made my choice," he said. "I have decided it is better to die on the highway than to make a butchery of my conscience.... We've gone too far to turn back now. We must let them know that nothing can stop us—not even death itself. We must be ready for a season of suffering."

CHAPTER 30

A Second Attempt

BY MIDMORNING TUESDAY, LEROY COLLINS HAD ARRIVED IN SELMA aboard an air force jet from Washington. The gray-haired former governor of Florida was a moderate on racial issues and had been appointed by President Johnson after he had promoted integration in his home state. Collins met first with John Doar, US assistant attorney general for civil rights, who had been in Selma since Sunday. Doar, who had escorted James Meredith to enroll at the University of Mississippi and quelled violent crowds after Medgar Evers's death, was never pushy or ostentatious about his important position at the Justice Department. After meeting with Doar, Collins went to the home of a local black dentist where King was staying and found King still in his pajamas. Collins again asked King to call off the march, but he refused.

That afternoon, King clasped arms with other leaders at the front of a mile-long line headed toward the Edmund Pettus Bridge. Behind them, all sorts of different people—including young blond beatniks, wives of congressmen, and dignitaries—braced themselves for the worst. But they were boisterous and animated, carrying signs that read "Police intimidation enslaves us all" and "Silence is no longer golden." I followed alongside the procession.

Law enforcement presence was more subdued than on Bloody Sunday. Four hundred state troopers were based at the armory on the edge of town until shortly before the march. Once it began, troopers wearing helmets lined the streets, but no posse men were present. Clark, who was wearing a brown suit and olive-colored felt hat rather than his traditional uniform, kept his deputies in the background. There were no horses, tear gas, or gas masks.

As King and about 1,500 marchers approached the bridge, a US marshal stepped in front of them and read the judge's order barring the march. King told him they wanted to proceed, and the marshal stepped out of the way. At the crest of the bridge, they saw a battery of troopers blocking the highway but advanced to within a hundred feet of them. It looked as if King were leading his soldiers into a trap. Major Cloud used his megaphone to inform the marchers they were forbidden to continue. King told Cloud they wanted to march to Montgomery to give the governor their petition, and then moved forward another fifty feet. Cloud repeated his orders, and the troopers stood firm with poised nightsticks as the marchers kneeled to pray and sang, "We Shall Overcome."

Suddenly, Cloud ordered the troopers to move aside and open the highway. None of the marchers moved until King suddenly turned and led them back to the church. They were confused and some were even angry, but they followed him. At a news conference at the church, King explained what happened. He said he had told Collins during his visit that the march would go on as planned, but he agreed to turn back when ordered by state police because civil rights lawyers had advised King that by doing so he would probably not be violating the injunction. He could also buy time until Thursday's hearing with the hope of getting federal protection. Collins had then taken this plan to Lingo and Clark, who also agreed. Although Wallace denied that any deal had been made, he ordered Clark's posse disbanded, and Baker was put in charge of the city streets.

A source who witnessed the meeting between Collins, Lingo, and Clark told me, "Colonel Lingo said the state did not want violence, and there would be none if the marchers turned back at the designated point." Collins would not comment on the meeting but said, "The president is extremely anxious to avoid a clash of the nature of that which occurred the other day. . . . I think good people on both sides were anxious to avoid violence." The arrangement was face saving for all sides.

Only a handful of leaders knew about the agreement and the limited danger when they led the mass of marchers to the Edmund Pettus Bridge. "We agreed that we would not break through the lines," King said. "In all frankness, we knew we would not get to Montgomery. We knew we would not get past the troopers." The day became known as "Turnaround Tuesday," and King set his sights on another march.

Selma was getting exactly the kind of traction King wanted. "We had the greatest demonstration for freedom today than we've ever had in the South," he said. The brutality witnessed by the nation on Bloody Sunday resulted in demonstrations in more than eighty cities. More than ten thousand people demonstrated in Detroit, thousands congregated in front of the White House, and others staged a sit-in outside Katzenbach's Washington office. The federal government sent twenty FBI agents and half a dozen Justice Department lawyers to Selma, and sixty members of Congress called on President Johnson to send them a voting rights bill.

Some said Bloody Sunday had as much as or more impact than the Birmingham church bombing or the Philadelphia murders. Thousands more religious, medical, and civil rights representatives, many of them white, arrived in Selma by buses, cars, and planes. They included the dean of the Yale Divinity School, four hundred out-of-town white ministers from every denomination, and fifty white Alabama residents. One day I saw a group of white nuns from Chicago, dressed in habits, pressed against the police as they attempted to control the crowds. One sister, her lips pursed in a prayerful smile, was squeezed belly to belly against a hefty deputy sheriff. Another day, I felt a tug on my sleeve. "John Herbers! What are you doing here?" When I turned around, I was surprised to see a white minister from the church I had attended when I lived in Washington.

"I'm working," I replied. "What are you doing here?"

"What does it look like?" he said. "I'm also working. I'm here to demonstrate."

Another clergy member who arrived was Reverend James J. Reeb, a thirty-eight-year-old white Unitarian minister from Boston. He was the son of a wealthy oil-well distributor in Wyoming and earned degrees at St. Olaf College in Minnesota and Princeton Theological Seminary. Reeb moved to Boston with his wife and four children to oversee a low-income housing program in a troubled black neighborhood. When he watched the beatings on television, he felt compelled to come to Selma. His wife pleaded with him not to go, but he said white clergy could bolster the cause. It was his first trip to the Deep South.

After the peaceful trek to the Edmund Pettus Bridge, Reeb and two other white ministers left a local café after a fried chicken dinner and quickly got lost in a poor white neighborhood. As they walked through the dark streets, five white men wearing sports clothes and carrying clubs yelled at them. The ministers stepped up their pace but were overcome by the jeering men, who began beating them. One of the ministers curled in a ball to protect himself as he had been taught by the civil rights organizers. But the attackers clubbed

Reeb on the back of his head and fled. The two ministers took Reeb to a local hospital, where he fell unconscious. His injury was so severe that doctors sent him to a Birmingham hospital one hundred miles away.

On the way to Birmingham, Reeb's ambulance blew a tire, but Reeb finally arrived in time for surgeons to remove a large blood clot on the left side of his head. He had multiple skull fractures and was in critical condition. Once news spread about the attack, organizers quickly assembled at Brown Chapel to hear King give a passionate speech condemning the beatings. "Selma had to show its true colors," he said. "It was cowardly work done by night." Ralph Abernathy announced that there would be more marches the next day to the courthouse despite a new city-issued ban.

As promised, the protesters assembled again the next day, and I watched as the city girded itself against a series of attempts to reach the courthouse. Selma mayor Joseph T. Smitherman, a slender thirty-five-year-old business-man serving his first term in office, appeared outside the church to make an appeal. "We have had eight weeks of continued demonstrations," he said. "We have tried to maintain the peace. We have called on civil rights leaders not to march today." His plea fell on deaf ears.

Six smiling nuns from St. Louis led a procession of five hundred protesters only to meet Clark a half block away from Brown Chapel. He was wearing a white riot helmet and a lapel button on his business suit that read, "Never." He was joined by Smitherman, Baker, one hundred state troopers, and a line of city policemen. Crowds of white spectators watched from their front porches. "You have had opportunity after opportunity to go to the court-house," Smitherman told them. "It has got to the point where we are not going to have any more demonstrations." Reverend L. L. Anderson, a black leader, said that some of the demonstrators wished to address the authorities. Sister Mary Antona Ebo, a black nun, was the first to speak. "I feel privileged to come to Selma," she said. "I feel that every citizen has a right to vote." She was followed by Sister Earnest Maria, a white nun, and a succession of ministers from Yale, Harvard, and Princeton. Thirty of them spoke for more than an hour, lecturing the authorities on the mistreatment of blacks in Alabama. But Smitherman did not stay to hear them. He returned to his office and left Baker in charge. The nuns prayed and then marched back to the chapel.

Five minutes later, two hundred children and teenagers tried to march from another nearby church. Baker hurried to the scene in his white Chrysler. Troopers arrived and gently nudged the youths with nightsticks. Ministers from the first march arrived and urged the youths to return to the church, which they did after a few tense moments.

Meanwhile, three white men were arrested for assault in the attack on Reeb and a fourth surrendered the next day. The men, ranging in age from thirty to forty-one, all worked at a local used car lot. They were released on bonds of $7,500 each but were immediately rearrested by the FBI on federal charges of conspiring to violate Reeb's constitutional rights. The men were again released on lesser bonds. Reeb's condition was worsening—twice, his heart stopped—and his wife arrived from Boston to be at his bedside.

As darkness approached, more demonstrators attempted a third march from Brown Chapel. King, who stayed in seclusion in the rear of the church, knew that night marches were more dangerous than at other times, but he gave his blessing. Then he left for Montgomery to prepare for the court hearing the next morning. Abernathy led three hundred youths and adults out of the chapel only to meet Baker and state troopers half a block away. When ordered to stop, the demonstrators opened sleeping bags and inflated air mattresses to stage a "sleep-in." "We're going to stay here all night until the state troopers move aside and let us through," Abernathy said. They settled in for the night. The police strung a rope across the street, which the demonstrators called "the Berlin Wall." On one side of the rope, demonstrators slept soundly. On the other side, scores of sleepy-eyed troopers, city police, and state conservation agents kept guard in patrol cars. Baker sat in his Chrysler all night.

"My main objective at all times has been the safety of citizens and visitors to Selma," he told me. "[T]here are many ministers here from all states. These white ministers have been most unreasonable. They have stated they feel someone else must die in Selma to bring this movement to its climax. I do not ever want to be in the position of prejudging anyone, nor do I feel a minister of God should come in and prejudge us. I call on them to show that they are men of God and want peace."

There was a brief flurry of excitement when fourteen troopers searched the church for a reported bomb. When they emerged finding nothing, the sleep-in demonstrators sang, "We love everybody . . . We love George Wallace." One of the troopers snapped his fingers in rhythm with the music. It was the first relaxed moment during a long day of confrontations. Tensions were also eased by emissaries recruited by Collins's Federal Community

Relations Service. One of those was a South Carolina newspaper publisher who talked with Clark one minute and with a SNCC leader the next. Collins had also met with eight white business leaders and members of the city council. "These men are very interested in finding ways to solve the problem," he had told reporters during a press conference. "I have been informed, too, that state business leaders are interested in establishing better race relations." That was a statement not heard often in Alabama.

I went back to the hotel to get a few hours of sleep and woke the next morning to a light rain. I rushed back to the sleep-in, where demonstrators lay under sheets of transparent plastic and tents. They stayed all day and sang, "The Berlin Wall, the Berlin Wall, the wall will come crumbling down." At the end of the day, Baker, unshaven and bleary eyed, shouted, "Take the tents away. You can't have tents in the streets—fire regulation." The demonstrators removed the tents, set them up on a grassy median, and stood in the rain singing, "We Shall Not Be Moved." Five nuns arrived from Chicago and joined the sleep-in. One of them, Sister Mary Peter, told me, "We came because a lot of religious leaders from the North were having to return and we didn't want to leave these people to the mercy of the troopers."

That night, Baker stepped out of his automobile and announced, "Reverend Reeb has died in the hospital in Birmingham." A silence fell over the crowd. There was disbelief and consternation. This was the second casualty in the Selma campaign. John Lewis, looking forlorn, told the demonstrators, "We will hold one minute of silent prayer for our fallen brother."

On hearing the news, King said that Reeb "now joins the ranks of those martyred heroes who have died in the struggle for freedom and human dignity." Both King and Baker had been bracing for the possibility of Reeb dying. When Baker had received word earlier that Reeb's death was imminent, he asked one of King's assistants, "Can you control your people when it happens?"

"We can control ours," the assistant replied. "The question is: Can you control yours?"

It was a valid question. Baker had beefed up his police force, and it recently stopped and questioned three carloads of armed men, some from as far away as St. Augustine. "The scum is starting to come in here from all over," he told me. The four men involved in Reeb's beating were arrested a third time, this time on murder charges, and released on bonds of $25,000 each.

Months later, an all-white jury acquitted all of them. Almost half a century later, the Justice Department reopened the case, but most of the witnesses had died, and by 2016 all four men were dead as well.

The day after Reeb's death, the mayor arrived at the sleep-in wearing a large overcoat. He was frustrated and disturbed. "I have lost patience with agitators. No marches or demonstrations will be permitted in Selma as long as the present threat of violence to our citizens exists," he told the crowd huddled under umbrellas and plastic. "If you want to hold a memorial service, you are free to go back to the church, which would seem to be more appropriate." Demonstrators had been in the streets for almost forty-eight hours and vowed to remain until they could march to the courthouse. Black teenagers and white ministers took turns moving from the street, which was muddy and littered with soggy debris, to sleeping on pews in the church.

Then Baker visited the outdoor sleep-in. His face was flushed as he sprang from his car, took out a pocket knife, and cut the single strand of rope that he had stretched across the street. Two hundred surprised demonstrators broke into cheers and chanted, "Freedom, we've got freedom." But the exultation was short. The weary Baker had simply eliminated a token, not a barrier. "You are not going to march," he said. The demonstrators cut the dangling rope into small pieces for souvenirs and created new lyrics to the tune of "The Battle of Jericho":

The invisible wall
Is a Berlin wall
In Selma, Alabama

The troopers' cars
Are a Berlin wall
In Selma, Alabama

Baker angrily told reporters, "I put it up on my own and I cut it on my own. I put it up there for their [the demonstrators'] benefit to prevent any unnecessary confrontations, but it got to be a symbol of some kind."

CHAPTER 31

What Killed James Reeb?

SIX DAYS AFTER BLOODY SUNDAY, TENSIONS CONTINUED TO FLARE AS more newcomers—mainly white—joined the demonstrations. Seventy nuns, priests, and laypersons from the Catholic Interracial Council of Chicago arrived by plane, joined by sixty Unitarian ministers from their denomination's Department of Social Responsibility. The streets of Selma were filled with thousands of demonstrators when President Johnson held a thirty-minute televised press conference from the White House to address the crisis. Someone in a nearby apartment building turned up a radio so that demonstrators could hear Johnson's hearty endorsement of their goals. "It is wrong to do violence to peaceful citizens in the streets of their town. It is wrong to deny Americans the right to vote," he said. "The events of last Sunday cannot and will not be repeated, but the demonstrations in Selma have a much larger meaning. They are a protest against a deep and very unjust flaw in American democracy itself." Johnson said the answer was "not in armed confrontation but in the process of law," which he planned to correct by introducing a Voting Rights Act to enforce the Constitution's Fifteenth Amendment requiring that no Americans be denied the right to vote based on race or color.

The president's words incited an hour-long face-off between law enforcement and demonstrators, including some neatly frocked and determined nuns. Reverend John J. Cavanaugh, a former president of the University of Notre Dame, found himself chest-to-chest with Baker during the shouting and shoving. I pushed my way closer to hear as Cavanaugh and other ministers engaged Baker in a theological argument about the movement.

"I am amazed at ministers of God committing violence like this," Baker told Cavanaugh.

"I have never committed violence in my life," Cavanaugh shot back. He was a small bespectacled man and at least a head shorter than Baker.

When another Catholic priest called for eliminating barriers for black voters, Baker responded, "I too stand for morality. The place to redress grievances is in the halls of Congress, not out here pushing and shoving." Some demonstrators became restless and moved along the police line in search of openings. Crowds of white citizens gathered behind the police and shouted insults at the demonstrators. Baker held up his hand and shouted, "Hold it."

"We're tired of holding it," one demonstrator yelled back.

"Yes, the president has stated today that we are in our legal rights," shouted another.

"The president has issued no such orders to me," Baker said. "If he'll write me a note, I shall so honor it."

"Does he have to write you a private letter?" a demonstrator asked. The dialogue distracted Baker long enough for a small band to break from the crowd, and Baker and his men ran after them. I ran behind the police and heard Baker plead with the demonstrators. "I ask you to stop—please stop."

"Why?" a protester asked.

"Because I cannot guarantee your safety," he said. "I've been saying that all day."

"But maybe the federal troops will guarantee our safety," another demonstrator said. "Mr. Baker, why don't you have your troops protect us, instead of just saying you can't guarantee our safety?"

Any answer Baker might have offered was interrupted when state troopers came forth with nightsticks. I tried to stay clear of the crush. One band of disruptive demonstrators broke through the police line but got no farther than the other side of the street when troopers shoved them back. Black leaders moved in to discourage demonstrators from breaking the police line. "We must not hold any hatred for these men," said Reverend C. T. Vivian. "It is the system we are fighting, not them." But he could not control them all. Twenty demonstrators broke the blockade and reached the courthouse, where they met Clark's posse, who in turn shoved demonstrators away from the entrance with nightsticks. The demonstrators retreated but faced a gang of white men, who shouted curses and threats. Within minutes, Baker arrived with one of his assistants. "Go on. Get out of here," Baker yelled at the white gang. "We've had enough trouble in Selma." The gang dispersed and Baker walked the demonstrators back to the church. By nightfall, demonstrators bedded down for a fourth night of a sleep-in. They dubbed the site "the thirty-eighth parallel," referring to the latitude dividing North and South Korea.

The next morning, city officials continued to debate over what to do next, but they agreed that new tactics were needed. The Selma campaign was in its ninth week, and people were still arriving to join the demonstrations and attend Reeb's memorial service. Smitherman and Clark issued a joint statement saying they would make mass arrests rather than use force. Baker replaced his rope with a flimsy wooden barricade and joked, "I wanted to give them something to sing about."

He also announced that demonstrators would be allowed to go to the courthouse in small numbers. Smitherman said the city football stadium, with 7,500 seats, was available for Reeb's service if Brown Chapel was too small. The service was ultimately, and more fittingly, held at the chapel on the afternoon of Monday, March 15. The attending dignitaries included an impressive yet disparate array of congressmen, high-ranking leaders of national and international religious denominations, government officials, and even the president and representatives of the United Automobile Workers labor union. Some showed up eager to claim association with the movement without having soldiered on the front lines in the previous weeks.

King's eulogy unified the thousands in attendance. After praising Reeb's "sensitive religious spirit" and martyrdom, King challenged the crowd by asking, "Who killed James Reeb?" He said the answer was "misguided men who have the strange notion that you express dissent through murder." But, King said, the more penetrating question was, "What killed James Reeb?" His answer here included many of the same reasons he had named at Jimmie Lee Jackson's funeral, including a disconnected church, irresponsible elected officials, a brutal system of law enforcement, a timid federal government, and indifferent black citizens. But he warned against despair and bitterness of the heart. "We must work passionately, unrelentingly, to make the American dream a reality, so he did not die in vain," King said.

One speaker announced that the final portion of the service would be held at the courthouse because a federal judge, with Collins's urging, had issued a special clearance. A cheer went up, and people poured from the chapel to form a three-person-wide line as prescribed by the judge's order. King took the front row, flanked by a Greek Orthodox priest wearing a traditional black robe and *kalimavkion*, Andrew Young dressed in dungaree jeans and a work jacket, and Ralph Abernathy in a suit and tie. King carried a giant wreath of palm leaves, white daisies, and pink roses. At least two thousand people followed behind them.

Clark met them at the courthouse, and I saw him break his steadfast vow. He allowed the demonstrators to approach the courthouse, which he deemed "a temple of justice," and took no swift action against anyone lacking proper reverence for the building. King laid the wreath at the door of the sheriff's office. "We are here to affirm our commitment that racial segregation is evil and the nation will never rise to its maturity until we get rid of it," he said. "This witness will help transform dark yesterdays into bright tomorrows." The media swarmed around him, clicking pictures to capture the moment.

That evening, President Johnson appeared before a televised joint session of Congress to urge adoption of his Voting Rights Act. Seventy million Americans watched and listened as the president stressed the gravity and urgency of the movement. "At times history and fate meet in a single time in a single place to shape a turning point in man's unending search for freedom," he said in his forty-five-minute speech. "So it was at Lexington and Concord. So it was a century ago at Appomattox. So it was last week in Selma, Alabama." He said universal suffrage was not an issue of constitutional, moral, or states' rights. "There is only the struggle for human rights," he said. He ended with a grand gesture by reciting the name of the movement's key anthem, "We Shall Overcome."

The next morning, Clark arrived at the chapel wearing a suit and his "Never" lapel button to face another march to the courthouse. He said the judge's order allowed the march, but because Baker was at the barbershop getting a haircut, it would begin that afternoon. By then, storm clouds had spawned tornados in northern Alabama that brought wind, rain, and lightning. Hail the size of marbles bounced off the heads of six hundred demonstrators. Clark was nowhere around, but Baker and his police force met the marchers at the courthouse. Baker was pleased when, shortly after, they returned peacefully to the chapel. But thirty-six white adults, including two women and mostly ministers, bolted from the chapel to picket in front of Smitherman's home. Baker, who felt the marchers were violating an agreement, arrested them for picketing in a residential neighborhood.

"This is stupid," I heard Baker shout at Harry Boyte, a white SCLC staff member. "You told me if you went to the courthouse there would be no

further demonstrations today. You ought to call your organization the Southern Stupid Leadership Conference."

"Wilson, I forgive you," said Boyte, a quiet man with a white mustache.

"Harry, I don't forgive you," Baker shot back. "Christianity has reached a
new low."

As Smitherman's children and neighbors looked on, the demonstrators
were herded into a yellow school bus and driven to the city jail, where twenty-
one of them refused to sign a $200 appearance bond so they could stage a
sit-in on the second floor of the courtroom. Back at Brown Chapel, Reverend
Hosea Williams announced to a cheering crowd that the long-awaited march
to Montgomery would begin in five days under protection of a federal court
order.

CHAPTER 32

A Climactic End

WHILE PREPARATIONS FOR THE MARCH WERE UNDERWAY, I HURRIED home to Atlanta, eager to see my family after spending so many weeks in Selma. The *New York Times* had assigned numerous good reporters to Selma and Montgomery, so I felt no pressure to be there. I had written about so many marches by this time and was glad to be relieved by eager new correspondents.

It was a brilliantly sunny, cold day that warmed to the mid-forties by the time thousands of people gathered at Brown Chapel to hear King deliver his pre-march sermon. He praised President Johnson for his support and encouraged the marchers to keep hope in the midst of despair. I went to church in Atlanta that morning, looking for my own spiritual inspiration, and followed events of the march through television and newspaper reports.

I read in the paper that King left Brown Chapel joined by national religious leaders, a United Nations representative, Jimmie Lee Jackson's grandfather, John Lewis, and other organizers. Behind them were 3,200 marchers. President Johnson sent 1,800 federal troops to protect them and posted another 2,000 officers on standby. Two trooper cars escorted the procession across the Edmund Pettus Bridge. In the lead car sat Major John Cloud, who had turned back the marchers on two previous occasions.

Marchers walked seven miles the first day, and although some protesters held signs reading "Too bad Reeb," the atmosphere was festive and peaceful. Ralph Abernathy joked, "When we get to Montgomery, we are going to go up to Governor Wallace's door and say, 'George, it's all over now. We've got the ballot.'" The court had ordered a limited number of marchers, so when the highway narrowed to two lanes, all but three hundred marchers returned to Selma by bus and train. For days, the marchers walked through barren farmland toward Montgomery, sleeping under big-top tents along the way. Churches provided meals, President Johnson erected a seventy-five-bed medical station, and some people who lived along the route opened their homes.

By the fifth day, the marchers reached the state capitol in Montgomery, where they were joined by an estimated twenty-five thousand people from across the nation. State and Confederate flags waved from the pristine, whitewashed capitol dome. A delegation of eighteen black and two white Alabamans tried unsuccessfully to deliver their petition to Wallace. They found his office closed with a message that he would meet them at a future time. The delegation said it was undeterred and would return the next day. They said a wait after a fifty-mile trek was minor compared to three centuries of "suffering and hardship" to proclaim freedom.

King spoke to the masses, saying, "No wave of racism can stop us now." Wallace peeked through the venetian blinds of his office window and heard the crowd cheer when King proclaimed, "The confrontation of good and evil compressed in the tiny community of Selma generated the massive power that turned the whole nation to a new course." The Selma campaign had reached a climactic end, but King urged the crowds to move forward without defeat or humiliation of the white community.

At the end of the day, organizers shuttled people back to Selma. One volunteer driver, Viola Gregg Liuzzo, a thirty-nine-year-old white mother of five children from Detroit, was halfway between Selma and Montgomery when she stopped for a seventeen-year-old black hitchhiker. As he rode with her in the front seat of her 1963 sedan, a carload of men drove by and shot Liuzzo in the head with a high-powered rifle, sending her car careening off the road. She was killed, but the hitchhiker survived. The murder shattered an otherwise peaceful day. President Johnson appeared on national television to condemn Liuzzo's death and announce that four Alabama Klansmen had been arrested for the murder. He said the Klan used "the rope and the gun and the tar and the feathers" to terrorize people.

"He's a damn liar," KKK imperial wizard Robert Shelton countered on a New York radio broadcast. "This organization has never used tar and feathers and a rope. I think he's got it reversed. He's got the shoe on the other foot." Shelton was the KKK leader I had spent time with years before, so I called him in his office in Tuscaloosa for an interview. He refrained from saying more about the president but talked a lot about the shooting and the march. "If this woman was at home with the children where she belonged, she would not have been in jeopardy," he said. He would not say whether he knew the defendants but said other arrests of his members were part of a larger plan of intimidation by the federal government. He also said the march was "an assembly of degenerates, nuts, and beatniks."

I returned to Selma the next day to write about how Wallace finally met with the march organizers to receive their petition. He promised to give it careful consideration. I was not sad that this would be my final trip to Selma. I wanted time to write more reflective and interpretive articles explaining the evolution and ramifications of the movement. I also needed time to figure out my next role as a reporter. Selma was the summit, and the movement and news coverage would now migrate far beyond Alabama and the South.

One narrative was what blacks and the nation might expect with the anticipated passage of the Voting Rights Act, which Johnson called "radical surgery." While systemic barriers to racial justice could not be erased with a single piece of legislation, the bill's historic significance and the gains made in the early 1960s were far-reaching. Between 1960 and 1964, almost one million blacks were added to the voting rolls, but the Southern Regional Council estimated that about three million blacks were still not registered. The bill was not a panacea, but it called for banning literacy tests, providing federal oversight in places where less than half the nonwhite voting population was unregistered, and allowing the US attorney general to investigate poll taxes in state and local elections. For the first time since Reconstruction, blacks might gain a small voice in government institutions, even the Mississippi legislature. The bill undoubtedly gave both Republicans and Democrats an incentive to court the black vote on the national and local level.

Mass migrations of blacks to the North, however, had left the South with blacks constituting just 23 percent of the voting population. There were some communities where blacks predominated—like Lowndes County, Alabama, with three thousand whites and twelve thousand blacks—but whites still had firm and unchallenged economic control, and blacks remained in the minority in almost every city and state.

In some cases, federal efforts had produced tangible results without legislation. Macon County, Alabama, had been a stronghold of the planter elite that refused to tolerate black participation in government. But it had sturdy black organizations centered around the Tuskegee Institute and a veterans' hospital where black professionals worked. Rather than stage disruptive street demonstrations, people in these organizations joined with the US Justice Department to sue the state to provide adequate means for blacks to register. Their legal efforts were successful, and five moderate candidates—three whites and two blacks—were elected to the Tuskegee city council by defeating their white supremacist opponents. One of the council's first acts was to pave and light streets in black neighborhoods, and the city hired several blacks for jobs formerly reserved for whites.

Another narrative was the movement's drastic change since its inception. Black professionals and local black citizens had finally heeded King's call and joined in large numbers. But more striking had been the arrival of whites from around the nation, mostly middle class, including members of the clergy and general sympathizers. Whites brought national influence and attention, and without them the movement may never have evolved from a regional black protest. The white presence also tamped down some of the violence. While the police disliked all outsiders, they nevertheless treated white middle-class protesters with more deference than blacks. "Remember one thing," a SNCC leader had told me. "They aren't about to beat up white people. What do you think will happen to the Negroes when the white folks leave?" One of King's assistants told a group of blacks who wanted faster results from the marches, "As much as I dislike middle-class whites, we need their help." King welcomed outside help, no matter what color. But the movement took on a different tone with whites' arrival. The southern novelist Walker Percy wrote later that the civil rights movement had been especially successful for whites, who were freed from their obsession with race and realized that the world would not end when blacks were treated more equally.

The movement always gained renewed vigor when celebrities showed up. Baseball legend Jackie Robinson and the singing trio of Peter, Paul, and Mary attended rallies and marches. Activist and writer Dick Gregory and seven people accompanying him were arrested at a Holiday Inn in Selma for disorderly conduct after they were refused rooms. The white evangelical preacher Dr. Billy Graham called for a spiritual and racial awakening at an Easter service in Birmingham that drew an integrated crowd of thirty-five thousand people. The stars of the popular television Western *Bonanza* canceled an appearance at the Jackson fairgrounds after a student at the mostly black Tougaloo College wrote to the cast members alerting them that the audience would be segregated. The college, first founded for freed slaves, had a white president, and about half its faculty was white. The college admitted its first white student in 1961, and by 1964 there were nine white students. The mayor of Jackson, incensed over the student's action and the cancellation, retaliated by calling on thousands of Mississippians to boycott the show, saying although he enjoyed *Bonanza*, it would never again be watched in his home. The state legislature also introduced a bill to revoke the college's accreditation. A Tougaloo faculty member and his family were threatened on their way to church by a group of men, one wearing a stocking pulled over his face and wielding a pipe.

Over time, the movement saw institutional changes as well. The rift between black leaders widened, not just over waning adherence to nonviolence but also due to power struggles. The money and influence that accompanied the swelling presence of whites and celebrities in the movement fueled a growing antagonism among black leaders. Some of this was rooted in the basic structural differences of various organizations. For instance, the SCLC was organized vertically under King, followed by his assistants. Their detractors claimed that King moved into a city, conducted demonstrations, and then departed with King's image bolstered but without signs of significant progress. "No one ever quite knows what the SCLC and Dr. King are going to do next," a member of a rival civil rights organization told me. "They are a bunch of preachers, all heart and no business acumen." But the SCLC had strong financial support from the North, and King's growing prestige and power added to the organization's coffers. The group maintained a strong religious orientation and consisted mostly of ministers, seasoned professionals, and middle-class blacks.

SNCC, on the other hand, was loosely organized and drew much of its support from college campuses. It had no single high-profile leader and worked primarily with poor blacks and youths. Many of its field workers were white, but they dressed down and made no attempt to emulate middle-class values. Despite the two groups' differences, they had worked well together up through the early days of the Selma campaign.

Over time, however, the connective tissue began to fray. SNCC leaders were angry that King had secretly maneuvered the turnabout on the Edmund Pettus Bridge and believed he should have tested the troopers' mettle rather than retreat. Some SNCC leaders also felt they had built the foundation in Selma during the previous years only to have the SCLC and King, with his commanding international presence, snatch the credit. Some SNCC leaders wanted more militant demonstrations. SCLC leaders called that idea "irresponsible in terms of nonviolence" and criticized SNCC demonstrations for having a "foolish kind of radicalism" that lacked the capacity for reconciliation. In the last days of Selma, SNCC leaders, who had always shared information with me, began cutting me off without seeming to care what I wrote about them or that continued media coverage might facilitate the fulfillment of their goals. King and other SCLC leaders constantly reminded demonstrators that the nonviolent approach, although frustratingly slow, was effective. Reverend James Bevel, an SCLC leader who wore denims, a white shirt, a tie, and a skullcap on his shaved head, pointed to the thousands of people arrested in Selma as evidence of impact. "We are testifying. Remember that," Bevel said. "Some people have a hard time understanding nonviolence. They try to spread the teachings of Jesus by using Caesar's methods."

Thomas Merton, an American activist and a Catholic writer, said about the movement at the time, "It is . . . possible that as the movement gains in power, the reasonableness and the Christian fervor . . . will recede into the background and the movement will become more and more an unreasoning and intransigent mass movement dedicated to the conquest of sheer power, more and more inclined to violence."

After Selma, leaders faced dilemmas about the future of the movement. "It is time to start thinking about where the movement is going when we are through in the Alabama Black Belt," Bevel said. "We will go to Harlem and do something about housing and income. Then we will go to South Africa and start a movement there. After that we want to find a way to use nonviolence instead of war and armaments in international relations."

The plans were ambitious but reflected King's own thinking. After hearing Bevel's comments, I tracked down Andrew Young of the SCLC, who confirmed that leaders were planning a campaign in a northern city for the upcoming summer and considering expanding to South Africa. Work in America's South, however, would not be abandoned, he said, and local affiliates of black organizations would lead voter education campaigns. Young warned, however, that all plans were subject to change. He pointed to the Selma campaign as an example. When it began, some leaders were predicting that street demonstrations were a thing of the past because more southern cities were adjusting to them. "In the past, the movement has been sustained more or less by violence," he told me. "But when you get a cordial welcome from the sheriff, it may be time to spend more time on organizing and educating than marching." The reception in Selma, of course, had made street demonstrations imperative, and the tired little town hosted a victory for the movement.

Yet, now that Selma was over, attention was shifting to a national stage. King appeared in cities all over America, and thousands of people staged protests from Bangor, Maine, to Honolulu, Hawaii. In Harlem, fifteen thousand people marched and held a rally to protest racial strife. "You can expect us in Baltimore, Philadelphia, Detroit, Los Angeles, and Chicago," King declared at a fund-raising rally in Baltimore. "We will have to work out the structure and the format, but I can tell you we will take the nonviolent movement all over the United States."

CHAPTER 33

Still Standing

FIFTY YEARS AFTER SELMA, ONE OF MY DAUGHTERS ARRANGED A RE-
union with John Lewis at an assisted living facility where I lived in Washington, DC. We had not seen each other in years, but he still appeared young. I
was ninety years old; he was only seventy-four.

The two of us had trodden varied paths since Selma. Despite enduring
more than forty arrests and physical attacks during the civil rights era,
Lewis had remained faithfully devoted to the philosophy of nonviolence.
The impact of this strategy cannot be overstated. President Johnson signed
the Voting Rights Act within months after the march on Montgomery, and
the Justice Department immediately eliminated literacy tests in seven states
so that blacks could quickly register to vote in large numbers. Blacks were
given greater access in legal and public arenas than ever before. For the
first time since Reconstruction, Mississippi elected a black state legislator,
Charles Evers became the first black mayor in Mississippi, and Hartman
Turnbow testified before Congress about how he had been terrorized in
Holmes County for attempting to register to vote. Freedom Summer organizer Fannie Lou Hamer helped found the Mississippi Freedom Democratic
Party and led a delegation to a 1964 Democratic National Convention that
included the Clarksdale pharmacist Aaron Henry and Turnbow. Mississippi has sent a racially integrated delegation to every Democratic National
Convention since then. In Mississippi, where 90 percent of blacks were
barred from voting in the early 1960s, more than 80 percent of blacks were
registered to vote in 2016.

When the nation elected Barack Obama as its first black president, younger blacks voted in greater proportions to whites for the first time ever. Selma

changed, too. In 1966, enough blacks voted to defeat James Clark and elect Wilson Baker as county sheriff, and by 2017, Selma was 80 percent black and had elected a black mayor, police chief, and many city council members. The city water tower bears the slogan, "Selma: A Nice Place to Live."

Selma had been a pivotal point for Lewis and the movement. "Something was born in Selma during the course of that year, but something died there, too," he wrote in his memoir. "The road of nonviolence had essentially run out. Selma was the last act. It had been Selma that held us together as long as we did. After that, we just came apart."

The campaign lost momentum once many of the overarching legal barriers to equality were removed. The SCLC's James Bevel said that when President Johnson signed the Voting Rights Act, he "signed the civil rights movement out of existence." There was also a rapid polarization among sympathizers and organizers and a continued divisiveness among the black leadership. Old-line organizations such as the NAACP and the Urban League remained committed to nonviolence and integration, while CORE and SNCC adopted radicalism and separatism. Lewis was dismissed as SNCC chairman and replaced by Stokely Carmichael, who advocated retribution as a road to revolution. SNCC also expelled whites who had worked in the protest trenches. King and the SCLC tried to steer a middle course, but King's influence was on the decline.

Black power, with its more radical tilt, was on the rise. Less than a week after President Johnson signed the Voting Rights Act, the Watts neighborhood of Los Angeles erupted in flames as blacks railed against poor housing, limited job opportunities, and police brutality. In five days, thirty-four people died, a thousand were injured, four thousand were arrested, and six hundred buildings were destroyed. For four successive summers, riots broke out in hundreds of cities across the country; King's vision of a national nonviolent movement did not hold. He was persistently hounded by the FBI and the KKK. Young turks who disagreed with his tactics called him Martin "Loser" King. He faced opposition from political and civil rights leaders in the North who felt their communities did not need new leadership.

King was also criticized for diluting the movement when he expressed opposition to the Vietnam War and took on the "triple evils of racism, economic exploitation, and militarism." Two weeks after the march to Montgomery, 1,400 marines landed in Vietnam and 15,000 demonstrators in Washington opposed the American bombing of North Vietnam. King said it pained him to shift his focus to antiwar efforts, but he said he had no choice when people of color in Asia were being abused by the United States. Although President Johnson called for a renewed effort to help blacks secure rights now promised by the new laws, his priority was to win the war in Southeast Asia.

This new focus drained the energy and assets of America's civil rights struggle. And over the years, many whites came to view the plight of blacks as a southern problem or a black problem. Ultimately, we as a nation did not live up to the goals of achieving racial equity. In *The Lost Priority: What Happened to the Civil Rights Movement in America?*, I wrote that the campaign had

> always held out a great promise for white America, a spiritual dimension that one could feel in the silent marching feet on the dark streets of St. Augustine; in the courage and selflessness of the [Black] Panthers; in the freedom songs heard in thousands of churches, parks, and courthouses; in that special kind of compassion seen on black faces; in the "soul" that sustained Watts, Harlem, Hough, and backroads rural communities; in the jazz of Preservation Hall in New Orleans.

Lewis, however, never changed the steady course of his ship. As one of the "Big Six leaders" of the civil rights movement, he became director of the Voter Education Project, which registered four million people of color to vote. In 1977, President Jimmy Carter appointed him to oversee a quarter million volunteers working for ACTION, a federal volunteer agency. Then Lewis entered the political realm himself. He became an Atlanta city council member and, in 1986, was elected to the US Congress representing Georgia's fifth congressional district. He still held the seat in 2017 as a leading Democratic member of Congress. Because Lewis stayed true to the nonviolent movement, I believe he is more admired and respected than leaders who opposed it, except for a few figures like Malcolm X.

I also considered Selma my departure point. The strain of recording social upheavals, violence, and hatred for a decade was taking its toll on my family and me. As understanding as Betty and my daughters were about the importance of my work, it was eroding our family life. I was dedicated to covering this historic period in America, but I also valued family unity and loyalty. I had not an ounce of strength left in me, and my family was more important to me than any assignment, or even remaining in my homeland of the South.

My fatigue had been exacerbated by trying to balance work with family life. During the Mississippi Summer Project, for example, editors refused to give me one day off to move my family from Atlanta to Memphis even though I had requested time off in writing six weeks earlier. Betty handled the move by herself while also caring for our four daughters.

As much as I cherished working for the *Times*, I began looking for other newspaper jobs. Fortunately, Clifton Daniel, managing editor of the *Times*, intervened and arranged my transfer to Washington to cover civil rights as it moved through the legislative and administrative process. I think that Daniel, as a fellow southerner, understood me. The son of a pharmacist and mayor in the small lumber-mill town of Zebulon, North Carolina, Daniel had risen from modest beginnings during the Depression to the highest levels of the *Times*. He ruled with a gentlemanly style. Daniel described himself and his wife, Margaret Truman, the daughter of President Harry Truman, as "citified small-towners."

Many of my colleagues did not understand why I would give up covering the South—one of the best beats at the paper. But I had witnessed more than my share of pivotal and historic events. The South still ran through my blood, but it no longer penetrated to my core. I had outgrown its parochial ways. The comforts of tradition and identity that soothed most southerners were lost for me. Faulkner's character Quentin Compson failed to answer his roommate's nagging question about the South, and his inability to find peace led to his ultimate suicide. My course was not so dramatic, but I acquired a fuller understanding about why the novel was named after Absalom, the biblical son of David, who rebelled against his father. Although I was never unable to fully resolve my conflicted identity as a southerner, I was ready to leave and make the nation's capital my home. This time, as I headed north, I did not look back.

It proved to be an excellent choice for my career. I wrote about the systemic complexities and failures of the federal government, initiatives rising from the states, grassroots political movements, the impact of inner-city riots, and rapidly changing demographics as white flight propelled emerging suburbs at the expense of the central cities. Some of these assignments were more nuanced and not as tangible in their immediate impact as covering events in the South. These trend stories were oozing rather than breaking. The stories included analyses of the rising importance of politics and government at the local level, a growing public distrust in government, a resistance to tax increases, and a voting system that prevented the election of a president most people wanted. I did not know then that these patterns would become the framework for current politics and government. I wrote dispatches from all fifty states and fifteen foreign countries, and I was the *Times'* White House correspondent during two presidential administrations. I served as the *Times'* assistant chief in the Washington bureau and worked as an assistant national editor in New York. During my twenty-four years at the *Times*, I had the privilege of covering some of the most important moments in American history.

To this day, I cannot shake the jungle of my memories, good and bad, of the events I witnessed: sitting in the White House surrounded by armed marines as billows of smoke from the burning city obscured the sky after the assassination of Martin Luther King Jr.; enduring three months of dawn-to-midnight travels on Robert Kennedy's relentless campaign for the presidential nomination, including one night when he sarcastically reassured reporters aboard a rocking airplane, "Don't worry, fellows, you're safe. You're with a Kennedy"; watching Robert Kennedy lie mortally wounded on the kitchen floor of the Ambassador Hotel in Los Angeles as his wife, Ethel, implored the crowds to stand back while his guards struggled to restrain the slight assassin on a metal table; smelling the stinging stench of tear gas in Chicago during the 1968 Democratic National Convention as police pushed war protesters through plate-glass windows on Michigan Avenue; gazing upon the beauty of Texas wildflowers that nurtured Lady Bird Johnson even as her husband was sending young men to die in Vietnam; watching the sadness of the burned-out centers of major cities, where children and old men picked their way through the ruins; laughing at a vodka party with other Western journalists and Soviet naval officers aboard a ship in Vladivostok harbor in 1974 while American and Soviet officials debated what to do with nuclear armaments; running too slowly from police as they hurled tear gas canisters at Vietnam War protesters on the lawn of the US Capitol; getting hit in the head by a flying rock during President Nixon's inaugural parade after escaping injury for years at civil rights protests in the South; seething with frustration and then circumventing Nixon when he cut off press access to White House information as the Watergate scandal closed in around him; and writing a front-page story topped with a giant ninety-six-point-type headline: "Nixon Resigns."

Memories of Pop hung with me through these assignments. After he died, I took home some of his possessions including the handkerchiefs from his dresser, old-fashioned ones of the softest cotton with colorful borders that had come from his store and somehow retained the fragrance of his bedrooms in the houses he and Mother had made into homes. I cherished using these handkerchiefs when I traveled on assignments to faraway places. Once in Minneapolis, where I was writing a story on urban poverty in the 1970s, I put on Pop's gray wool sweater and strolled outside to size up the surrounding neighborhood. Walking through a downtown park, I came upon a man on a bench, disheveled, dirty, drunk on cheap wine, and begging for money to buy more. He would not listen to my suggestion that he could find real help nearby, so I plunged my hands into my sweater pockets for a small bill to give him. Suddenly I felt surrounded by Pop's love, assuring me of my well-being even as the man on the bench may have never known paternal affection. For one tied so closely as a mere observer to the physical world of communities and nations, I nevertheless became increasingly aware at that moment of the spiritual world around me and how its messages come to us in metaphors. The invisible, unspoken work of a spirit, seemingly unrelated to natural law, sustains humans and ties them together.

I also realized that the most meaningful and gratifying part of my thirty-six years as a journalist had been writing about the civil rights movement in Mississippi and the South. When historians and filmmakers called me for interviews, they didn't want to talk about Nixon or the Kennedys, but the civil rights movement, past and present. My years in Washington were fulfilling and exciting because I was at the center of extraordinary national events. But the most visceral moments were witnessing the cheers and songs that sprang from black churches across the South as the long-delayed promise of liberty seemed within reach. The nation withstood a historic revolution that forever changed us all, especially a native son of the South like me as I learned to defy conventions and norms integral to my heritage and tradition. Paradoxically, the glorious confines of a small southern town, which had been my source of confidence and hope, empowered me to reject the myopic tendencies of inclusiveness and adopt a more expansive and worldly perspective. The quiet, genteel society of my upbringing had infused me with the strength I needed to write story after story about raw and brutal acts of violence. Covering these news events was perversely stimulating in one sense, but the depressive effects were overwhelming. I survived because I possessed a pervasive sureness of a bright future instilled in me since childhood.

Even after I left the South, I was drawn back time and again to report on race in America. I wrote about school desegregation, the difficulties of enforcing the Civil Rights Act in jobs and housing, and a US House of Representatives inquiry into KKK activity that resulted in indictments against Robert Shelton and six other KKK members for contempt of Congress. In the 1980s, I wrote a series of articles about how black poverty in the old city centers was spreading despite the public and private social programs designed to curtail it. Also in 1980, I reported that Jackson, Mississippi, seeking to repair a racist image that had severely damaged its economic growth, had the most integrated schools, neighborhoods, and politics among Southern state capitals. The state had a progressive Democratic governor, and even the Hederman publishing family and former senator Eastland had moderated their tones. Certainly, conditions were not perfect, but it was far different from the South I had known during my early reporting days.

"I think about those days in the 1960s and how fast things were moving," I told John Lewis during our reunion. He agreed, and we talked about the changes over fifty years but also about how many untrod roads lay ahead. A year before our reunion, the US Supreme Court had invalidated sections of the Civil Rights Act, and many states were instituting voter identification restrictions. Our meeting was before Donald J. Trump was elected president, but I saw Lewis on television after the election expressing concerns for the future. "I feel like I'm living my life all over again—that we have to fight some of the same fights," he said in a speech. "To see some of the bigotry, the hate, I think there are forces that want to take us back."

During our meeting, Lewis and I traded stories about how we each had in recent years returned to the Deep South. In 2012, Lewis attended a worship service with a former governor and secretary of state at the small church in Philadelphia, Mississippi, that had replaced the one burned in connection with the murders of the three civil rights workers. "It was a different Philadelphia," he said. "It's a different place. It was wonderful to see the audience that turned out for the service at the church. It was unbelievable. There were so many local people. Blacks and whites. It was very moving to me."

Lewis noted that another difference was that the church's Methodist pastor was a woman, and he regretted that the civil rights movement had not made room for more women leaders. "I think we should have treated women better in the roles they played," he said. "The students in the sit-ins, the great majority of participants were young women who, with a few exceptions, could not emerge as leaders." He said one reason women were overlooked for leadership roles was because many of the male civil rights leaders were ministers, and they treated the movement like it was a church. "Women didn't play that role in the church then," he said.

Lewis also returned to his hometown of Troy, Alabama, on John Lewis Day, a special event that featured marching bands and an honorary degree from Troy University, which had rejected his original letter for admission almost thirty years earlier when the institution was called Troy State College. It was symbolically paramount to Lewis that the university chancellor who bestowed the degree had once been a friend of Governor Wallace.

My visits to the South revealed that the past holds no grasp on time or place. I often traveled from Washington to visit Mother in Crystal Springs during the 1970s. She lived in a modest home, and a maid named Essie came to her house once a week to clean, iron, and cook. During my visits, I drove to the countryside to visit Essie and her family, who lived in the middle of a cotton field in a weathered, bare-wood cabin with dirt floors and no running water. My children played with her children in the back fields while I sat on Essie's front porch and distributed used clothes and shoes from my mother. Essie wanted to hear about Washington and asked when I thought change would come. Her people were Mississippi poor and didn't trust the system to be fair. I always wore my objective reporting hat while still trying to give her hope for the future. I think she was disappointed I didn't answer with more dedication or conviction, but she always sent me home with freshly shucked black-eyed peas and lima beans.

On one trip, I visited Greenwood, Mississippi, and stopped by the city cemetery, where the veterans of four wars, beginning with the Civil War, were buried beneath ornate tombstones. As a young man, I found this place to be a beautiful setting with the cooling deep shade of giant oaks and magnolias. But upon my return, I found the cemetery sacked, most of the tombstones removed, and the grounds unkempt. These were acts of retribution by those held in bondage too long and who were finally free to live in formerly all-white neighborhoods.

I was always overwhelmed by the enormous change, but some things remained as bleak as always. On a visit to Rosedale, Mississippi, in the mid-1970s, I stopped at a gas station where the clerk held the keys to three un-marked restrooms. He gave one key to white women, another to white men, and a third to blacks, both men and women. But a man who had left the state to make his fortune returned and bought the grand 1840 plantation home where his ancestors had been slaves. And I discovered that blacks in Memphis participated in a wide range of civic and political activities and lived in fine old homes near the city's downtown, which whites had abandoned during the riots following King's assassination.

I asked Lewis during our meeting to repeat his story about how, as a five-year-old boy, he had preached daily to his family's flock of sixty chickens. While his family regarded the farmyard birds as smelly stock, Lewis viewed them as outcasts entrusted to his care. To me, this story defined his character and explained how he withstood police beatings and public defeats without growing embittered or cynical.

"They were like an audience or a congregation," he said. "I would start preaching. Some of the chickens would bow their heads. Some of the chickens would shake their heads. Some of the chickens tended to listen to me just like some of my colleagues listen to me in Congress."

Lewis said his mother had written him a letter in college to discourage him from protesting, saying, "Boy, we sent you off to get an education. You need to get out of that mess before you get hurt or killed. You have a hard head. You won't listen." He and I laughed that his hard head may have been what saved his life on Bloody Sunday. He sighed, "I'm still standing, by the grace of God."

Lewis had lost none of his modesty or humility over the years. When my son-in-law, who attended our reunion, commended him for being a pioneer for change, Lewis deflected the compliment. "But this man here had to tell the story," he said, pointing to me. "He used the pen." He turned to me and quietly said, "Thank you for all you did." I felt humbled, yet unworthy of praise from someone who had made much more valiant sacrifices. Betty finally settled the score. "Your shoes walked in the same place," she said.

"Without the press, the civil rights movement would be like a bird without wings," Lewis persisted. "There were many brave young men and women using the pen and using the camera to tell the story."

We shook hands and embraced at his departure. As I watched him walk to his car with his congressional aide, I remembered him as a younger man leading multitudes into uncertain danger with those long-ago southern voices singing, "Be still my soul; when change and tears are past, all safe and blessed we shall meet at last."

THE END

Acknowledgments

THE MOST DIFFICULT PART OF COMPOSING THIS BOOK WAS URGING MY father to write about himself and explain how he reacted to these tumultuous news events, because it was not in his nature to be a character in the story. He said journalists were public servants, the eyes and ears of the people, and subjectivity could compromise credibility. He also dismissed the celebrity status associated with journalism, especially for himself, even though he relished the impact his stories might have on society. He admired the writings of Richard Schickel, who in the 1980s described how Americans' obsession with celebrity "bends our minds," leaving us divided between those people who are celebrities and those who are not, even as they try to become so.

This book could never have been published without a community of people who played integral parts. My mother, who died six weeks before my father in 2017, was his greatest love and source of strength. He could never have earned the headlines without her behind-the-scenes support, humor, and get-up-and-go attitude.

My husband, Perry, enabled me to commit time and energy to this book, provided wise and studied insights, and always put a smile on my face. My sisters, Claudia Slate and Mary Herbers, were ready with emotional support and quick eyes for accuracy. My children, Emily Farris and Ray Farris, contributed the unique and youthful perspectives of a third generation.

Those who lent encouragement and expertise include Nathan Abse, Michael Anderson, Ira Chinoy, Hope Coulter, Karen Davidov, David Davies, Emily Nichols Grossi, Paul Hendrickson, Hank Klibanoff, Bill Kovach, Kathryn Kranhold, John Lewis, Michael Lewis, Neil Lewis, Lewis Lord, Barbara Matusow, Jerry Mitchell, Eugene Roberts, Risdon Slate, James Stein, and

Robert Stone. David McCraw and Andrew Rosenthal at the *New York Times* assisted in gaining permission to reprint some of the material in this book that originally appeared in the *New York Times*. UPI also granted permission for use of its articles.

Troves of written materials consulted include, but are not limited to, the *Nieman Reports*, the *Jackson Daily News*, the Greenwood *Morning Star*, *Collier's Year Book*, John R. Tisdale's *Oral History Review* interview, Ann Waldron's *Hodding Carter: The Reconstruction of a Racist*, Adam Nossiter's *Of Long Memory: Mississippi and the Murder of Medgar Evers*, the Library of America's *Civil Rights Reporting*, Syracuse University's *Civil Rights and the Press Symposium Opening the School House Door* (which includes Stephen Clark's oral history interview), and Mrs. George Fuller's *A History of Camp Beauregard*.

My editors—Craig Gill, Katie E. Keene, Mary Heath, Norman Ware, and all the staff at the University Press of Mississippi—recognized the importance of this book and were not timid about embracing a story about dark periods in Mississippi history.

Accumulating archival and factual information was possible because of several institutions including the Sixth Floor Museum at Dealey Plaza; the Philip Merrill School of Journalism at the University of Maryland; the Stuart A. Rose Manuscript, Archives, and Rare Book Library at Emory University; the Lyndon B. Johnson Library in Austin, Texas; the National Civil Rights Museum in Memphis, Tennessee; the National Museum of African American History and Culture in Washington, DC; and the Newseum in Washington, DC.

ANNE FARRIS ROSEN

Index